Ego-Alter Ego

UNC | COLLEGE OF ARTS AND SCIENCES
Germanic and Slavic Languages and Literatures

From 1949 to 2004, UNC Press and the UNC Department of Germanic & Slavic Languages and Literatures published the UNC Studies in the Germanic Languages and Literatures series. Monographs, anthologies, and critical editions in the series covered an array of topics including medieval and modern literature, theater, linguistics, philology, onomastics, and the history of ideas. Through the generous support of the National Endowment for the Humanities and the Andrew W. Mellon Foundation, books in the series have been reissued in new paperback and open access digital editions. For a complete list of books visit www.uncpress.org.

Ego-Alter Ego
Double and/as Other in the Age of German Poetic Realism

JOHN PIZER

UNC Studies in the Germanic Languages and Literatures
Number 120

Copyright © 1998

This work is licensed under a Creative Commons CC BY-NC-ND license. To view a copy of the license, visit http://creativecommons.org/licenses.

Suggested citation: Pizer, John. *Ego-Alter Ego: Double and/as Other in the Age of German Poetic Realism*. Chapel Hill: University of North Carolina Press, 1998. DOI: https://doi.org/ 10.5149/9781469656533_Pizer

Library of Congress Cataloging-in-Publication Data
Names: Pizer, John.
Title: Ego-alter ego : Double and/as other in the age of German poetic realism / by John Pizer.
Other titles: University of North Carolina Studies in the Germanic Languages and Literatures ; no. 120.
Description: Chapel Hill : University of North Carolina Press, [1998]
  Series: University of North Carolina Studies in the Germanic Languages and Literatures. | Includes bibliographical references.
Identifiers: LCCN 97030010 | ISBN 978-0-8078-6582-8 (pbk)
  | ISBN 978-1-4696-5653-3 (ebook)
Subjects: German fiction — 19th century — History and criticism.| Realism in literature. | Doubles in literature. | Split self in literature.
Classification: LCC PT763 .P65 1998 | DCC 833/ .70927

This book is dedicated to the memory of
Ernst Behler, a true mentor.

Contents

Acknowledgments   xi

Introduction   1

1. Gender, Childhood, and Alterity in Annette von Droste-Hülshoff's Doppelgänger Thematic   20

2. The Double, the Alter Ego, and the Ideal of Aesthetic Comprehensiveness in "Der poetische Realismus": Otto Ludwig   40

3. The Oriental Alter Ego: C. F. Meyer's *Der Heilige*   60

4. Duplication, Fungibility, Dialectics, and the "Epic Naiveté" of Gottfried Keller's *Martin Salander*   76

5. Guilt, Memory, and the Motif of the Double in Theodor Storm's *Aquis submersus* and *Ein Doppelgänger*   95

6. The Alter Ego as Narration's Motive Force: Wilhelm Raabe   113

Conclusion   133

Notes   135

Works Cited   145

Index   153

Acknowledgments

Three of the chapters of this book were previously published elsewhere, though all have been substantially revised. Chapter three originally appeared under the title "Double and Other: C. F. Meyer's *Der Heilige*" in *Seminar* 30 (1994): 347–59. Chapter four, "Duplication, Fungibility, Dialectics, and the 'Epic Naiveté' of Gottfried Keller's *Martin Salander*" was first published in *Colloquia Germanica* 25 (1992): 1–18. Chapter five, "Guilt, Memory, and the Motif of the Double in Theodor Storm's *Aquis submersus* and *Ein Doppelgänger*," can be found in its initial form in the *German Quarterly* 65 (1992): 177–91. I appreciate the permission of the editors of these three journals for their permission to republish.

I would like to thank the College of Arts and Sciences at Louisiana State University for granting me a sabbatical research semester in the spring of 1995. This greatly facilitated my work on the project. My thanks are due as well to my friend and colleague at LSU, Irene Di Maio, for her suggestions for the final chapter. I am also indebted to Professor Clayton Koelb, the former editor of the series, to Paul Roberge, the current editor of the series, and to Brian MacDonald, the book's copyeditor. The readers of the initial manuscript provided many valuable suggestions. I also appreciate the assistance provided me by the staffs of the libraries of LSU, Tulane University, Portland State University, and the University of Texas. Finally, I would like to express my gratitude to my wife Patricia for her patience and understanding while I was completing the project.

Ego–Alter Ego

Introduction

From early Hellenic drama to contemporary screenplays, the figure of the Double has been one of the most widely employed motifs in world literature. It can be used to create a comical confusion of identities, a device already popular in Greek and Roman comedies such as *Amphitryon*. In narratives of the Far East, authors have employed the Double in order to illustrate the dialectic of mutability and unity that the philosophy of this region sees imbuing all phenomena. In Wu Ch'eng-en's sixteenth-century tale *Journey to the West*, semidivine and magical subterfuge allow enchanted figures to assume many shapes. More contemporary Western writers often use the Double in exploring what they regard as the human individual's innately divided psyche, torn between the extremes of good and evil, avarice and selflessness, hatred and love, serenity and emotional chaos. These modern authors utilize nondivine but often fantastic stratagems to create two Beings from one. To cite two of the more popular examples in English language literature: Robert Louis Stevenson used a chemical compound to make, seemingly, two men out of one in *The Strange Case of Dr. Jekyll and Mr. Hyde* (1886), and Oscar Wilde employed a painting in representing a dual persona in *The Picture of Dorian Gray* (1891). The Double is in many works a physically manifested projection of a tortured soul's imagination; the most celebrated instance of this variation on the Double motif is Feodor Dostoevski's *The Double* (1846). Countless detective novels and films create plots in which an innocent individual is implicated in a crime committed by a look-alike. These works need not rely on fantastic devices, since the guilty party is an actually existent, physically and spiritually discrete individual, though many movies use the same actor or actress to play both criminal and innocent accused.

Given the huge range of works that employ the Double motif in its many manifestations, the seemingly infinite variety of techniques and plots connected to its enactment, and the enormous amount of scholarly attention already devoted to this theme as a general feature in world literature,[1] what legitimates a project purporting to shed further light on the Double as a literary device when the project restricts itself to a single period and to a body of work written in a single language? Albert J. Guerard has argued with regard to the word "Double" that "no term is more loosely used by casual critics of modern literature. As almost any character can become a Christ figure or Devil archetype, so almost any can become a Double," though he concedes this figure is a "crucial literary and psychological phenomenon" (204). Paul Coates has argued with some cogency that all literature can be viewed as informed by the presence of the Double and the Other when the dynamics of both reading and writing are taken into account. An innate desire to identify with literary protagonists, "to discover in the apparent foreignness of another person the lineaments of one's own aspirations and hopes," inspires, to a great extent, the act of reading fiction. The reader thereby turns the fictive work's Other into his or her Double. Writing constitutes the mirror image of this dialectic, since figures in literature crystallize elements in the authorial ego. The various characters are fragments of the author's self. However, once another self attains discrete existence within the literary work, "the Double assumes independent life as the Other" (1).

Coates's assertion that the Double and the Other are inherently imbricated manifestations of the authorial psyche evident in all fiction lends some weight to Guerard's claim that the Double has been misappropriated and globalized in literary criticism. The same can be said of the term "alter ego," often used interchangeably with "Double" by Germanists and others who write on literature.[2] Most dictionaries define "alter ego" as a "second" self, an intimate friend or associate, or as a unique facet in an individual's personality. However, the literal translation of the Latin expression is "the other I." If one adheres to the precise nuance inherent in the original Latin, the alter ego must be seen as governed by a relationship of radical alterity to the primary ego. Thus, when one juxtaposes the two figures in a dialectic synthesis, the entire spectrum, the broad range of human personality traits is revealed. Opposing, indeed antithetical qualities are thereby fused and united like the colors in a rainbow.

Such ego–alter ego relationships are only informed by the Doppelgänger motif when the two oppositional entities manifest a physical identity, or at least a close physical resemblance, as in *Dr. Jekyll and Mr. Hyde* and *The Double*. In German Romanticism, most ego–alter ego pairs were also Doppelgänger. However, as Wilhelmine Krauss has indicated in her book on the German Romantic Doppelgänger, this figure is truly a physical "Abbild" of a primary ego, whether in the form of a mirror image, artistic representation, imaginative-poetic vision, or a discrete corporeal Double (6). This was often the case in the age of German Poetic Realism as well, but even when it was not, the writers of the period discussed in the body of my text, with the singular exception of Gottfried Keller, employed ego–alter ego pairings to evoke in their texts the psychic totality, the broad range of human emotions and attributes brought forth through the sort of character dialectics evident in the previously mentioned works of Stevenson and Dostoevski. When such antithetical pairs are not bound by the physical resemblance inherent in the word "Doppelgänger," their liaisons are forged through close collegial relationships, familial ties, friendship, and/or similar personal histories. As we will see, the representation of psychological comprehensiveness was a key telos of German Poetic Realism, one of its most definitive attributes. In this period, the alter ego was often the near physical duplicate of the primary ego, but, even when this was not the case, it stood in a position of radical "alterity" to the original "I." Hence my modification of Coates's thesis; German Poetic Realism's "Others," its "alter egos," frequently functioned *as* "Doubles," but Double *and* Other are not, in my view, inevitably interchangeable terms.

In order to understand Poetic Realism's character dialectics, and its particular manifestations of the Doppelgänger motif, one must first understand how this motif was constelled in the period of German Romanticism. German Romantic writers played a unique role in developing the figure of the Double as a modern literary manifestation. Even Coates acknowledges the existence of "stories that deal explicitly with the Double" (2) quite distinct from those emerging in the universal space of the author's projections and the reader's identifications, and the explicit thematization of the Double in works of modern literature received its primary impetus from German Romantic literature. The term "Doppelgänger" is often used in critical studies when a scholar wishes to bracket the Double as a phenomenon immanently specific to a fictional work or a cluster of fictional works, and it was first coined by the German Romantic writer Jean Paul Friedrich Richter in his novel *Siebenkäs* (1796–97). C. F. Keppler has said of the Double that in spite of certain obvious influences, "this strange figure . . . seems to have no history whatever" and "that he is the product not of tradition but of individual experience" (xii–xiii). He acknowledges Jean Paul as the inventor of the term "Doppelgänger," but feels this term and the English term "Double" have been rendered vague and overly elastic through loose and imprecise usage, although he finds both words inevitably suggest a material and/or spiritual duplication (2–3).[3] However, though one cannot situate the historical origin of the Double with Jean Paul and his Romantic contemporaries, they were the first writers to utilize fully the motif's *psychological* possibilities, to explore the conflicted recesses of the immanent psyche by making them visible, as it were, in the form of Doppelgänger. The subjective idealism of the period, particularly in the philosophical writing of Johann Gottlieb Fichte and Friedrich Schelling, inspired the Romantics with the notion that the solipsistic ego is capable of infinitely varied self-replication. When this solipsistic ego encounters any form of strong resistance to its desires in the external world, an oppositional Double to the ego is projected and externally manifested.[4]

Though Doppelgänger in Western literature after Romanticism are often devoid of the demoniac quality evident in the early period, when one of the two selves was frequently associated with dark, fantastic, and/or underworld forces, the use of the device as a means for exploring the many nuances in the individual soul continued (and continues) to predominate. The psychological element in the German Romantic Doppelgänger not only directly and indirectly influenced writers as temporally, nationally, and linguistically diverse as Stevenson, Poe, Dostoevski, Claude Farrère, Franz Werfel, Friedrich Dürrenmatt, Bruno Schulz, and H. G. Wells, but it was seminally inspiring to Freud and his school, as we will see. Though the figure of the Double continues to crop up in infinitely varied costumes, we can say, contrary to Keppler, that he does have a modern history, and it begins in the German Romantic age.

If the possibilities for exploring psychological nuances first realized in German Romanticism have continued to exercise a predominant influence on subsequent generations of writers in their employment of the Double and the closely related ego–alter ego relationship, what are the special significance of these motifs in the age of German Poetic Realism? How do their enactments become transformed from the earlier period to the later one? Most importantly, how does this alteration help to *define* Poetic Realism as a unique epoch in German literary history? Attempts to establish Poetic Realism as a discrete movement have led to endless rounds of debates concerning which writers should be included in its pantheon, what time frame constitutes its temporal borders, what, if any, are the sociopolitical attitudes and thematic interests shared and explored by its authors, and whether the term "Poetic Realism" itself is adequate to define the age.[5] Before elucidating how a discussion of the Doppelgänger and the alter ego in this age can positively contribute to this debate and concomitantly help to enhance a historical understanding of the motifs themselves, we can first take note of a relatively noncontroversial fact: the Double as a literary figure tended to lose its supernatural aura in the transition from German Romanticism to German Poetic Realism. This loss was not only gradual during the transition as a whole; the strong influence of Romantic demoniac elements on the seminal writers of the period can be seen in the presence of these elements in these writers' individual works. Particularly in the case of Otto Ludwig, whose essays (according to some scholars) gave Poetic Realism its name,[6] but in authors such as Theodor Storm as well, we will find Romantic metaphysical elements strongly evident in some works but generally diminished in their later oeuvre. Elisabeth Frenzel is accurate in noting that, while the Doppelgänger motif continued to be resilient in mid and late nineteenth-century Realism, such Romantic devices as shadows, purely imaginative Doubles, Doubles generated by mirror images, and personal Doubles were in a state of flux during the later period (106). Fluctuation between these devices, their mingling, and an ebb and flow in their employment particularly characterize the writing of Annette von Droste-Hülshoff, a transitional figure explored in the next chapter.

Most critics who believe Poetic Realism may be defined as a legitimate and coherent movement in German literary history situate its beginning in the year 1848 and its conclusion at the close of the nineteenth century. In his *German Poetic Realism*, for example, Clifford Bernd begins his chronology of the movement with events of this revolutionary year (13). Roy Cowen's *Der Poetische Realismus* also anchors the era's onset in 1848, though with a legitimate caveat: "Wie das allgemeine deutsche Streben nach 'Realismus' in der Literatur, beginnt der 'Poetische Realismus' als Konsequenz der mißlungenen bürgerlich-liberalen Revolution von 1848; er läßt sich jedoch nicht lediglich vom Soziopolitischen her erfassen, denn als geistesgeschichtlich und ästhetisch bedingte 'Bewegung' reicht er über mehrere Epochen- und Periodengrenzen hinaus" (29). Certainly, sociopolitical elements often constitute a merely latent presence in the works associated with German Poetic Realism and are sometimes almost elided.

This is also the case in much of the aesthetic writing of German Poetic Realism's two chief theorists, Otto Ludwig and Julian Schmidt. The frequent abnegation of political themes in the literature of this period—its tendency to avoid the representation of overt social, class-based conflict—distinguishes the movement from its chronological precursor, the resolutely ideological epoch that stands between Romanticism and Poetic Realism, the *Vormärz* or *Jungdeutschland* phase. However, the relative absence of pronounced political ideology in the aesthetics of the *Nachmärz* period (the term signifying the temporal frame of Poetic Realism) may perhaps be explained by the fact that it emerged in a milieu of the most profound social disillusion. Indeed, Poetic Realism was born in, and is deeply resonant with, an ethos of strong political disappointment, which sometimes manifests itself as resignation in works by authors such as Gottfried Keller and Adalbert Stifter. The "humor" critics such as Cowen (29) and Wolfgang Preisendanz[7] see as Poetic Realism's most fundamental unifying stylistic feature is often merely a compensatory mechanism for coping with the era's dashed political hopes.

To be sure, a sociocritical consciousness is not absent in the literature of Poetic Realism, as our investigation of the period's individual writers will make clear. However, in a programmatic statement in 1850 influential to Poetic Realism's subsequent development, Schmidt dismissed Young Germany's striving for universal freedom and equality as illusory, and argued that the revitalizing of art, the rebirth of poetry, must occur inwardly: "Vielmehr muß die Regneration [sic] eine innerliche sein." Shortly after this refutation of the political idealism of the "Märzpoeten," he goes on to dismiss the Romantic telos of universality as superficial and the Romantic technique of irony as lacking an impulse toward conceptual totality (Bucher, et al., ed., *Realismus und Gründerzeit* 2:78–79). Schmidt's critique of Romanticism is based primarily on the same abnegation of the fantastic we will find in Ludwig's seminal essays defining Poetic Realism. Nevertheless, the principle of approximating universalism and totality through an immanent aesthetic idealism betrays the strong influence of the Romantic school. Friedrich Schlegel's famous *Athenäum Fragment* 116 strives precisely toward the conceptualization of an aesthetic totality through an ideal fusion of all genres in the context of a "progressive universal poetry." This comprehensive activity takes place immanently, that is to say, in the unfettered artistic spirit. As Ginette Verstraete has noted in commenting on this fragment: "This plural universality Schlegel describes as poetry's 'state of becoming,' dictated by no other law than the absolute freedom of the artist's will. Poetry's ideality is to be situated in the creative freedom of its producer as much as the autonomy of the latter's imaginative power is to guarantee the infinity of Romantic poetry" (29). Corollary to the unlimited creative freedom granted by Schlegel to Romantic authors in the pursuit of aesthetic universalism and totality is subjective idealism's postulate that the individual's immanent superego is capable of unlimited cognitive self-replication, a postulate that found artistic expression in the Romantic Doppelgänger motif.[8]

As Schmidt's essay begins to make evident, the telos of aesthetic totality was as much an ideal for Poetic Realism as it was for Romanticism. In a review of some of Ludwig's creative prose, Schmidt praises his coarchitect of Poetic Realism's theoretical base by highlighting Ludwig's "Streben nach einem harmonischen Dasein." Schmidt argues that this search for life's ideal harmony and totality motivated Ludwig to anchor his works in the milieu of (putatively) uncorrupted German provincial life (*Realismus und Gründerzeit* 2:191). Poetic Realism's yearning for utopian social unity, concord, and integration underlies its theoretical and creative predilection for "Dorfgeschichten" of the sort praised in this essay by Schmidt, a predilection sometimes linked by critics to a tendency toward political conservatism within the movement's ranks.⁹ However, though perhaps tied to political tendencies, Poetic Realism's embrace of "Dorfgeschichten" transcended the merely reactionary; it had a metaphysical dimension as well. Helmut Kreuzer has cogently argued that "Der Realismus des Nachmärz hatte, in Fortführung älterer Tendenzen, das Göttliche aus der Transzendenz zurückgeholt, es der Natur und der Geschichte einverleibt. Damit war nur in der Immanenz, im erfahrbar Wirklichen des Lebens, die Möglichkeit von Glück und Sinn gegeben" (64). Some Poetic Realists, such as Jeremias Gotthelf, found divine nature and an overarching meaning, happiness, and sense in life only in the German village milieu.

Poetic Realists did not uniformly embrace all the social and aesthetic predilections they found in the "Dorfgeschichte" genre, and the body of literary criticism produced by this movement shows conflicting opinions regarding individual writers who created these popular village tales. Considering the enormous stylistic, linguistic, and content variations in works associated with the genre, and the highly incongruous typologies these divergences have inspired "Dorfgeschichten" theorists to create,¹⁰ such differences among the Poetic Realists who took an interest in these tales are not surprising. Schmidt, for example, excluded Berthold Auerbach's *Schwarzwälder Dorfgeschichten* (1843, 1848) from the pantheon of Poetic Realist works because they were so narrowly focused. Although Auerbach succeeds in artistically representing the colorful local details of life in the depths of the Black Forest, Schmidt believed such provincialism inevitably failed to portray reality in a comprehensive manner.¹¹ Keller, on the other hand, praised Auerbach in the course of his writings on Gotthelf (1849–55) for imbuing the *Schwarzwälder Dorfgeschichten* with, among other things, a beautifully rounded quality. This allows Auerbach's narrative material to be "ennobled" (*veredelt*) without any diminution in its truthful character (3:921). Even in their disparate judgments of Auerbach as a writer of village tales, we can see how both Keller and Schmidt valorized the combination of precise realistic detail with a wholeness, a fullness of expression in content and style. This exemplifies what Poetic Realists intended in articulating the ideal fusion of aesthetic, "poetic" totality with a realism tied to precise, concrete, expository descriptions.

With regard to Gotthelf, Keller expressed ambiguous views. He lauded his countryman's great diversity in characterization and his ability to bring forth well-crafted epic, lyric, and dramatic moments in *Uli der Knecht — Uli der Pächter* (1849) (3:934–35). However, much of his analysis contains extended criticisms of Gotthelf's obsessive moralizing and his narrow, reactionary religious and political views. Jürgen

Hein has accurately summarized Keller's ambivalence as mediated by the examination of the "Widerspruch zwischen epischem Realismus und protestantischem Konservatismus" Keller saw at the core of Gotthelf's oeuvre (74). Keller's reviews of Gotthelf thus belie the sweeping tendency of some critics to associate Poetic Realism's predilection for "Dorfgeschichten" with a pronounced political and theological conservatism. However, Keller's praise of comprehensiveness in Gotthelf's work with regard to characterization and genre nuances does illustrate once again the emphasis Poetic Realists placed on the creation of aesthetically integral ("epic") but realistic narratives.

The belief that an author should create images of aesthetic totality immanent to genuine life, thus "poeticizing" the "real," is a core feature of the period's aesthetics, and not just to be considered in connection with Poetic Realism's special "Dorfgeschichte" genre. This ideal played a substantial role in Ludwig's conceptualization of the term "Poetischer Realismus," as we will see. The reason Schmidt, Ludwig, and their followers felt literature must establish an ideal but reality-based totality is once again grounded in a political perspective. Hermann Kinder has shown that Schmidt's belief in the need for the artistic representation of an ideal comprehensive harmony in the world, for evoking images of "die Totalität einer mit sich versöhnten, einer nicht entfremdeten Wirklichkeit," was based on his realization that the time for a free and united Germany might lie in a still distant future. The artist must lay the groundwork for this future by aesthetically prefiguring it in his literary representations (178–79). As with the related fondness for the stable, orderly, harmonious, and traditional that Schmidt and his circle perceived in German village life, the evocation of which they valued in "Dorfgeschichten," the promotion by these Poetic Realists of a nonfactual absolute in the artistic sphere does not simply betoken illiberalism and insularity. For, as Peter Uwe Hohendahl notes, "The poeticization of reality, of which German realism is so often accused, had less to do with narrow-mindedness than with the belief that a still imperfect empirical-historical reality had to be brought to harmonious perfection in the aesthetic sphere. The work of art was to create a totality reaching beyond the empirical elements of reality" (113).

The *Nachmärz* telos succinctly summarized by Hohendahl that art must complete and perfect the empirical through a projective totality is not so very different from Romanticism's most cherished ideals. In his essay on Poetic Realism's primary hypotheses, Preisendanz has established a continuity between Romanticism and Poetic Realism in their mutual rejection of Aristotelian mimesis in favor of the idea that one must represent nature in its innate doubled character. The artist must evoke the world's objective *and* subjective, external *and* internal features. Both Romantics such as Jean Paul and Poetic Realists such as Stifter, Keller, and Wilhelm Raabe saw a "double reality" in need of aesthetic expression (Preisendanz 1963:192, 206). Hohendahl may be right in asserting that Preisendanz's essay overlooks the radically different nature of authorial autonomy in the two historical periods encompassing these literary movements (114), but Preisendanz's analysis allows us to see that Poetic Realism and Romanticism are united in their hypotheses concerning both the dual nature of reality and the necessity for representing this "doppelte Wirklichkeit" through the framework of an imaginative (or "poetic") totality. This aesthetic common ground facilitated Poetic Realism's adaptation of the Romantic Doppelgänger motif, a motif that allows the artist to mirror the bifurcated character of nature, cognition, and emotion.

The embrace by Poetic Realists of an organic, harmonizing totality as their guiding aesthetic telos finds parallels in the same philosophy of subjective identity that gave rise to the Romantic Double figure, though Hegel, rather than Schelling and Fichte, provided the greatest influence on Ludwig, Schmidt, and other leading theorists of the period in this regard.[12] Nevertheless, given Poetic Realism's belief that Romantic fantastic devices were inappropriate for literary employment in a dawning realistic age, how could its adherents make use of the Doppelgänger? How is this figure evident in Poetic Realism's ego–alter ego juxtapositions? Certainly, the usefulness of such an appropriation would be evident given the period's telos of artistically representing totalities. The Doppelgänger motif provided the Romantics the opportunity to develop their protagonists in a psychologically comprehensive manner. If a character was intimidated, limited by bourgeois conventionality, and frustrated artistically and/or romantically, writers of this generation previous to Poetic Realism, such as Jean Paul, Ludwig Tieck, E. T. A. Hoffmann, and Adelbert von Chamisso could introduce vital, bold, free-spirited, and often demoniac second selves for him from an arsenal of imaginative techniques: shadows, mirror images, conjurations, surreally sympathetic identifications, and a playful, if unbelievable, confusion of identities heightened by the deliberately bewildering diversions thrown at the reader by an ironically intrusive narrator. This blending, indeed frequent conflation of Doubles (and, concomitantly to Romanticism, of ego and alter ego) imbued Romantic characters with the stamp of an all-encompassing spiritual wholeness obverse to the ideal of aesthetic totality. Both Poetic Realism and Romanticism tended to reject onesided characterizations, and wished to consistently portray the "double reality" (Preisendanz) they saw immanent in the psyche of all individuals. Indeed, both movements shared the telos of artistic comprehensiveness, particularly in the area of characterization.

Because most Poetic Realists turned away from the panoply of the Romantic fantastic, the authors associated with the later movement usually employed a dialectical approach in their characterizations. Physically discrete figures who are nevertheless identical or at least closely resemble each other externally are often juxtaposed. The juxtaposition of corporeal similarities in the two protagonists often underlies a certain elective affinity, but their endowment with dichotomous psychic, spiritual qualities turns them into Double *and* Other. We will see this process at work in Ludwig's oeuvre. In Conrad Ferdinand Meyer's *Der Heilige* (1879), where parallels in personal history and background tend to take the place of physical resemblance, the primary ego–alter ego relationship is not marked by the Doppelgänger motif. Second selves in Theodor Storm's oeuvre are often imbued with supernatural, demoniac qualities indicative of Romanticism's continued influence, but his novella *Ein Doppelgänger* (1886) lives up to its name not through a resort to fantastic devices or irony, but by means of an onomastic sleight of hand. John Hansen is given the name John Glückstadt as the result of serving time in the Glückstadt town prison. Storm uses this onomastic doubling to evoke this character's deeply divided psyche; Hansen is a loving father to a daughter who recalls her childhood in the story's contemporary narrative frame, while Glückstadt is used in association with this character's antisocial, indeed psychopathic, tendencies, with what contemporary psychology would call his "dark side."

Gottfried Keller reverses the dialectic pairing of temperamentally antithetical Beings in the Doppelgänger and ego–alter ego enactments of Ludwig, Meyer, and Storm by bringing forth a set of twins who are not only physically but also spiritually identical in his novel *Martin Salander* (1886). This unusual twist in the Double motif, which so robs each twin of any individuality that they are both manifested as characterless and quite vacuous, allowed Keller to evoke and subtly to condemn what he saw as the moral and spiritual emptiness of his time. In *Pankraz, der Schmoller* (1856), Keller expressed a clear rejection of the ideal of psychological totality in characterization. Indeed, in the case of *Martin Salander*'s twins, psychologically comprehensive characterization is turned on its head, for they represent a totality of ethical absence and spiritual lack.

Such subtle social criticism is also evident in the work of Annette von Droste-Hülshoff. Her Doppelgänger usually exist in a milieu imbued by the preternatural but also tinged with a gritty, hard-edged realism. This ambivalence marks her as perhaps the key transitional figure between Romanticism and Poetic Realism; for this reason she is the object of this book's first chapter. Its last chapter is devoted to Wilhelm Raabe, whose alter egos are usually created to vitalize, and dialectically complete, a hesitant, sometimes faltering, first-person narrative voice. The third-person Other both inspires the narrator to begin, continue, and finish his story, and acts as the dynamic counterpart of his inquisitive but tepid, or at least introverted, persona. In some ways, Raabe marks the end of Poetic Realism, for his increasing insights into life's fragmentary quality led him ultimately to turn away from the movement's emphasis on evoking an ideal aesthetic totality.

In *German Poetic Realism*, Bernd summarizes quite well the strict criteria Schmidt established for the writing he considered worthy of inclusion in the movement's canon: "On the one hand, literary excesses of fancy and escapism were condemned; on the other, realistic literature was to be shunned if its poetic substance had withered to a state of artificial incrustation" (26–27). We have seen that both Schmidt and modern analysts of the movement saw Poetic Realism's chief aesthetic telos as the evocation of a harmonious whole; poetic substance is vital rather than withered only if it strives toward this totality. This totality must also be evident in narrative characterization. Although (with the obvious exception of Ludwig) their knowledge of Schmidt's and Ludwig's theoretical writings is questionable, the five Poetic Realists treated in the body of this text—Ludwig, Meyer, Keller, Storm, and Raabe— wrote in a manner consistent with Schmidt's rigid dictums. All were influenced by German Romanticism in varying degrees, and it is this book's principal thesis that these writers adapted the Romantic Doppelgänger motif in order to approximate such comprehensiveness in the psychic, spiritual realm.

The Poetic Realists discussed in this book attempted to keep their works realistic by stripping the Doppelgänger motif, again in varying degrees, of the "fancy and escapism" they believed imbued it in the German Romantic age during which it emerged as a significant psychological technique in literature. Sometimes their realism involved eliding the Doppelgänger motif altogether, so that only the related ego– alter ego relationship remained. Droste-Hülshoff, the only writer discussed in the following chapters who was born in the eighteenth century (1797), and who died in the year (1848) most critics cite as the first in Poetic Realism's history, is included because her writing begins to develop the tendencies later enunciated as the movement's theoretical ideals. The book's final chapter examines some of the novels of Raabe; he is the only one of the five Poetic Realists substantively treated in this book to have died in the twentieth century (1910). Raabe's last work, the novel fragment *Altershausen*, published in the year following his death, betrays a decline in confidence that Poetic Realism's telos of an aesthetic harmonious whole can be sustained, and thus signals this movement's demise as a vital literary period. The overarching goal of my book is, then, twofold: to achieve a better understanding of Poetic Realism's predilections, priorities, and techniques, and to explore the Doppelgänger and ego–alter ego figures as literary devices in the age when writers first significantly utilized them after the Double's Romantic heyday, outside the context of Romantic fantasy and irony.

In order to perceive how the motif of the Double was altered or sometimes elided in the transition from German Romanticism to the ego–alter ego dialectics of Poetic Realism, it is necessary to examine, at least cursorily, how the Doppelgänger functioned in the Romantic period itself. I will therefore conclude this introduction with a brief look at three exemplary Romantic works where Doppelgänger play a significant role. The first is Jean Paul's *Siebenkäs*, chosen partly because this novel coined the term "Doppelgänger," but also because it constitutes a paradigmatic instance of the motif's instantiation through playful irony and identity confusion, hallmarks of Romanticism. The second narrative to be analyzed is *Die Elixiere des Teufels* (1816). I examine this novel by E. T. A. Hoffmann because no work better illustrates Romanticism's proclivity for creating Doubles with preternaturally demoniac attributes. The last work selected is Heinrich Heine's one-act tragic drama *William Ratcliff* (1823). The radical foregrounding of the chimeric quality in this play's Doppelgänger signals the finale of the Double as a construct inscribed by subjective idealism, and, indeed, it indicates the demise of the Romantic movement itself. Against this backdrop, Poetic Realism's unique achievements in reconstellating the figure of the Double, or making it disappear into antithetical pairings stripped of physical resemblance, can be more adequately considered.

It is interesting to note that in terms of plot, *Siebenkäs* has been considered a powerful literary instance of psychological realism.[13] The book presents a highly compelling, painful case of a marriage gone sour due to poverty and incompatibility. Firmian Siebenkäs is an advocate to the poor and a restless, ambitious writer given to flights of fancy and somewhat capricious deeds. One of these deeds costs him his inheritance. He and his equally impulsive and nonconventional friend, Heinrich Leibgeber, had legally exchanged names as students, and this allows Siebenkäs's rather nasty guardian to block Siebenkäs's access to his familial estate. When Siebenkäs's wife Lenette learns this news, her deep sense of hurt and loss deals the marriage, already betraying signs of stress due to the couple's fundamentally discordant personalities, an almost fatal blow. Most of the novel portrays the slow dissolution of their relationship, a dissolution intensified by Siebenkäs's need to sell off their possessions in order to maintain a minimal access to food and shelter. Its near breaking point stems from jealousy caused by Lenette's attraction to another man, the preacher and man of letters Stiefel, and Siebenkäs's love for a woman he meets in his travels with Leibgeber, the aristocratic Natalie. Finally, Siebenkäs fakes his death and reassumes Leibgeber's identity so that Lenette may obtain widow's insurance. As Leibgeber, he obtains employment with a count in Vaduz. This allows Leibgeber to indulge in the vagabond life-style he prefers. The vividly described, incrementally intensifying agony brought about by so much interpersonal dissonance, devoid of all the usual eighteenth-century sentimentality, which might otherwise sugarcoat this distress, provides the novel a sharp psychological edge lacking even in many Realist stories.

To be sure, *Siebenkäs* is also full of playful digressions and Romantic irony, as well as humorous scenes made possible by the eponymous protagonist's near physical identity with his friend Leibgeber. Leibgeber is literally Romanticism's first "Doppelgänger." The term is used initially in connection with courses of food served at the wedding of Siebenkäs and Lenette, where "nicht blos Ein Gang aufgetragen wurde, sondern ein zweiter, ein Doppelgänger" (32). This is a typical Jean Paul witticism, a pun that tacitly affiliates excess in eating and in human behavior. Too much is served and consumed at the nuptial banquet, and Siebenkäs and Leibgeber go too far with the pranks allowed by their corporeal resemblance. The word "Doppelgänger" is first employed in connection with these two characters, who also share the sort of deep, innate, sympathetic attachment that often typifies Romantic Doubles, as the friends are about to part one evening. The look-alikes come before a pillar representing a paradigmatic tableau of sisterly reunion, which mirrors the two friends' own coming together on the occasion of Siebenkäs's wedding. Jean Paul defines the term here as referring to "Leute, die sich selber sehen" (54–55).

Jean Paul's definition is unquestionably apt in the case of Siebenkäs and Leibgeber; they see in each other a reflection of their own respective selves. Such self-duplication becomes intensified and multiplied later in the novel, when they not only stand before a mirror together, but Leibgeber squeezes his eye in such a manner that a manifold reproduction takes place (495). Aglaja Hildenbrock has said of Leibgeber in connection with this key mirror scene: "Die Spiegelszene, in der er sich selbst vervierfacht sieht, ist Ausdruck seiner emotionalen Verunsicherung, die es ihm erschwert, sein eigenes Ich als einheitlich und intakt zu erleben und gegen die Außenwelt abzugrenzen" (8). The endless multiplying of the ego mused upon by Leibgeber in this scene, and the identity crisis, accurately summarized by Hildenbrock, to which this leads, is a fictively clothed critique of Fichtean subjective idealism.[14] The loss of an intact sense of self it implies represents the dark side of identity confusion suggested to Jean Paul by Fichte's concept of an, at least in potential, infinitely self-replicating superego. This confusion is treated with playful irony elsewhere, as when the two friends use their similar appearance to disconcert Siebenkäs's disagreeable guardian.

The two men are so much alike in body and spirit that even their differences are, as Ralph Tymms notes, "like contrasting, but complementary, sides within one complex nature" (30). The many ironic digressions from the novel's plot, in the form of treatises, notes to the reader, framing devices, and the like, further heighten the novel's play with subjective idealism's construct of a self-regenerative, identity-blending superego. For example, at the end of the first volume, the narrator remarks: "Ich habe oft ganze Bücher über das Ich und ganze Bücher über die Buchdruckerkunst durchgelesen, eh' ich zuletzt mit Erstaunen ersah, daß das Ich und die Buchstaben ja eben vor mir sitzen" (123). Leibgeber playfully closes a letter to Siebenkäs with the salutation "Dein, nicht mein Ich" (323).

While the enactment of the Double motif and the concomitant ego–alter ego pairings of Poetic Realism were largely generated through the dialectical juxtaposition of opposites, self and Other are brought together in *Siebenkäs* through Romantic irony (in the form of the intrusive presence of the narrator) and Fichtean concepts of self-reflexivity. As Leibgeber's crisis of self makes evident, the novel's ground-breaking Doubles require no psychological energy to fuse their identities. Instead, the typically Romantic challenge facing them is the opposite one, the maintenance of discrete and self-contained individualities. Their failure to meet this challenge generates both the novel's humor and its tragic crises.

Hoffmann's *Die Elixiere des Teufels* is the story of a young man who decides in adolescence to lead the chaste, virtuous, and religious life of the Capuchin order, under the tutelage of which he spends his formative years. His resolve stems from experiences in childhood tinged with revelatory mysticism and his desire to act in accordance with what he perceives are his pious mother's wishes. However, the monk Medardus's deeply sensual nature, evident even before he takes his vows, becomes corrupted and debauched after he quaffs elixirs supposedly concocted by the devil to tempt St. Anthony. A mission to Rome frees him from the bonds of his cloistered confinement. Medardus's subsequent life in the external world, the narration of which constitutes the bulk of the text, alternates between episodes of violent carnal indulgence and equally tormented, baroquely extravagant bouts of remorse. This fissure in his soul is enhanced by his physical resemblance to the decadent Count Viktorin, whose identity he effortlessly assumes after plunging the count to his apparent death from a precipice when he tries to rouse his look-alike from a perilous somnolence at the cliff's edge.

The count's putative death allows Medardus to replace him as the lover of the beautiful Baroness Euphemie. Because only Euphemie and the count's hunter take him for Viktorin and assume his religious garb is a disguise, he can use his monkish aspect to pursue the pious, chaste Aurelie, with whom he was already smitten when she came to him for confession at the cloister. However, his feints do not fool Aurelie's brother Hermogen, whose insanity gives him extrasensory insight into the deep duplicity of Medardus's soul and deeds. After Medardus murders Hermogen as the latter discovers him trying to ravish his sister, the Doppelgänger motif takes on a preternatural, demoniac aspect, which becomes the novel's primary movens. Viktorin begins to haunt Medardus, and their personas become so intertwined as to be, at times, indistinguishable for the reader. This identity confusion is enhanced when Medardus, imprisoned *on suspicion* of being the criminally insane runaway monk, tells his jailers he is the nobleman Leonard Krczynski and concocts a story about his aristocratic Polish background. His assumption of *this* role allows him, upon his release as the supposedly innocent victim of a mix-up, to become betrothed to the blueblooded Aurelie, whose own passion (revealed to the monk during her confession at the monastery) blinds her to Krczynski's true self. During his incarceration, he receives nocturnal visitations from his spectral Double, and this exemplary mise-en-scène of the Doppelgänger motif in its *Schauerromantik* aspect continues up to their wedding day. As they prepare to exchange vows, Medardus sees Viktorin being taken away to be executed for the crimes committed by the monk.

This sight regenerates the true Medardus's madness; he delivers Aurelie a violent (and, he believes, fatal) blow with his knife. He runs into the woods, where the escaped count leaps on his back. When he awakens from his struggles with his Double, he finds himself in Italy. There, after further adventures, while engaging in extravagant repentance for his deeds at a Capuchin monastery near Rome, he comes into possession of a book written by the mysterious painter whose appearance at key moments of his life made him aware of a personal culpability extending even beyond his crimes. He had learned earlier that he and Viktorin were the sons of one father, and the painter's book reveals that Aurelie (still alive) is the daughter of his father Francesko's former paramour. He comes to realize that only his and Aurelie's celibacy can bring a conclusion to his family's propagation, necessary because all its members carry the strain of an incest-tinged debauchery. His passion for Aurelie becomes spiritualized, and she becomes his guiding light, especially after her murder at the hands of Medardus's ever-present demoniac Double, Count Viktorin. This deed occurs while she is taking the vows that would make her a nun, and turns her into a saint.

Like *Siebenkäs*, Hoffmann's novel is full of bizarre plot twists, ironic framing devices, and thorough identity conflation typical in the Romantic instantiation of the Doppelgänger figure. Pictorial representations lend further macabre touches to this motif, turning Aurelie, for example, into the Double of St. Rosalia. The ghostly haunting of the self by its Doppelgänger, brought on by the self's own guilty imagination, creates fantastic scenes transcending Schmidt's prescriptions for a *realistic* poetry, as when Medardus's alter ego digs his way from underground into the monk's jail cell and confronts him with the "naked truth" of his own Being: "Der, der unten war, drückte wacker herauf. Vier, fünf Steine lagen zur Seite weggeschleudert, da erhob sich plötzlich ein nackter Mensch bis an die Hüften aus der Tiefe empor und starrte mich gespenstisch an mit des Wahnsinns grinsendem, entsetzlichem Gelächter. Der volle Schein der Lampe fiel auf das Gesicht—ich erkannte mich selbst—mir vergingen die Sinne" (2:172). Such preternaturally demoniac tableaux will themselves haunt Poetic Realism's narratives, but when such Doubles are conjured, their imaginative, illusory quality will be foregrounded.

This underscoring of the spectral Doppelgänger as a fictive construct already takes place in Heine's tragedy *William Ratcliff*, and thereby marks Heine as an underminer of Romanticism. Like Medardus, the title character of this play is possessed by dark passions inherited from his father. His obsessive love for Maria, daughter of the Scottish Lord Mac-Gregor, is a reprise of his father Edward's obsession with Maria's mother, Schön-Betty. While Maria was an infant, Mac-Gregor saw Schön-Betty stretch her arms longingly toward Edward, who prowled the lord's castle. The jealous lord then either killed Edward, or had him killed, and Schön-Betty died of shock three days later. All this is revealed at the play's climax; William Ratcliff does not comprehend the matrix of the forces that drive him to murder surreptitiously Maria's first two betrothed when his own courtship is thwarted. However, he is haunted by constant visions of two vaporous figures who vainly try to embrace. When he first sees Maria, he comes to believe he is the vaporous man and she the vaporous woman, not realizing the two figures might also represent his father and Schön-Betty. William Ratcliff's ardor for Maria is at first reciprocated, but she comes to reject him. Haunted by the ghosts of his first two victims during a duel by sword with Maria's third fiancé, Count Douglas, Ratcliff's battle ends in his humiliating defeat and a blood-chilling apparition of his foggy Doppelgänger, who seems to command the murder of Maria. After committing this deed on his beloved's wedding night, he attempts to duel his own spectral self. The commotion attracts Mac-Gregor to the scene, whereupon Ratcliff kills his father's killer. His sense of mission fulfilled, he then ends his own life in order to join Maria in death. The final appearance of the previously thwarted foggy lovers after this suicide suggests this union, impossible in life, is fulfilled after death: "Die zwei Nebelbilder erscheinen von beiden Seiten, stürzen sich hastig in die Arme, halten sich festumschlungen, und verschwinden" (374).

Tymms has argued that the element of paternal destiny driving William Ratcliff's deeds and his tormented Double visions was probably inspired by Heine's reading of *Die Elixiere des Teufels* (75). Wilhelmine Krauss has also noted Hoffmann's probable influence on this play, but points out a significant difference between the two works; while frustrated earthly love is fulfilled on a spiritual, imaginative plane in Hoffmann's works (including *Die Elixiere des Teufels*), Heine was infused with a pessimism, indicative of Romanticism's decline, which recognizes no such duality (119–23). Thus his Doubles create all the anguish but possess none of the revelatory impact, leading to a transcendent adoration, which imbues Hoffmann's Doppelgänger. Medardus's fulfillment of self in the Romantic universal cannot be reenacted in *William Ratcliff*, for this play's Doppelgänger are only chimeric phantoms. Such products of imaginative, sometimes ancestral memory, evanescent representations of the dead constellated through a distorted recollection, are evident in much of Heine's oeuvre. At the conclusion of the prose fragment *Florentinische Nächte* (1836), for example, the narrator Maximilian describes his nocturnal visions of significant figures from his past as "Zerrbilder," who play out a "Schattenspiel" and who, like the Doubles in *William Ratcliff*, are "wie Nebel zerquirlend" (614). In Heine's oeuvre, which often subverts the techniques of the Romantic age, Doppelgänger lose their configuration as substantive figures capable of imbuing fiction with an aesthetic totality and inscribing the narrated ego with a comprehensive character, though they may indicate his or her destiny. Poetic Realism would have to work out alternative strategies, theoretically distant from the Romantic fantastic, in order to create new kinds of Doubles and/or alter egos capable of helping to achieve these goals.

Sigmund Freud was inspired by Hoffmann's Doubles to articulate the threshold phenomenon implied by the term "uncanny" in his famous essay of that name ("Das Unheimliche," 1919). He maintains that this word describes a feeling one experiences as the result of an event both odd, even bizarre, and yet familiar, expected, such as déjà vu, when an episode analogous or even identical to a previous one seems to be repeated. Freud felt Hoffmann was particularly adept at evoking the sorts of ego disturbances that lead to uncanny sensations, representations that, in Hoffmann's oeuvre, make extensive use of the Doppelgänger motif. Regarding such psychic derangements as portrayed in Doppelgänger relationships, filiations largely responsible for creating uncanny impressions in Hoffmann's readers, Freud notes: "Es handelt sich bei ihnen um ein Rückgreifen auf einzelne Phasen in der Entwicklungsgeschichte des Ich-Gefühls, um eine Regression in Zeiten, da das Ich sich noch nicht scharf von der Außenwelt und vom Anderem [sic] abgegrenzt hatte" (12:249). Such uncanny moments, and such regressions to primal stages in the ego's development of a discrete identity, are rare in Poetic Realism, though evident in the oeuvre of Droste-Hülshoff, as we will see. Rather than using the figure of the Double to elide the border between ego and Other, most of the works we will explore in the following chapters use Doppelgänger and alter egos to *enhance* this division, thereby creating clearly distinguishable, indeed antithetical, character types. With or without employing the Double motif, Poetic Realists strove to engender a sense of radical alterity between primary egos and figures in the narrative with whom they are closely linked externally. This dialectical praxis allowed these writers to imbue their texts with a sense of psychic totality, encompassing the extreme range of emotions, moral attributes, and personality types.

David Perkins has asserted that one of Julian Schmidt's "splendid feats" as a literary historian was "to display the history of German literature as the unfolding of a political and ethical ideal. Thus he both unifies the texts under a concept and also integrates the long temporal span he surveys" (49–50). My book strives to achieve the more modest feat of looking at the social, aesthetic, and psychological principles governing the brief temporal span of the movement which found in Schmidt its greatest lobbyist. In so doing, I, too, unify the texts I examine under the lens of one technique: the juxtaposition of ego and alter ego. Often, this dialectic is informed by the motif of the Double, or Doppelgänger. In using these words interchangeably, I follow the lead of Robert Rogers, who in his psychoanalytic study of this motif notes that "no matter what terms are used, we can argue that man does have a double—or multiple—nature" (2). Although the psychoanalytic ramifications of this nature were first thoroughly explored scientifically by

Freud, the first group to fully exploit its artistic possibilities was the German Romantics. By integrating key works and authors of the nearly subsequent, Poetic Realist, period within the framework of the Doppelgänger and related ego–alter ego motifs, I hope to facilitate a better understanding of this movement's ideals and goals, its own authors' individual dilemmas and accomplishments, and an insight into how these motifs could be positively utilized to show man's "double or multiple nature" despite the constraints placed on the aesthetic imagination by the dictates of a new realistic age.

1. Gender, Childhood, and Alterity in Annette von Droste-Hülshoff's Doppelgänger Thematic

The decision to incorporate Annette von Droste-Hülshoff into a book centered on German Poetic Realism is bound to meet with controversy. Those who define Poetic Realism in its narrowest sense, as consisting of the explicit and implicit followers of the movement as it was theoretically articulated by Julian Schmidt, tend to reject emphatically Droste-Hülshoff's status as a Poetic Realist, particularly given Schmidt's tendency to deny the supernatural as a fitting theme in realistic literature.[1] Indeed, Schmidt himself disliked Droste-Hülshoff's most famous work, the 1842 novella *Die Judenbuche*; he was put off by its abundant preternaturally gruesome details.[2] Some critics have no reservations about including Droste-Hülshoff among the leading Poetic Realists.[3] Still others regard her, as I tend to do, as a transitional figure between Romanticism and Poetic Realism.[4] Of all the writers treated in this book, Droste-Hülshoff is the most celebrated for her frequent and highly nuanced employment of the Doppelgänger motif, and one could argue that her Doubles and mirror images betray more than any other individual structuring motifs in her oeuvre a strong affinity for the Romantic supernatural.

While recognizing the validity of those arguments which hold Droste-Hülshoff's predilection for the uncanny, her religiosity, and indeed a certain political conservatism (exemplified by her rejection of Young Germany politics) tend to put her into the pantheon of late Romantics rather than among the Poetic Realists, her Doppelgänger thematic is articulated in a manner consistent with its employment or its ego–alter ego adaptation by those writers included in this book who are universally accepted as Poetic Realists: Ludwig, Meyer, Keller, Storm, and Raabe. For in spite of the supernatural element in her Double and mirror images, they tend not to be Fichtean-inspired products of a single consciousness, a cognitively all-encompassing subjectivity that simply divides itself into two physically identical but spiritually antithetical physical shapes. Her Doubles, in spite of their uncanny features, are more mundane than those of the Romantics. In *Die Judenbuche*, for example, she creates two completely discrete (albeit often misidentified, given their common appearance) individuals, Friedrich Mergel and Johannes Niemand.

Bernd Kortländer has indicated E. T. A. Hoffmann and other Romantics used the motif of the Double to create an atmosphere evoking the complete loss of personal identity. The loss generating the division of one identity into two reflects the irreconcilable gap in the Romantic world between the poetic and everyday realms. One of the two corporeal entities in the Doppelgänger relationship is the routine, stultified, quotidian self, while the other is his or her socially, sexually, and aesthetically suppressed but latently manifest subterranean Being. Even in poems such as "Das Spiegelbild," also written in the early 1840s, where the attempt to evoke an unearthly, ghostly atmosphere is most extreme, the absolute division between the mundane and poetic found in most Romantic works is absent; there is no attempt to sublate the "banal" into a "higher reality." As Kortländer puts it: "Die Droste strebt im Gegenteil eine Versöhnung der als dämonisch und sündhaft erfahrenen poetischen Sphäre mit dem Bereich des Alltäglichen auf einer Ebene der Mitmenschlichkeit an, sie setzt der romantischen eine biedermeierliche Lösung des Konflikts entgegen" (174). This transformation of a central Romantic trope is consistent with Poetic Realism's shift in interest from exploring the creative imagination's ability to transcend the confinements of everyday life to themes with a broader socioethical purport: class conflict, the problems of crime and punishment, guilt and repentance. As we will see, these veritable dilemmas rather than the abyss between art and humdrum existence are what animate Poetic Realism's engagement of the Doppelgänger motif, or its reworking of the motif into an ego–alter ego dualism. This is the reason the transformation of the motif both clearly illustrates Poetic Realism's agonistic relationship to Romanticism and significantly constitutes it as a discrete literary movement.

Whether one sees in Droste-Hülshoff's stylistic and thematic blending of the uncanny Romantic "poetic" realm and the more concretely socioeconomic "real" everyday sphere a "reconciliation" like Kortländer or the juxtaposition of irresolvably conflicted elements like Ulrich Gaier, it is safe to say the two realms are more inextricably intertwined in her oeuvre than in those writers universally accepted as Poetic Realists. In their works, the uncanny is usually manifested quite subtly (as in Storm) or elided altogether. With regard to the Doppelgänger motif, the most frequently and powerfully enacted literary device in Droste-Hülshoff's otherworldly pantheon, the "poetic" and the "real" can be seen to intersect most consistently and profoundly in the domain of childhood and gender. To be more precise, Droste-Hülshoff's Doubles are almost always divided into the antitheses of male and female and child and adult. In *Die Judenbuche*, we will see how gender plays a role even in structuring the novella's famous, seemingly all-male, Doubles: Friedrich Mergel and Johannes Niemand. Although nineteenth-century German literature's only canonic woman writer has inspired some outstanding feminist-oriented scholarship,[5] even this research has largely ignored the roles of gender and childhood in Droste-Hülshoff's enactment of the Doppelgänger motif. While Romantic writers created Doubles in order to represent a breaking free from the constraints of everyday, empirical reality, Droste-Hülshoff's mirror images show the struggle for liberation from the spiritual, sexual, and indeed physical corsets placed upon women in the conservative German Restoration period during which she penned her works. But we will see her Doppelgänger are ultimately constituted and framed by loss and absence—of girlhood, innocence, and, in the end, unconscious feminine power.

Droste-Hülshoff's career ended before Poetic Realists developed the ideal of aesthetic totality, which is reflected in much of the period's creative output. Nevertheless, the related desideratum of comprehensive characterization which lay behind the movement's employment of the Doppelgänger motif (as well as its non-Doppelgänger ego–alter ego pairings) can also be glimpsed in Droste-Hülshoff's configuration of her Doubles. What is striking in her employment of Doppelgänger as a means for completing the narrated ego is the consistent presence of the element of gender. Citing the work of Elke Frederiksen, Cora Lee Nollendorfs has noted that "in both *Bertha* and *Ledwina* Droste's heroines criticize their male counterparts as ruled by rationality alone, whereas they demand a holistic approach which includes reason and feeling from both sexes" (325). Droste-Hülshoff's Doubles are a seminal element in her own holistic approach to characterization; ego and alter ego combine to imbue protagonists with what their author regards as male and female attributes, allowing them to emerge as psychically total individuals. However, this effect primarily serves to heighten the sense of these characters' spiritual limitations and psychological deficiencies when they are considered apart from their Doubles.

Without explicitly discussing Droste-Hülshoff's Doppelgänger motif, Patricia Howe has indicated one of the significant social circumstances driving its inspiration. Drawing on the work of John Berger, she notes how woman's image of herself tends to be divided between an external observer internalized within her psyche into a sort of masculine observer who makes sure she conforms to certain stereotypes, and the observed figure who really represents her essential feminine self. The watchful male superego reacts with disapproval when the observed female attempts to transcend the restricted sphere into which she is cast by striving for achievement in traditionally male domains. Howe believes Droste-Hülshoff, like all women writers, is aware of this inward, twofold identity, and sees this awareness manifested in the early dramatic fragment *Bertha oder die Alpen* (1813–14), when Bertha's sister Cordelia tells her that women who seek to transcend their own wisely circumscribed limits are really fleeing their "own better self." Women who would explore the intellectual realm traditionally reserved for male exploits are not truly women, but androgynies (26–28).

Throughout the dialogue between Bertha and Cordelia, tropes of upward and downward movement are used to signify "masculine" ambition and an antithetical drag upon the spirit into an oppressive aquatic realm. Just prior to Cordelia's assertion that a woman who would climb "masculine" heights loses her own better self and can no longer be followed by the female gaze, Bertha complains: "Mein Geist ist unstät und hinweggezogen / Wird er gewaltsam wie von Meereswogen." (6/1:68). She responds to Cordelia's reproach by asserting it is not her masculine ambition that causes her suffering, but a gentle and melancholy feeling: "Es hebt mich nicht auf Schwingen mehr empor / Es drückt mich nieder macht mich muthlos krank" (6/1:69). She dares not reveal even to her sister this melancholy's real source; it is caused by the noble Bertha's socially impermissible love for a wandering minstrel. Though Bertha's dejectedness is misdiagnosed by her sister, the scene makes clear Droste-Hülshoff herself was aware of an observing masculine superego present in her authorial psyche, reflective of the external world's disapproval at a woman's intellectual ambition. Thwarted love, guilty ambition, an awareness (though not an overtly expressed disapproval) of a rigid, stultifying social stratification: these afflictions pluck the spirit from the heavens and pull it down with the force of oceanic waves. Not much later in her poetic career, Droste-Hülshoff's Doubles are actually engendered by and tarry at this liquid realm.

One of Droste-Hülshoff's early water-generated mirror images occurs early in the novel fragment *Ledwina* (1820–25). Like several such tropes in her oeuvre, the presence of death is so thoroughly imbricated with the reflection at its description's very outset that the implication of narcissistic demise seems divorced from narcissistic vanity: "Ledwinens Augen aber ruhten aus auf ihrer eignen Gestalt, wie die Locken von ihrem Haupte fielen und forttrieben, ihr Gewand zerriß und die weißen Finger sich ablösten und verschwammen und wie der Krampf wieder sich leise zu regnen begann, da wurde es ihr, als ob sie wie todt sey und wie die Verwesung lösend durch ihre Glieder fresse, und jedes Element das Seinige mit sich fortreiße" (5/1:79). Ledwina's enchanted gaze down into a watery second self whose wavy motion inscribes this Double with beckoning death is the logical downward progression of Bertha's split persona toward the fluid realm. She, like Bertha, suffers from being a woman of vision who must exist within a closed, hierarchic society. Like Bertha, Ledwina is made miserable by the prospect of having eventually to marry a young man from her narrow class circle. Guided like Bertha by conflicting external pressures to conform and a questioning inward spirit, she senses her immanent self is threatened by the suffocating Restoration milieu—hence her vision of a death-inscribed Double.

Ledwina's ominous pondering of her own water reflection naturally cannot be entirely disassociated from the concept of narcissism. But it represents a variation on what Ludwig Pfandl refers to in an early Freudian article on this concept as a "Verdichtung" of the Narcissus myth. Like Otto Rank and Freud himself, Pfandl believes the Doppelgänger thematic and the Narcissus theme in its many forms belong essentially to the same psychopathological matrix. He regards authors such as Tolstoy, Oscar Wilde, Strindberg, and Nietzsche, whose works often feature self-obsessed characters, as marked by an abnormal interest in their own persons. This neurosis can lead to a split in the self-perception of one's personality. The division is what Pfandl characterizes as the Doppelgänger "complex," and such writers often creatively sublimate this complex in their own works. This abnormal self-love represents an inability to transcend primitive narcissism, the infantile autoerotic state in early personality development prior to the transference of love to one's parents. Rank and Freud developed similar arguments in works cited later in this chapter, but used primarily German Romantic writers as examples of such psychic abnormality. These writers are seen to sublimate their pathology by creating Doubles in literature.

However, despite her lingering gaze at her image in the water, and though she is quite introspective, Ledwina cannot be regarded as such a creation. Pfandl notes that the classic tale of Narcissus is extremely compressed; there is no development of his personality, no progressive plot. His entire tale is constituted by a single powerful experience (301). This is even truer of Ledwina's early pseudonarcissistic act, for it is devoid even of self-enchantment. To be sure, the occurrence is but one scene in a fragmentary novel rather than, like the Narcissus myth, an aesthetic totality. Still, this absence of exaggerated *amour propre* is consistent in Droste-Hülshoff's Doppelgänger tableaux, and indeed generally characteristic of Poetic Realism's Doubles and alter egos. The loving lingering at a reflection, the endless musing on the self and its fantasies, an egotism that generates alter egos—all these narcissistic and pseudonarcissistic elements are "compressed" out of Droste-Hülshoff's Doppelgänger. Ledwina's water reflection creates no premonition of a narcissistic *Liebestod;* it only suggests unsublimated mortality.

The figure of the Doppelgänger occurs a second time in *Ledwina,* during the title character's churchyard dream. Underway to a theatrical performance with a large group of friends and relatives, she is told by an insignificant acquaintance to watch out for freshly dug graves. As the torches in the churchyard thereupon suddenly flare up, she is driven by a vague fear to start digging up the earth between the graves. Suddenly she finds herself observing her Double as it performs the act of digging, deathly pale and with wildly blowing hair. The cognating self then once more becomes the digger, who falls through the coffin slats, finds the skeleton of her beloved, and performs acts of devotion. As she awakens, the shadows in her room undulate upon her blanket, leading her to imagine she is underwater. This sensation once again causes her to imagine her dead second self, after she first sees herself as an Undine; she observes the corpse sinking under the river and being dissolved by the water as her parents vainly cast out a net in order to rescue her (5/1:96–97). Clemens Heselhaus has refuted those critics who see echoes of Romanticism in this scene by noting it represents not the illustration of Romantic ideas but their refutation; the dream images are "Halluzinationen und Schreckbilder des Romantischen, die den Geist des Lebens wecken sollen" (74).[6]

This view is lent credence by the mortification attending these Doubles. To be sure, Romantic Doubles are often revealed to be lifeless—one thinks of Achim von Arnim's golem in *Isabella von Ägypten* (1812) and Olimpia in Hoffmann's *Der Sandmann* (1817). Nevertheless, this lifelessness is only gradually revealed, and, in works such as *Isabella,* Double and original are often rendered confluent through deliberate identity confusion. The water Doubles in *Ledwina* are marked by death from their very outset. A playful confusion of identities such as the one found in *Isabella* (discussed in the chapter on Meyer) is thereby rendered impossible. As was noted, the uncanny in *Ledwina*'s dead aquatic images is devoid of the narcissism associated with Romanticism's great water Doubles, such as the reflected lake image that haunts the eponymous protagonist in Nikolaus Lenau's cyclic poem "Anna" (1838). The Romantic Doubles may be resonant with death, but *Ledwina*'s Doppelgänger are from the start (and without the Romantic narrative retardation that impedes the revelation of the grinning death's skull behind the beautiful aquatic image) the intimations of her mortality. Droste-Hülshoff's refusal to use Romantic irony to introduce a playful imbrication of Double and original is what turns the Romantic

Double motif into something truly frightening, a shock that would awaken life's spirit, as Heselhaus suggests. Ledwina's Doubles are unadorned death, death incarnate. But as we will see, Droste-Hülshoff is not averse to employing a confusion of identity between Double and original in *Die Judenbuche*.

Droste-Hülshoff's detachment of the narcissistic from the uncanny in her water Doubles represents a significant departure from Romantic allegoresis. In his essay on the uncanny, Freud drew heavily on German Romantic works in elaborating his view that Doppelgänger in primitive cultures represented an attempt to insure the survival of individual egos. According to Freud, the Doppelgänger thus finds its origin in self-love, and is a phenomenon of primary narcissism (12:247–48). The Double may often incorporate the ego's wish for immortal youth and beauty, a wish spawned in its turn by an underlying fear of death. While the Baroque age was fond of vivid *vanitas* tropes, which show death lurking behind a beautiful facade, Romantic Doubles often link this facade to a *fear* of such mortality. Lenau's "Anna" is a paradigmatic instance of Romanticism's use of a beautiful second self to link narcissism to the ego's survival instinct.

Based by Lenau on a Swedish legend, the tale tells of a lovely young woman who, at the poem's outset, is lost in the reflection of her image in a lake. A gust of wind causes the image to dissipate. The distortion of her water image leads her to reflect not on the transience of life, as in *Ledwina*, but of beauty. Driven by her all-consuming narcissism, she allows herself to be rendered infertile by an old sorceress in order to retain her youthful comeliness forever. She wishes to marry a knight, whom she would have born seven children had there been no magical intervention. Their souls are sacrificed through the sorceress's incantation. Seven years later, the knight curses his wife as he notices she casts no shadow in the moonlight. Overcome by guilt and fear, Anna confesses her sin, and her husband exiles her. After another seven years of wandering, she enters a church, where her children's unborn but physically objectified souls reveal themselves to her: "Sieben leichte Lichtgestalten / Jetzt an ihr vorüberziehen / Und mit stummem Händefalten / Vor dem Altar niederknien" (385).

The poem narrates a complex Doppelgänger metamorphosis driven by Anna's narcissism. Because she is attached to her beautiful water image by a vain self-love, the sorceress horrifies her with the prospect of gazing at herself in the water after she has sacrificed her youth to her children: "O dann frage deinen Schatten: / Wangen, seid ihr mein, so bleich? / Augen mein, ihr hohlen, matten? / Weinen wirst du in den Teich" (374). Like another great Romantic character, Adelbert von Chamisso's Peter Schlemihl, she is willing to sacrifice this shadow for a vain cause. At first the vision of an ominously aged Double, the shadow is forfeited by Anna so she can retain her immaculate water image. However—a material manifestation of the return of the repressed—the shadow comes back as her unborn children's spirits; shade is transformed into light. Bathed in this light, Anna is forgiven and redeemed. Freud indicates in "Das Unheimliche" that such complex interplay between Double and original is characteristic of Romantic Doppelgänger. Indeed, the dissolving of borders between the two, found, for example, in Arnim and Hoffmann, is a symptom of primary narcissism. The redemption of the original is also a Romantic phenomenon; one finds it not only in Lenau, but in Chamisso's *Schlemihl* (1814) and Arnim's *Isabella*. What moves *Ledwina* into the realist mode is the lack not only of Freudian narcissism—her water image suggests a death drive[7] rather than the instinct for self-preservation—but also of a redemptive element in the story's Doppelgänger motif. Rather than metamorphosing into a force for ultimate salvation, her dream of her second self's drowning is transformed, as she awakens, into the witnessing of a real-life drowning. There is only a brief narrative transition from fatal revery to fatal actuality; she observes the tragic accident begin to unravel immediately after she rises from her bed and gazes out her window (5/1:97–100). In Poetic Realism, uncanny Doubles are rarely involved in supernatural acts of salvation. If Droste-Hülshoff's water reflections do not evoke death, they at least, as in *Die Schlacht im Loerner Bruch* (1837–38) point to conflict, flight, and exile.[8]

Brigitte Peucker has suggested Ledwina's dream represents an attempt to reanimate what we today would call the "inner child"; the buried skeleton is the dreamer's "wild self," and the child who sells Ledwina flowers in the dream is "a mute and regressive self, which nevertheless provokes creative activity" (388). This journey to the past is more overt in the poem "Doppeltgänger" (1844), where the Double who pays the poetess a nocturnal visit is apparently her childhood self, a painful embodiment of that part of the heart where youthful memories, past spirits, are buried. The poem's opening evokes an atmosphere conducive for establishing what Freud described as the key site for the uncanny, that liminal situation where the commonplace and the expected collide with their opposites, the supernatural and incredible. Another element of Freud's definition, influenced by Schelling, holds that the uncanny represents the emergence of secrets one expects to remain hidden (12:236–37). These two circumstances are strongly manifested in "Doppeltgänger."

The threshold ambience ideal for bringing about the dialectical confrontation between the "heimlich" and the "unheimlich" is created in the poem's opening lines, when the poetess rhetorically asks if the reader has experienced the blissful hours when one hovers between dreaming and waking. This psychic border creates the interstice where the Freudian uncanny is ripe for self-disclosure in the form of long-buried secrets and memories. They gradually take on phenomenal form, gliding along the poetess's cheeks as a moist darkness, beginning to emit tone and light. They then swim before her eyes like the daguerreotype pictures just then becoming popular commodities. Given the newness of photographs at this time as an artistic phenomenon, as well as Droste-Hülshoff's deep immersion in popular Westphalian folklore, one can understand their invocation in this poem as something ghostlike and preternatural, engendering by themselves a fearsome mysteriousness of the sort described by Otto Rank in his discussion of non-industrialized people's reactions to such images (65–66). To be sure, Droste-Hülshoff did not actually share this fear; she even promised a friend in a letter composed the same year the poem was written to send her a daguerreotype of herself if the reproduction was accurate (10/1:206). Nevertheless, she was able in an only dawning age of Poetic (and photographic) Realism to exploit the "shock of the new" by using the daguerreotype image to prefigure the poem's apparent title figure, who makes her appearance in the same stanza as the daguerreotypes, a beautiful and serious child. The child's soul seems to flow forth from its gaze. Consistent with the poem's pervasive liminality, the child alternates between expressions of pain and ecstasy. Intensely hearkening for something, for a communication, it climbs to the poetess's shoulder and disappears. The last lines of the apparently incomplete poem indicate all these apparitions are products of her own heart: "Doch nur mein Herz ist ihre stille Gruft / Und meine Heiligen, meine einst Geweihten / Sie leben Alle, wandeln Allzumahl / Vielleicht zum Segen sich doch mir zur Qual" (2/1:67–68).

This poem shares much of the imagery and atmosphere of another lyrical work from 1844, "Durchwachte Nacht." The same borderline between night and day, sleeping and waking, is evident in its first two stanzas. Later in this longer poem, the same preternatural lights, tones, and daguerreotype images flit across the ceilings, and this again leads to the appearance of the soulful, mysterious child (1/1:351–53). A comparison of the two works has led Margaret Mare to conclude "that the child is a vision of Annette's young self" (145), and given the flood of youthful memories it triggers in "Doppeltgänger," this assessment seems justified. Nevertheless, the poem's title creates a certain ambiguity, for its lack of an article makes it impossible to determine whether "Doppeltgänger" is singular or plural. The elegiac conjuring of deceased spirits is absent in "Durchwachte Nacht," while they become ambulatory living presences once again in the poet's heart in "Doppeltgänger." These are perhaps the poem's true Doppelgänger, ghostly Doubles of Droste-Hülshoff's dear departed. They attain this status not through a Romantic, preternatural ego division, but simply through narrative memory. The overriding mood in the engendering of these Doubles is not Romantic playfulness, but monumental pain. The intertwining of memory and the creation of Doubles in Droste-Hülshoff anticipates a tendency in the age of Poetic Realism; a similar connection will be explored in the chapter on Storm. What is unique here is the personal character in the lyrical blending of memory and doubling, the intense subjective pain the poetess feels as she "blesses" the dead by providing them artistic immortality.

The child in "Doppeltgänger" and the spirit it evokes are manifestations of less troubled, more carefree days. The loss of innocence assumes a more ominous form in the ballad "Das Fräulein von Rodenschild" (1841). We find this maiden at the outset of the poem in a state of budding, aroused sexuality. Spring has sprung inwardly and outwardly, and her blood is seething. As in "Doppelgänger," the poem's milieu is doubly liminal; its action takes place at the moment when the clock strikes twelve and announces Easter Sunday. The poem's restless protagonist is at the threshold of childhood and maturity. She attempts to break free of the confinements this emerging womanhood imposes on her in a conservative Catholic society, literally and figuratively loosening the bands of her corset. There is a setting of dreamy wakefulness and dark distorted shapes. While confusion and oppressiveness reign as the house servants gathered to welcome Easter surround and gaze up at the balcony, the maiden of Rodenschild glimpses her Double. The vaporous figure, which causes the maiden premonitions of insanity and death, flows down the steps. Rodenschild follows the phantom until she stands spellbound in front of the room storing the family archives. The Double begins to mirror the original as though she was the maiden's mirror image. This twofold doubling—in action and appearance—has catastrophic consequences:

Langsam das Fräulein die Rechte streckt,
Und langsam, wie aus der Spiegelwand,
Sich Linie um Linie entgegen reckt
Mit gleichem Rubine die gleiche Hand;
Nun rührt sich's—die Lebendige spüret
Als ob ein Luftzug schneidend sie rühret,
Der Schemen dämmert,—zerrinnt—entschwand.

The poem ends with an image of the maiden in her later years. She keeps her frozen right hand gloved, and appears to be insane (1/1:260–63).

As in "Doppeltgänger," the difference embedded in the identity of

Double and original in "Das Fräulein von Rodenschild" emerges at the boundary between childhood and maturity. However, the latter poem is informed not by an epic elegiac tone, but by a sense of drama and immanent crisis evoked through its balladic form. Winfried Freund's interpretation underscores the work's personal and sociocritical elements. It was inspired, according to Freund, partly by Droste-Hülshoff's unhappy relationship with Heinrich Straube, but also offers a thinly veiled critique of a conservative society, which includes the suppression of erotic feelings as part of its rigid behavioral code. The Double, in this view, represents the maiden's unleashed sexual self. Through an act of extreme self-discipline, the maiden overcomes this threatening manifestation of her emerging sexuality. But her frozen hand indicates that this surrender to social mores (her presence at a dance at the poem's conclusion indicates she has succeeded in achieving acceptance and integration) comes at a cost, for it symbolizes the loss of her inner vitality.

Freund also indicates the poem may have been partly inspired by Droste-Hülshoff's reading of Ludwig Tieck's Romantic novel *William Lovell* (1795–96). The shift from Romanticism to Poetic Realism is indicated by the identity of the two works' respective protagonists. The figure in Tieck's novel driven mad by a Double who incorporates the rift in the ego between the intellectual-spiritual and physical-sensual spheres is the poet Balder, and his musings are thus intimately tied to the Romantic obsession with creative, artistic fantasy. Rodenschild's vision lacks this dimension; her Double is the product of an obvious adolescent sexual crisis driven to an extreme by social rigidity. As a girl on the verge of womanhood, she is made to feel an outcast. Her alterity is symbolically imposed upon her by the servants who welcome Easter's arrival below her balcony but seem to stand guard, isolating her until she can prove worthy of integration into her proper circle. Through a too great sacrifice, this integration occurs at the ballad's conclusion. Hers is not a poet's dilemma, but one faced everyday by thousands of young women in repressive Restoration Germany.

In the poem "Das Spiegelbild" (1842), another mirror image filled with an unknown phantasmic power observes the narrator from a crystal. The maiden of Rodenschild engaged in a tenacious battle of wills with her Double before banishing it—and thus her sexual side—from the right to existence. The narrator of "Das Spiegelbild" resists her mirror image at the outset simply by refusing to acknowledge it is truly her Double. She calls it a "phantom," not really her equal, the product of a dream and lacking genuine physical resemblance. As she begins to recognize there is an identical quality after all, she wonders if she would love or hate the Doppelgänger should it actually emerge from the crystal. There are elements in the image both attractive and repulsive; the eyes are full of a cold deadness, but the mouth possesses a gentle, childlike quality. Her ambivalence carries over into the penultimate stanza, where she once again expresses certainty the image is not really her genuine self, but asks God's mercy should the image's soul actually dwell latent within her. Finally, she decides the attitude she would adopt should the vision leave the crystal and stand before her would be one of mourning:

> Und dennoch fühl ich, wie verwandt,
> Zu deinen Schauern mich gebannt,
> Und Liebe muß der Furcht sich einen.
> Ja, trätest aus Kristalles Rund,
> Phantom, du lebend auf den Grund,
> Nur leise zittern würd ich, und
> Mich dünkt—ich würde um dich weinen!
>
> (1/1:168–69)

The narrator of the poem stands clearly beyond the liminal dangers destructive to the maiden of Rodenschild. The poem is elegiac like "Doppeltgänger"; the first-person narration conjures the Double from a lyric rather than a balladic stance. Because she is not plunged into a crisis, the narrator can observe the ambiguity in her crystal vision; the Double itself seems inscribed by a duality, by a chilly deadness and a childlike innocence.[9] This alternation or ambiguity reflects the unconscious level at which the events described seem to be played out. In her analysis of the poem, Christa Suttner has shown how Droste-Hülshoff's elucidation of an inherently unconscious process reflects the emergence of Realism from late Romanticism taking place in the 1840s. The image's dualistic daemonism, the narrator's concomitant acknowledgment and disavowal, inclination and rejection with regard to the emanation, its unfathomable power—these factors point to the idea that the crystal allows the viewer a glimpse into her own unconscious. Suttner's article argues that the realization of the unconscious as an essential element in the personality's construction marks Droste-Hülshoff not only as a significant figure in the transition to (Poetic) Realism, but as someone who expressed in literature what contemporary pioneers of psychoanalysis were discovering about the human mind.

The poem's tentative ending—the conditional tense predominates in the last stanza—indicates the narrator is not only afraid of the apparition's latent, unknown force, but of its forfeiture should the image leave the unconscious realm, stand concretely before the narrator, and show her it is not—in part or whole—her indwelling being. Seen in this light,

"Das Spiegelbild" shares with "Doppeltgänger" and "Das Fräulein von Rodenschild" the theme of possible or actual deprivation. In these three poems, the Doppelgänger is constituted by loss and absence—of girlhood and childish innocence ("Doppeltgänger" and "Das Fräulein von Rodenschild"), sexual vitality ("Das Fräulein von Rodenschild"), and, finally, unconscious feminine power ("Das Fräulein von Rodenschild" and "Das Spiegelbild"). This dispossession is clearly related thematically to the ultimate human loss suggested by *Ledwina*'s water Doubles, namely, that of human life itself. From both personal experience and an awareness of social circumstances in 1840s Germany, Droste-Hülshoff makes her Doppelgänger express her own elegiac mourning for vanished possibilities. For she did not share the Romantics' faith, inherent in their own Doubles, in the poetic imagination's transformative force.

Precisely this kind of loss informs the motif of the Double in *Die Judenbuche*. Prior to his falling under the sway of the relentlessly masculine Simon Semmler, the young Friedrich Mergel was usually as gentle and docile as a deer, albeit a bit stubborn. His mother Margreth had essentially raised him as a daughter. This is revealed at the moment Simon, Margreth's brother, comes to adopt the youth. She listens patiently and reacts passively to her brother's proposal: "Margreth ließ sich geduldig auseinandersetzen, wie groß der Vortheil, wie gering die Entbehrung ihrerseits bei dem Handel sey. Sie wußte am besten, was eine kränkliche Witwe an der Hülfe eines zwölfjährigen Knaben entbehrt, den sie bereits gewöhnt hat, die Stelle einer Tochter zu ersetzen. Doch sie schwieg und gab sich in Alles" (5/1:11).

Even Friedrich's aggressive outbursts prior to his adoption provide evidence of his feminine side. Nollendorfs has noted Margreth's profound emotional loyalty toward her family was intended by Droste-Hülshoff to be seen as a feminine characteristic, opposed to male tendencies to engage in the self-serving rationality that can lead to a betrayal of loved ones. Friedrich's battles with other children in defense of his father's memory thus reflects his mother's typically female sense of obligation and devotion to kin.[10]

Most readings of *Die Judenbuche* tend to regard Friedrich's early feminine upbringing in a negative light. Even feminist readings of the novella such as Patricia Howe's merely see it as one of many elements that combine to create an instability in his identity (38). However, given the rapaciousness and brutality that characterize the male Mergels and Semmlers, the distancing of Friedrich from the feminine component in his rearing when he is on the verge of adolescence must be seen as contributing to his ultimate downfall. The withering or stripping away of the childlike *and* the feminine is associated in the four poems discussed earlier with displacement, profound loss, and, indeed, disaster. The circumstance that Friedrich is a male does not mean he is immune to the problems caused by the very same metamorphosis. When he is adopted by Semmler, he casts off his graceful, innocent, and gentle persona. It does not rearise as a narrative haunting of the sort found in "Durchwachte Nacht" and "Doppeltgänger," where the ghostly girl's pristine, emotionally vital, and wondering gaze comes forth intact from the narrator's distant childhood. Instead, it reemerges, distorted, in his Doppelgänger, Johannes Niemand.

Niemand is introduced to the narrative in a manner reminiscent of the appearance of the ghostly Doubles in Droste-Hülshoff's poetry. In the novella as well, the Double first haunts the story in the evening, when a confusion of identities is most likely. This confusion is enhanced when the narrator ironically drops her omniscience and refers to the figure Margreth sees in her dark kitchen *as* Friedrich, albeit transformed into a wretched figure lacking vitality: "Als sie wieder in die dunkle Küche trat, stand Friedrich am Herde; er hatte sich vorn übergebeugt und wärmte die Hände an den Kohlen. Der Schein spielte auf seinen Zügen und gab ihnen ein widriges Ansehen von Magerkeit und ängstlichem Zucken. Margreth blieb in der Tennenthür stehen, so seltsam verändert kam ihr das Kind vor" (5/1:13).

Margreth's bafflement and fear increase when the figure she takes for her son responds incoherently to questions she poses. Finally convinced the child before her is not her offspring, she calls out Friedrich's name. Only then does he appear, with a new vigor, ambition, and self-confidence which stand in marked contrast to Niemand's pathetic feebleness. As Friedrich approaches Niemand right after Margreth calls out his name, Niemand is described as Friedrich's "verkümmertes Spiegelbild" (5/1:13–14). As Heinz Rölleke has noted, this scene represents Friedrich's casting off of his childhood self. The "larva" of the boy raised as a girl takes on life as Johannes Niemand, who is Simon's illegitimate offspring. Friedrich, in turn, begins to take on the physical attributes of his uncle (1970:225–26).

In Niemand, Friedrich's early gentle femininity is turned into its shadow side, abject and passive victimization. Johannes is abused by Mergel junior much as Margreth had been abused by Mergel senior. Mergel junior becomes the dynamic and aggressive masculine Other as he emerges into adolescence from childhood. In Jungian terms, Friedrich's abandonment by the external female with whom he has a primary bond causes him to reject his inner female. This process is heightened through the absolute lack of a developed anima in the man who adopts him. To be sure, as Gertrud Pickar indicates, "criticism directed at Margreth for allowing Simon to assume the custodianship of her fatherless child fails to take into account that, in the world Droste depicts, it was not unusual for the paternal role to be taken from the mother and given to a male authority figure" (87, n. 22). But regardless of the justification one might grant Margreth in this case, the fact remains that such an act must exercise an enormous psychological impact on the child. The puberty Friedrich was undergoing at the time would have created personality changes at any rate, but the added shock of adoption by a man whose spirit was absolutely antithetical to that of his mother brings about a virtually dialectical transformation. Friedrich's Doppelgänger represents his cast-off feminine persona, the inner female twisted into its most grotesque form through the violent suddenness with which it is discarded.

Friedrich loses more than a well-functioning anima when he experiences his metamorphosis. In his essay on the uncanny, Freud notes that the representation of the Doppelgänger is not purely a phenomenon of primitive narcissism. In the personality's later developmental stage, a discrete, second or double ego may develop, split off from the first. The primary ego will then treat the second ego as an object. This objectified Double is known to our conscious mind ("Bewußtsein") as moral conscience ("Gewissen") (12:247–48). Given his abject behavior in Margreth's presence—he acts as though guilty of some abysmal deed—we may also characterize Johannes Niemand as the objectification of this moral conscience shed by Friedrich. Johannes is, in such a reading, guilt in its pure form, pure because unmotivated by any actual crime. Only later in the tale does Johannes commit a theft; given his role as Friedrich's Double, we may regard this offense as a prefiguration of the tale's ultimate, far greater misdeed.

This image of Johannes Niemand as Friedrich Mergel's turbulently cast-off anima and moral conscience is consistent with his secretive nature. As Benno von Wiese has observed, *Die Judenbuche*'s tendency to conceal secrets and thereby communicate them is especially acute in the scenes involving Johannes. But as he goes on to note: "Der Doppelgänger, der Schatten oder Halbschatten Johannes, hat zwar nichts von dem Mysteriösen der romantischen Dichtung. Johannes ist ganz real der uneheliche, vom Vater verleugnete und mißbrauchte Vetter des Friedrich" (163–64). Contrary to the Romantics, Droste-Hülshoff does not heighten the aura of the uncanny mystery surrounding this Double in order to highlight his alterity vis-à-vis the outside world and a more quotidian primary ego. Instead, his murky or shady character helps imbue the novella with an ambient mystery designed to allow its central mystery to strike the reader with maximum effect: Who reappears in the village after years spent in Turkish captivity? Who hangs himself on the Jew's beech tree? Niemand's ambiguity allows Droste-Hülshoff to increase the impact of the confusion of identities. But as von Wiese indicates, Niemand is quite prosaically realistic in his role as the neglected bastard of Simon Semmler and as Friedrich Mergel's abused cousin. There is a subtle condemnation here of the way Restoration Germany's illegitimate offspring were treated, a social criticism more in line with Poetic Realism's priorities than those of Romanticism.

The uncanny configuration of Johannes and Friedrich in connection with mysterious criminality is introduced earlier in the tale, with Niemand's second appearance. Margreth has received the shocking news from a court reporter named Kapp of the forester Brandis's death. Friedrich has just responded to his mother's anguished reaction to this news by asking her to let him sleep in peace. Johannes enters the house, pale, skittish, and tattered, as when Margreth first saw him. He has come to fetch Friedrich and bring him to Simon Semmler, who has tasks for him. At first, Friedrich sarcastically refuses to accompany his cousin. But after Margreth briefly leaves the room, she returns to find he has changed his mind: "Sie ging auf einige Minuten hinaus; als sie zurückkam, war Friedrich bereits angekleidet.—'Was fällt dir ein?' rief sie, 'du kannst, du sollst nicht gehen!'—'Was seyn muß, schickt sich wohl,' versetzte er und war schon zur Thüre hinaus mit Johannes.— 'Ach Gott,'seufzte die Mutter, 'wenn die Kinder klein sind, treten sie uns in den Schooß, und wenn sie groß sind, in's Herz!'" (5/1:22). Through an unarticulated and inscrutable dynamic, Friedrich is persuaded to change his mind.

There is a gap in the text when Margreth leaves the room. The reader has no concrete clue about what brings her son to drop his bitterly expressed resolve to remain at home. But given the psychological forces Friedrich's maternal abandonment has set in motion, and knowing Johannes Niemand has become his Double, we cannot be surprised at his sudden about-face. Margreth's unexplained departure from the room triggers associations with her forsaking her son to a domineering male figure who exercises such complete sway over him that they have begun to attain a physical resemblance. The minutes alone with Johannes bring about the reconstellation of Double and original, the confused blending of antithetical but immanently enmeshed identities. Left alone, the Doppelgänger reconnects the primary ego's subservience to the masculine authority figure who dominates them both.

The difficulty in unraveling this entanglement and establishing their discrete and coherent psychic identities is the primary factor in generating the ambient uncertainty, ambiguity, and indeterminacy Heinrich

Henel characterizes as the dominant stylistic feature of *Die Judenbuche* in his highly controversial essay on the novella. Henel refers to "Das Spiegelbild" in this essay as Droste-Hülshoff's core poem, the key to comprehending her entire lyric output. As he notes, the features revealed by the mirror to the observer in "Das Spiegelbild" seem to belong to two completely antithetical and antagonistic souls, but nevertheless they blend together (167). Precisely this dialectic is at work in the relationship between Friedrich and Johannes. This is what brings about Friedrich's sudden change of mind in the previously cited passage, and what makes the novella's ultimate mystery so plausibly implausible to resolve.

The dialectic of subterranean division and merging, bonding and repulsion between Friedrich and his Double is manifested on an external level through their mutual but differentiated involvement in the generic activity that constantly drives the novella's plot: crime. Friedrich's possible complicity in the Brandis murder becomes most striking in his conflicted reaction to Niemand's awkward attempt to bring him back to Semmler; the dynamics of the exchange make us at least suspect Friedrich has been seduced by Semmler into a criminal life-style, is trying to pull away from his uncle and this criminality, but is drawn back into their vortex through a Double who seems to personify the primary ego's guilty conscience even though, at this point, the Double is still innocent of wrongdoing. When Johannes does commit a misdemeanor—the theft of a half-pound of butter—his ineptness immediately guarantees the crime's disconcealment; the butter drips through the handkerchief in which it is bound and through his pocket when he passes near a kitchen fire at a wedding dance. Friedrich reacts with rage to his cousin's botched pilferage, beating and kicking him. However, his domineering violence collapses into its opposite after he drives off his cousin. Feeling his dignity wounded by the incident, he displays an abject despondency and instinct to cower (he feels the urge to run and hide behind a bass viola) heretofore evident only in his Double. His humiliation becomes far more profound shortly thereafter when the Jewish peddler Aaron publicly accuses him of not yet having paid off a watch he has just displayed in order to counteract his shame at his cousin's theft (5/1:28–29).

Three days later, Aaron's murder is revealed by his hysterical widow. She discovers his corpse in the same Brederholz where Brandis was murdered, and where some in the local populace perceived the ghost of Friedrich's father, who, like Semmler, was a violent brute. The conjuration of the old Mergel's spirit in connection with Friedrich's public humiliation by Aaron hints at the younger Mergel's complicity. But

Droste-Hülshoff's subtle spiritual imbrication of Friedrich and his superficially antithetical Double Johannes Niemand causes the reader to hesitate at this conclusion, and our doubts concerning Friedrich's unequivocal guilt are confirmed by the circumstance that he and his Doppelgänger disappear from the village on the same day (5/1:35).

Maruta Lietina-Ray has argued convincingly that both Friedrich and Johannes are victims of class prejudice and a related judicial blindness. These social defects, subtly attacked by Droste-Hülshoff, rather than absolute textual evidence itself, are what implicate Friedrich as the unequivocal murderer and, later, suicide. One might add that not only Droste-Hülshoff's psychological intertwining of Friedrich with his Doppelgänger and their contemporaneous disappearance make it difficult to determine which "individual" is alone guilty, but their mutual marginalization through societal, class-based abuse further tends to conflate their identities. Indeed, when the individual who claims to be Johannes and whom most critics assume is really Friedrich returns to the village after allegedly spending years in Turkish slavery, the guilt-ridden abjectness of the Doppelgänger rather than any features one associates with Friedrich as a young man is the dominant external attribute described by the narrator: "Eine armselige Figur! mit schiefem Halse, gekrümmtem Rücken, die ganze Gestalt gebrochen und kraftlos" (5/1:36). If this is truly Friedrich Mergel, one must find that his guilt and repentance have completely transformed him, spiritually and physically, *into* his Double.

The willingness of the village to accept the prodigal son's assertions concerning his identity reflects a further social dynamic Droste-Hülshoff is able to articulate through her employment of the Doppelgänger motif. Wilhlem Gössmann has argued it is in the village's best interest to assume the pathetic stranger is telling the truth when he claims to be Johannes Niemand. The townspeople could not allow the execrated Friedrich Mergel back into their fold, but to condemn the wretched figure after so many years would call into question the presumed Christian charity and selfless love of one's fellow man professed by this patriarchal, class-driven society. By taking "Johannes" at his word, the town permits itself to be seen in a positive light, capable of showing pity to a pitiable, quasi-blameless figure (162–63). The use of the Double subtly to expose social hypocrisy is a hallmark of Poetic Realism; we will see this tendency at work in Keller and Storm, for example. By creating a Double shown to possess a genuine if marginalized place in the social fabric rather than being a product of poetic fantasy, Droste-Hülshoff can reveal how this society will act in its own best interest when forced to distinguish between two immanently conflated identities. The suicide's scar brings the village squire to proclaim the corpse belongs to Friedrich (5/1:42), but this belated recognition is rendered suspicious by its occurrence only at the first moment it no longer causes any inconvenience.[11]

Nevertheless, *Die Judenbuche* is not primarily concerned with social criticism, but with the problematic of personal guilt and repentance. Although the refugee from Turkish slavery is tolerated by the villagers and even treated with some generosity by the squire and his wife, his obviously unquiet conscience causes the noblewoman to prophesy his bad end (5/1:40). It appears the artificial Christian charity displayed to the murderer would allow him to live out his life quietly, but the forces that determine his fate are largely circumscribed by the Old Testament. As Rölleke (who assumes the suicide is Friedrich) remarks: "Mergel bleibt wesentlich im vor- und unchristlichen Raum befangen" (1968: 422). If the contemporary hypocrisy delineated by Gössmann permits an escape from retribution, then an earlier, implacable order—the law of the victim's people—must prevail. To be sure, contrition marks the refugee's very first act, his Canossa-like fall to his knees in the churchyard snow on Christmas Eve (5/1:35–36). New Testament associations with Johannes Niemand's name, as well as the timing of his return at Christmas, also point to ultimate divine forgiveness, redemption in the Beyond.[12] However, earthly justice must first be served. Johannes distortedly incorporates Friedrich's cast-off anima, his humility, gentleness, moral conscience, and tractability. The salvation signified by his name is Christian, but the salvation his deeds and his persona evoke in his role as Friedrich's Doppelgänger is resonant with the eternal feminine as Goethe understood it. Just as Margarete must die to redeem Faust, the refugee must die to resolve Friedrich's psychic imbalance. Double and primary ego become united through repentance, final retribution, and death at the end of a dialectical process that began as division engendered by damaged and abused childhood; this is why only one individual returns to the village though two had fled. Thus, the narrated ego finds integration through the refugee's repentance and death.

If the refugee's obvious contrition and the circumstance that he dies known to the world as Johannes point to salvation, what accounts for the novella's final bleak lines? We learn at the tale's conclusion that the corpse of the suicide is buried—as Friedrich Mergel—in a carrion pit. A touch of realism is added by alluding to the date of this allegedly authentic episode, and the story closes with a translation of the Hebrew writing on the beech tree, with its now fulfilled prophecy: "'Wenn du dich diesem Orte nahest, so wird es dir ergehen, wie du mir gethan hast'" (5/1:42). Heselhaus suggests one reason for this emotionally desolate conclusion. The novella's foundation was provided by the supposedly reality-based tale "Geschichte eines Algerier-Sklaven" (1818), penned by Droste-Hülshoff's uncle August von Haxthausen. Heselhaus argues Droste-Hülshoff's alteration of this tale's close—in Haxthausen's story, the lines on the tree become effaced by the bark's growth and the tree is cut down two years after the suicide—is an act of "lightly modified reality." He claims the admonishing Hebrew script illustrates an aesthetic concept penned by Otto Ludwig, one of Poetic Realism's most prominent theorists and the object of the next chapter. Ludwig argued the "metaphorical thought" ("bildlicher Gedanke") was the artistic device most suited to satisfying the contradictory demands of fantasy and reason, the conflicting pull of imagination and reality. In creating such a metaphoric thought in the script's warning, Heselhaus believes Droste-Hülshoff is able to create an irresistible suggestive power (163–64). The novella's conclusion is thus in line with Poetic Realism's priorities; Realism seeks to move the reader through credible symbolic signifiers rather than through a contrived "happy end" that might foreground the resolution of conflicts, especially when conflicts and their resolutions are engendered by fantastic devices such as Doppelgänger.

With regard to *Die Judenbuche*'s plot, one may seek a different explanation. Although Droste-Hülshoff's onomastics and the refugee's contrite behavior point to repentance for Aaron's murder, no suggestion is made that Friedrich atones for his depredations of nature. As with his possible complicity in the Brederholz murders, Droste-Hülshoff subtly places Friedrich into the sphere of the "Blaukittel," the poachers who practiced a horrendously destructive forest clear-cutting. The complicity is suggested mainly through Friedrich's conversations with Brandis shortly before the forester's murder. Thus the fulfilled prophecy of the Hebrew script signifies the warning of a doubled author: not just the village's Jews, but the beech tree itself, a metonym for the natural world. Stripped of his anima and his childhood, Friedrich devastates not only his mother, but mother nature. As her Doppelgänger poems suggest, the loss of the feminine and the childlike has painful consequences. In *Die Judenbuche*, these consequences are only partially obviated by a contrition enacted through the merging of Double and primary ego. This merging may point to spiritual salvation, but it cannot ward off nature's revenge.

2. The Double, the Alter Ego, and the Ideal of Aesthetic Comprehensiveness in "Der poetische Realismus": Otto Ludwig

While Droste-Hülshoff is often regarded as a transitional figure in the development of German Poetic Realism, Otto Ludwig is one of its most seminal figures.[1] Indeed, until Clifford Bernd's recent (1995) study treating the Scandinavian roots of Poetic Realism showed otherwise, most scholars assumed Ludwig's two brief essays on "Der poetische Realismus" gave the movement its name. In the second and more critically celebrated of the two treatises, Ludwig attempts to situate Poetic Realism between the extremes of Naturalism and Idealism. The Naturalist, according to Ludwig, is overly concerned with artistically representing the natural world in its variety, while the Idealist sacrifices too much of this rich variety in the attempt to evoke a spiritual, metaphysical unity. Poetic or artistic Realism, in Ludwig's view, would strike a balance between the two poles. While the Idealist is chiefly concerned with "Einheit" and the Naturalist is obsessed with "Mannigfaltigkeit," the Poetic Realist's desideratum should be the evocation of a "Totalität." Precisely by steering between the Scylla of Idealism and the Charybdis of Naturalism, the Poetic Realist can achieve such completeness. This middle course rejects both the idiosyncrasies of Romantic fantasy and the uncohesiveness associated with an exaggerated focus on the common and everyday. The Poetic Realist's dramatic world (both essays focus on the dramatic genre) is mediated by a "schaffende Phantasie." Ludwig was an accomplished musician, and he relies on musical terminology to explain how the dramatist can attain artistic totality. For example, dialectical comprehensiveness in dramatic characterization is described as "eine Polyphonie mit allen Arten doppelten Kontrapunktes" (S1:458–62).

Double counterpoint is central not only to Ludwig's drama theory, but to his own practice as both a creative dramatist and prose writer. Throughout the typological range of his oeuvre, Ludwig creates pairs of physically and spiritually antithetical characters as a primary technique of achieving the aesthetic totality he regarded as the central goal of Poetic Realism. Nevertheless, Ludwig consistently if unintentionally brings the representation of discrete but polarized protagonists as the key to artistic comprehensiveness into contiguity with the portrayal of a single but internally split persona. Edward McInnes has noted that Ludwig regarded the realistic novel as a genre ideally and primarily "devoted to the study of the divided self" (704), and often characters who seem to be mirror opposites in Ludwig's works are actually facets of one comprehensive poetic ego. Ludwig's first essay on "Der poetische Realismus" is, like the second, governed by the telos of demonstrating that the creative representation of totalities must guide those who would identify with the movement. The dramatist strives to portray a "Totalität des Gefühles" (S1:265), and must chiefly envisage what sort of "Totaleindruck" (S1:266) his or her drama would achieve. Here, too, Ludwig would have his readers believe that this ideal comprehensiveness can only come about when the dramatist avoids both a focus on coarse reality and an overreliance on illusory fantasy. An example of the Naturalist reality Ludwig disdains is the grossly corporeal. The dramatist must portray a protagonist's "natural soul" and allow the "pure body" to fall away: "Soweit die Seele den Leib schafft, sozusagen, die bloße Form des Leibes steht verklärt auf aus dem Grabe" (S1:265). This body-soul dichotomy is closely allied to Ludwig's Doppelgänger and ego–alter ego thematics in much of his prose oeuvre. One character's actions and personality are directed and developed by carnality and egotism, while his or her opposite is driven by exaggerated spiritual ideals. But a closer observation will reveal that these antagonists are but two sides of one coin, who together form the "totality" of a single persona.

In a letter dated 3 July 1857, Ludwig reveals the key reason his contrapuntal characters often seem to constitute a single personality, a dialectically comprehensive "Totalität." The letter was written to German Poetic Realism's other great theorist, Julian Schmidt, and shows that the effort to comprehend the world in its totality is, in actuality, the attempt to understand the self and its reasoning: "Ja, lieber Freund, Sie geben sich Mühe, einen vernünftigen Menschen aus mir zu machen; denn der Glaube an die Vernünftigkeit des Weltganzen ist am Ende nichts weiter, als Folge des Bedürfnisses, die eigene Klarheit auch außerhalb Unserer wiederzufinden und an dieser Weltvernünftigkeit wiederum unserer eigenen gewisser zu werden" (S2:393). Ludwig's letter shows his belief that the Poetic Realist must above all strive for the representation of artistic totalities is not primarily tied to the common dictum that such totalities alone result in aesthetic pleasure. The doctrine of art for art's sake celebrated by Poe, Coleridge, Walter Pater, and the French

Symbolist poets, who all stressed the importance of the artwork's comprehensive quality, was entirely foreign to Ludwig and the other German Poetic Realists.

Instead, the evocation of the world in its wholeness is designed to show the logic or reasonableness ("Vernünftigkeit") underlying its foundation and its operations. The need to believe in this logic stems from the need to believe that one's own personal universe, and one's own Being, are also governed by it. As Hans Steiner has indicated in his discussion of this letter, Ludwig confirms here a belief in a dynamic interchange between personal and subjective reason. Human nature is the starting point of both Ludwig's epistemology and his aesthetics. However, human nature in its relationship to nature as a whole can be defined in terms of the microcosm-macrocosm duality. The reason that moves and guides the universe moves and guides the individual as well (69). Given this perspective, it is not surprising that Ludwig invokes Goethe and Shakespeare in describing the contours of Poetic Realism: "Mit Shakespeare und Goethe finden wir immer die Naivität mit der höchsten Bildung, mit dem nach allen Seiten hin ausgebildetsten Geiste zusammen" (S1:460).

More importantly, the letter to Schmidt allows us to see why Ludwig consistently strove to create exhaustively circumscribed protagonists. The reason governing the world can only be glimpsed when we reflect on the world in its totality. On a microcosmic level, human nature must be considered and portrayed in a similarly comprehensive manner if the dynamics of subjective logic are to be understood. Ludwig notes, in agreement with Schmidt, "der Dichter solle in seinem kleinen Ganzen ein Spiegelbild des großen geben" (S2:394). By means of a dialectic we will also see at work in Meyer, namely, the narrative juxtaposition and synthesizing of primary ego and alter ego, Ludwig attempts to achieve such totality in his artistic representations of the individual.

How does the Poetic Realist achieve a wholeness of characterization in the literary work without succumbing to exaggerated Romantic fantasy or the Naturalists' bent for exhaustive detail? He or she must strive to represent the *typical* in a protagonist's personality: "Mit der reintypischen Behandlung ist die Geschlossenheit, Ganzheit, Einheit, Vollständigkeit, Übereinstimmung und Notwendigkeit, d. i. die *poetische Wahrheit* gesetzt" (S1:68, Ludwig's emphasis). If the artist focuses his or her fantasy on representing the *characteristic* behavior of specific personality types, then the confusion of the real world's complex individuals does not perplex the spectator or reader, for the endlessly manifold nature of genuine people will not have to be artistically delineated. The use of creative fantasy to separate the wheat from the chaff in literary figuration and in portraying the external world makes realism poetic for Ludwig.[2] If, in spite of the need for wholeness, clarity, and simplicity in this figuration, Ludwig also maintains that the realistic novel should explore the *split* self, a division caused by "those processes, often ambiguous and desultory, through which the individual was driven to adjust to external change and to the disruptive forces within his own unknown being" (McInnes 704), then we see another reason he adapted the Romantic Doppelgänger motif to his own Poetic Realism. Such split selves—physically discrete manifestations of a single ego—allow Ludwig both typological simplicity and psychological comprehensiveness in the development of his protagonists, and he can thus adhere to Poetic Realism's seemingly conflicting desiderata.

Nevertheless, Ludwig's early prose, written when he was most strongly and directly influenced by German Romanticism, is anything but a model of clarity with respect to characterization. *Die wahrhaftige Geschichte von den drei Wünschen* (written in 1842–43, first published in 1890) shuttles constantly back and forth from the quotidian reality of nineteenth-century Leipzig to fantastic Oriental tableaux. The repeated shifts from prosaic everyday life to settings imbued with the Romantic grotesque are inspired by E. T. A. Hoffmann; indeed, his influence is tacitly acknowledged by the primary narrator at the story's outset: "Weder die Tausendundeine Nacht noch ihr in Berlin verstorbener Vetter, der selige preußische Kammergerichtsrat Hoffmann, hat eine wundersamere Geschichte erdacht, als die ist, die ich selbst erlebt habe und die ich dir nun erzählen will" (1:109). As in Hoffmann, figures in the realistic scenes of this story possess Doppelgänger in the fantastic passages. The relationship between primary egos and their Doubles is underscored by the story's onomastics. For example, the publisher Jammerdegen is also the Indian wise man Jamadagni in the Oriental tableaux, as the primary narrator himself points out at the tale's conclusion (1:173).

Die wahrhaftige Geschichte von den drei Wünschen is, like Hoffmann's *Der goldne Topf* (1814–15), the story of love and ambition thwarted in the real world but fulfilled in the fantastic realm. The primary narrator, whose tale "Zu stille Liebe" weaves in and around the *Geschichte*'s numerous interpolations, is (like Ludwig at the time) an unsuccessful young author. He encounters three equally impoverished *Literati*, friends whose wildest erotic, professional, and material dreams are realized but quickly vanish into thin air when they violate promises they made to their Oriental princesses. These princesses turn out to be the same Indian nymphs constellated in three pages apparently translated from an ancient Sanskrit document possessed by the young author and primary narrator, who has his auditor read these pages at the tale's outset during moments when his emotions so overcome him that he cannot continue relating his tale.

The *Geschichte*'s Doubles, inspired by Ludwig's reading of Hoffmann, largely reflect his desire to engage in Hoffmann's late Romantic dialectics. Ludwig described this telos in a diary entry as follows: "Unsichtbarkeit—Doppelsichtbarkeit, so weit zu treiben, als dem Zauberer gefällt, so daß ein einziger ein ganzes Heer scheint" (1:xxxv). But while the reader of Hoffmann's Double visions effortlessly follows his seamless transitions from the real to the fantastic and back, the *Geschichte*'s five narratives packed into one brief tale are so jumbled and confusingly interpolated that it is quite difficult to tell who functions as a Doppelgänger for whom.[3] For example, the publisher Jammerdegen is onomastically associated with the wise man Jamadagni, and Jamadagni's daughter Vasantasena is also Fides, Jammerdegen's daughter and the object of the primary narrator's passion. Vasantasena and her sisters (who become the lovers of the three *Literati* in the *Geschichte*'s fantastic tableaux) live together, according to the Sanskrit manuscript, in the most perfect harmony until they accidentally abuse Chyavana, a wise man covered with ants after years of immobile meditation. They mistake his eyes for precious stones in an anthill and poke them out. He curses them to live apart, a curse that can only be lifted if a wealthy editor is willing to publish a manuscript by an unknown author and offers the author the hand of his only daughter in marriage (1:127–28). This putatively redemptive trio clearly exists in the *Geschichte*'s real-world sphere as Jammerdegen, the primary narrator, and Fides. Nevertheless, Jammerdegen also seems to function as Chyavana's Double, for he is portrayed as deeply contemplating the lowest of his five gold buttons in a manner almost identical to the way Chyavana contemplates his navel (1:127, 129).

Aside from Hoffmann's far greater adroitness in juxtaposing the real and fantastic worlds, along with the Doppelgänger who link these realms, the Romantic author tends to reconcile the two spheres in a manner allowing a satisfying resolution to the dualism. Heinz Puknus has shown that the fissure between the everyday and the fantastic in Hoffmann's oeuvre coincides with the confrontation between artist and bourgeois that generated so much late Romantic literature. This conflict, in whose interstice many of Hoffmann's Doppelgänger emerged, is resolved in favor of the aesthetic-imaginative realm in *Der goldne Topf*; this tale's happy ending places the poet Anselmus in the ultimately "higher reality" of Atlantis and poetic fantasy (54–55). In other tales, the bourgeois realm is given its due as the proper space of limited but productive life. In Hoffmann's last fairy tale, *Meister Floh* (1822), the two planes come together in ultimate harmony as the imaginative but sensible merchant's son Peregrinus Tyß becomes one with his Doppelgänger, the fantastic figure King Sekakis. But in these as in most tales of Hoffmann, love itself attains the power to resolve dissension between the prosaic and artistic, real and imaginative, ego and alter ego (60–61). Love's transformative force is often able to bridge the gap between Doubles and allow a cohesive, productive, and happy personality to emerge in this late Romantic writer's works.[4]

Inspired though it was by Hoffmann, *Die wahrhaftige Geschichte von den drei Wünschen* does not suggest the ultimate confluence of the quotidian and the fantastic. Rather, it ends on a discordant note, as the author-narrator's aesthetically lovely dream world is shown to be entirely illusory, indeed, the product of insanity. This narrator had prefaced his tale with the words "Ich kann's durchaus nicht ertragen" (this is the first sentence of the *Geschichte*), and what he finds unendurable is the resemblance of the present day to the one on which he first glimpsed Fides. He claims his tale would drive him mad "wenn ich nicht besser wüßte, wie es sich damit verhält" (1:109). What threatens his reason is the knowledge, revealed at the *Geschichte*'s conclusion, that the real life Fides has married someone else. The illusion that allows the narrator to avoid a plunge into utter despair is the belief that Jammerdegen-Jamadagni will eventually reunite him with his daughter Fides-Vasantasena. He believes her powerful yearning will achieve this wish and thereby fuse the prosaic Leipzig father and daughter with their fantastic Doubles, a success consistently achieved by Hoffmann's heroines. Indeed, this fusion had taken place in the narrator's dream, a dream that brings together all of the *Geschichte*'s primary Doppelgänger pairings in an ecstatic, erotic manner also reminiscent of Hoffmann's triumphant, synthetic tableaux (1:170–73).

What might have been the ultimate scene in a Hoffmann fairy tale is only the penultimate episode in Ludwig's. *Die wahrhaftige Geschichte von den drei Wünschen* ends with the narrator awakening from his dream in the same restaurant where he had heard the tales of the three *Literati*. He had entered the "Walderich'sche Restauration" in a highly feverish state, shortly after a friend had revealed to him that Fides was engaged to someone else (1:130). When he finds himself in this establishment after his synthetic vision, he asks Walderich what has become of its fantastic figures and Jamadagni, who he explains is Jammerdegen in his "Inkarnation." Walderich is astonished at hearing of the exoticisms experienced by the narrator, an astonishment that helps reveal that they are but a figment of the unhappy suitor's delirious imagination.

However, Walderich does note that Jammerdegen had visited his restaurant on the previous day with his son-in-law (1:173–74); this latter figure is the "Begleiter" the narrator had seen in Jammerdegen's company just before plunging into his synthesizing dream (1:171). The narrator doesn't understand Walderich's reference to a son-in-law until the restaurateur shows him an engagement announcement. His reaction to finding Fides a few weeks later in a list of newlyweds indicates his entire tale, "Zu stille Liebe," was what psychoanalysts now call a reaction formation, imaginatively invented to deflect the unbearable shock of the, for the narrator, tragic news: "Wüst' ich nicht, daß Fides-Vasantasena durch die Bitten und Tränen ihrer Sehnsucht ihren Vater bewegen wird, mich nachzuholen, so—nein! ich muß an andere Dinge denken sonst... erleb' ich's gar nicht einmal" (1:174).

Lee Jennings has noted "a profusion of Romantic elements and fairy tale motifs" in Ludwig's early (1840s) oeuvre, but he argues that "such Romantic elements as are present already show an orientation toward new realistic ideals" (1963:86). *Die wahrhaftige Geschichte von den drei Wünschen* confirms Jennings's analysis. I have concentrated on showing how one particular Romantic motif, the figure of the Doppelgänger as conceived by Hoffmann, is employed by Ludwig in this youthful tale. One can also find already in this work an initial attempt to approximate the ideal of typological comprehensiveness achieved by juxtaposing physically and emotionally antithetical individuals who together constitute an aesthetic totality of the sort upheld by Ludwig in his theoretical treatises on Poetic Realism,[5] a tendency predominant in his later work. But ultimately, Ludwig employs Hoffmann's devices not so much in support of still-to-be articulated Realist ideals as to deflate the ideals of late Romanticism. The artistic-fantastic realm valorized by Hoffmann and other Romantics as a creative and redemptive sphere emerges in the *Geschichte* as purely illusory, the product of a tormented mind seeking imaginative solace from harsh real-life disappointments. The use of the Doppelgänger motif to deflate Romantic priorities and to turn Romantic ideals on their head, and the treatment of fantastic Doubles as a product of escapist dementia brought on by disappointed love, anticipate Dostoevski's procedure a few years later in *The Double* (1846).

Ludwig's conflicted fascination with Hoffmann is also evident in his dramatic adaptation (written in 1848 and first published in 1870) of Hoffmann's novella *Das Fräulein von Scuderi* (1818). Ludwig's recasting of Hoffmann's tale as a drama naturally has consequences for his articulation of the Doppelgänger motif subtly enacted in the original version. Nevertheless, there are thematic and ideological variations evident in a comparison of the two works. Although Ludwig's theatrical piece retains Hoffmann's title, his central protagonist is not the eponymous heroine who risks her reputation at the court of Louis XIV to save young Olivier Brusson, assistant to the malevolent goldsmith René Cardillac and unjustly accused of the great artist's murder, from a seemingly certain execution. Instead, the internally tortured Cardillac himself is the axis around which Ludwig's drama revolves. In both the original and Ludwig's variation, Cardillac seems to possess two souls. The city of Paris knows only the positive side of his Double persona, his "day" side, the extraordinarily gifted artist and loving father to Madelon, who is herself the object of Brusson's passion. For most of the story, only Brusson is aware of Cardillac's evil, nocturnal aspect, the figure who murders his noble customers under cover of night in order to regain the artistic creations from which he cannot bear to part. Both Hoffmann and Ludwig create such a polarity in Cardillac's psyche that he seems to be two beings at once, constituted by a creative genius and his murderous Double. Through his Cardillac's dramatic monologue, Ludwig is able to highlight this Doppelgänger motif more forcefully than Hoffmann with his detached narrative description: "Nun ist es zehn erst—und kaum das.—Das ist / Mein Morgen; da wird meine Seele frisch / Und stark. Ein Anderer bin ich bei Nacht" (5:186).

Ludwig's Cardillac possesses two distinctly antipodal souls. In constellating the personality of his great jeweler, Hoffmann did not use such a radically "contrapuntal" approach (to borrow Ludwig's term—see S1:462—indicative of the proper technique for achieving a "poetically realistic" dramatic characterization). Indeed, Hoffmann wanted to show the powerful fusion between madness and artistic genius, a common late Romantic theme. To be sure, he also created two apparently discrete personas, a day and night Cardillac. However, his Cardillac is also possessed of a slyness, a base cunning that stoops even to obsequiousness when it serves his purposes, as when he fawns over Brusson when the latter discovers the truth about his night life (Hoffmann 3:688–89). This trait mitigates his radical dualism, but this radical dualism is evident in Ludwig's Cardillac. This later Cardillac is a truly tragic figure, whose split self is the result not of his demented virtuosity but of his lineage. Rather than fawning on Brusson when his assistant learns he is the murderer feared by the Parisian nobility, Ludwig's Cardillac admits to his assistant that he is a "Scheusal" (5:167).

In the course of this long monologue, Cardillac reveals that his father was an indentured servant with a gift for making jewelry and a pregnant wife whom his master found attractive. The master seduced Cardillac's mother with the father's own artistic creations. The master attempted to get the jewels back, thereby revealing the seduction, and

Cardillac's father was killed in the ensuing duel. The mother lapsed into insanity, becoming fixated on the ill-starred gems (5:168–69). Hoffmann's Cardillac is also cursed at birth; in her first month of pregnancy, his mother was seduced by a jewelry-bearing cavalier. As he embraced her, she grasped for his beautiful chain. At that moment, the nobleman died of a stroke. Despite her shock, she was successfully delivered of the infant Cardillac (Hoffmann 3:691–92). Both Cardillacs are thus imbued with their murderous fixation as a result of prenatal trauma and maternal madness. But as Expeditus Schmidt notes in his introduction to Ludwig's play, the origin of Cardillac's madness—his split or doubled personality—subtends a social critique, a hatred for the nobility lacking in Hoffmann's narrative (5:xxvi). This shift in the employment of the Doppelgänger motif as primarily an affect of aesthetic genius in Romanticism to its engagement in the service of a veiled social critique in Poetic Realism was also evident in Droste-Hülshoff's lyrical adaptation of a theme in Tieck's *William Lovell*, as was noted in the previous chapter. When we consider that Ludwig wrote his play amid the tumultuous social upheaval of the revolutionary year 1848, it can come as no surprise that his reworking of Hoffmann's novella is tinged with a political polemic absent in the original.

Of course, Ludwig did not intend Cardillac's revelations concerning his ill-fated origins to absolve him of guilt. Instead, they allow us to see the murders as stemming from *tragic* guilt. Ludwig's view of this dramatic movens has been well summarized by Helmut Schanze: "Tragik wird bestimmt als Kampf der Leidenschaft mit dem Bestehenden; immer entstehe sie in einem Schuldzusammenhang" (385). The passionate, irresistible bond that ties Ludwig's Cardillac to his bejeweled artistic creations, his psychological inability to part with them even after he has sold them to the noblemen who use the jewels to win the affection of their mistresses, is tied to his hatred of the existing social order. The murders he commits in the guise of his nocturnal Being stem from this hatred and constitute his "battle" against the status quo. The "nexus of guilt" that leads to his tragically split self—artist by day and assassin by night—is inexorably linked to a rage against the political hierarchy.

This rage suffuses Ludwig's Cardillac from his earliest childhood. While Hoffmann's Cardillac steals gold and jewels as a boy to satisfy his youthful fixation (3:692), Ludwig's Cardillac perceives the removal of any precious stones from his circle of vision as a theft by someone else. In addition, unlike the juvenile Cardillac in Hoffmann's tale, the boy despises "Alle, die genossen, / Ohne zu schaffen, während der Arbeiter / Aus seinem eignen Schweiß sein dürftig Brot / Nicht kneten darf, gibt er das Beste nicht / Dem faulen Dränger hin" (5:169). Although this contempt is often enunciated in Cardillac's sarcastic remarks to his noble customers and their servants, it mainly expresses itself in the activities of the goldsmith's deadly nocturnal second self. In representing a destructive fixation engendered prenatally by a web of guilt, which causes its bearer to passionately and murderously contest the ruling elite, the wealthy parasitic aristocracy, Ludwig's dramatic praxis here closely corresponds to his theoretical views on the tragic genre. His ability to achieve this harmony between theory and praxis is linked to his adaptation of Hoffmann's Doppelgänger motif to suit his political and aesthetic ideology.

To be sure, Ludwig was not an overtly political author, particularly after hopes for radical change were dashed as the year 1848 came to a disappointing close. Hermann Korte has even argued in his book *Ordnung & Tabu: Studien zum poetischen Realismus* that Poetic Realists, most prominently Ludwig, devoted their creative energies to masking fissures, disparities, and conflicts in Germany's social order. "Poetic" reality, in this view, has little to do with authentic life as most people experienced it. Rather, the movement presents a falsely harmonious and euphonic vision of mid-nineteenth-century existence. Thus Ludwig's Poetic Realism is "ein striktes Programm zur Harmonisierung und Glättung aller Widersprüche der Realität mit den Mitteln der Poesie" (17). Certainly, an overtly sociocritical stance is generally lacking in Ludwig's mature oeuvre. Nevertheless, in his exploration of the human psyche in later works, Ludwig highlighted to the greatest possible degree the contradictions and polarities existing between various antithetical types of people and, to a lesser degree, within individuals. Only by elucidating, and sometimes exaggerating, these contrasts did Ludwig feel it was possible to approximate the aesthetic totality he believed should be Poetic Realism's chief goal. Although he borrowed less from the Romantic repertoire of the supernatural, macabre, and fantastic—even refuting the grotesque elements of his erstwhile inspiration, Hoffmann (Korte 19), in pursuing his artistic ideals later in life—he intensified his use of a "contrapuntal" variation of Romanticism's Doppelgänger device. It was, indeed, his chief means for portraying the human soul in its comprehensive (as opposed to naturalistically variegated) complexity.

Ludwig's antipodal, or dialectical, approach is evident in the title of the first of his two most significant and acclaimed mature prose works, *Die Heiteretei und ihr Widerspiel* (written in 1854, first published in 1855–57). This opus actually consists of two separate stories, "Die Heiteretei" and "Aus dem Regen in die Traufe." There are characters common to both narratives, though their plots are quite discrete. The integrative title suggests that the respective heroines of the two tales are physical and psychological opposites, and, to a large extent, this is indeed the case. The "Heiteretei" (Annedorle) of the first tale is, as her name suggests, a relentlessly cheerful figure. She is proud to be able to support herself and her sister's illegitimate daughter by doing odd jobs and farm work. She scorns the attention of men, and nearly kills the strapping Holders-Fritz by acting on a serious misapprehension that results from the gossip of the prominent women in her imaginary town of Luckenbach in Thuringia (where both stories take place), to the effect that he is stalking her to avenge a humiliation at her hands. When it is believed that he did indeed drown in the brook into which Annedorle, in her fear, plunged him late one night, the women turn against her. Too proud to appease them and therefore quickly mired in poverty, she nevertheless sustains her hearty good nature in public, and ultimately marries Holders-Fritz when all the misunderstandings (including the events surrounding his disappearance) are cleared up.

Annedorle's "Widerspiel" in "Aus dem Regen in die Traufe" is indeed her antipode. Though also strong and self-reliant, she has dark features (she is only known as "die Schwarze") in contrast to Annedorle's blondness. Reversing Annedorle's diffidence, she uses her wiles to seduce the diminutive tailor Hannes Bügel into betrothal. Once she has achieved this goal, it becomes evident that her personality is diametrically opposite to Annedorle's. She is tempestuous, greedy, ill-humored, and so domineering that she intimidates even the tailor's equally forceful mother. Indeed, Hannes was largely attracted to "die Schwarze" because he saw in her a way to escape maternal violence, but it becomes clear that marriage to his authoritarian bride would create even greater physical danger for him. Only through the ruse of a prospective marriage to Hannes's wealthy apprentice is the tailor able to escape his fiancée and marry Sannel, the house's other occupant, whom he had overlooked as a potential partner until the apprentice's attraction to her awakened his own interest.

Annedorle and "die Schwarze" are not the only antipodes in the two Luckenbach stories. Hans-Heinrich Reuter has pointed out other characteristic contrasts and counterpoints in Ludwig's figuration of the tales. The tailor Hannes's intertextual relationship with Holders-Fritz mirrors the liaison implicitly existent across textual boundaries between Annedorle and Sannel. Hannes's intimidation finds its antithesis in the defiant manliness of Holders-Fritz, while Sannel's servility contrasts with Annedorle's stubbornly independent nature. Another contrapuntal effect is engendered by the two stories' respective plots; the "Heiteretei" invests much of her energy in avoiding marriage in order not to *lose* her independence, while the tailor's attempt to find a robust, energetic wife (before meeting "die Schwarze," he has designs on Annedorle herself) is motivated solely by his desire to *win* independence (345).

Jennings has noted this juxtaposition of opposites in some of the minor characters, for example, "an obese lady and an extremely thin one, who, taken together, represent the two poles of feminine girth" (1963:78). In both these examples, one can see Ludwig's striving for a dialectical synthesis in his representations, for the evocation of an aesthetic and psychological totality which lies at the core of Poetic Realism as he defined it. But if Annedorle-Sannel on the one hand, and Holders-Fritz–Hannes on the other, constitute antipodal pairings, then the *actual* couplings toward which the two plots each progress, and ultimately attain in their climaxes, must be tacitly informed by a bisexual Doppelgänger effect. Indeed, there is a remarkable congruence between Annedorle and Holders-Fritz. Both are physically imposing, defiant, and given to bravado. Both value self-reliance and freedom from the control of others above all, though Holders-Fritz only gradually acquires these traits as he falls in love. Sannel and Hannes are diminutive, often cowed, and constitutionally driven to interdependence rather than independence; even the tailor's dream of freedom relies on affiliation with a substitute mother figure.

One could argue, of course, that similarities between the two individuals in each couple simply foreground their compatibility, and make the nuptial unions with which each tale closes more plausible. However, when one observes them with Ludwig's own musically influenced aesthetic perspective in mind, the counterpoint effect of the two couples seen in their intertextual relationship can be regarded as harmonically balanced by the fusion of each protagonist to his or her sexual Other within the *intra*textual filiations. In other words, if the couples are to counterpoint each other across textual boundaries, man and woman must mirror each other within each text. In this structural sense, then, the Doppelgänger motif is enacted in *Die Heiteretei und ihr Widerspiel*.

This dialectic of Double and Other as a means for attaining the comprehensiveness Ludwig saw as Poetic Realism's chief goal is evident in individual passages of these polarized but twin texts as well. Annedorle's refusal to apologize to Luckenbach's leading women for throwing them out of her house after they reverse their sympathy and imply she is guilty of murdering Holders-Fritz virtually destroys her standing and the esteem she enjoys in the community, and this emboldens her sister, whom Annedorle had banished from their parental home, to come and attempt to visit her illegitimate daughter. Her appearance at the door inspires the following comparison with Annedorle, a comparison informed by the synthesis which the Double-Other dialectic enacts: "In der Tür erschien eine weibliche Gestalt, kleiner als die Heiteretei und ihr zugleich so ähnlich und unähnlich, als ein Mädchen dem anderen sein kann. Es waren zwei ganz verschiedene Worte, aber mit denselben Schriftzügen geschrieben. Eben das, worin ihre Ähnlichkeit lag, machte sie sich so unähnlich." There follows a series of contrastive physical descriptions designed to juxtapose Annedorle's chaste and virtuous nature with her sister's putatively wanton and dissolute sensuality.

The comparison ends with an extension of the contrasts to encompass the entirety of their Beings: "Und ähnlich verhielt es sich mit Denkart, Stimme, mit dem ganzen Wesen" (2:209–10). One is reminded here of Droste-Hülshoff's mirrors and reflective water surfaces, the refractions of which constitute Beings at once opposite and identical, though Ludwig, unlike Droste-Hülshoff, clearly valorizes the virginal in this coupling. There is even an uncanny quality to Ludwig's description; the sudden appearance of an overtly sexual woman after the bulk of this long tale had been almost asexual in its characterizations, and her juxtaposition with the diffident but now familiar Annedorle, bring about the clash of the strange and commonplace generative of the uncanny, the liminal atmosphere Freud associated with the scene of the Romantic Doppelgänger's emergence.

The dialectic between the strange and familiar also comes to the fore when Sannel attempts to persuade Hannes not to marry "die Schwarze" by comparing her with Annedorle in "Aus dem Regen in die Traufe." Parallels between the two women—their physical strength, resilience, independence, authoritativeness, and self-reliance—had been clearly perceived by the tailor. He finds either one would be an ideal wife, for either could protect him from his mother. In spite of their identical qualities, however, "die Schwarze" is not a fully fleshed-out character. Ludwig allows her background to remain largely a mystery, and her name in a deeply racist period in Germany's history would act as a cipher resonant with foreboding, obscurity, and latent violence for Ludwig's contemporary readership. From an intertextual perspective, she is indeed Annedorle's "dark" side, incorporating as she does all the threatening qualities the Occident saw—and many of its inhabitants continue to see—in a woman who is physically and emotionally stronger than most men, and who doesn't need their custodianship. Her "blackness" and relative foreignness in Luckenbach make her function as Annedorle's "Widerspiel," causing her to absorb these qualities. She thereby deflects them from the blond and cheerful Annedorle, whose status as post-Romantic nineteenth-century heroine is enhanced by her ultimate obeisance to Holders-Fritz.

Annedorle is not a protagonist in "Aus dem Regen in die Traufe." She is merely an object of discussion, as Hannes ponders her as a potential bride. This circumstance allows her to function as an implicit foil to "die Schwarze," a role evident in Sannel's gentle admonition to the tailor concerning the mystery woman: "Guck', wenn die Heiteretei hereingekommen wär', da wär' ich ruhiger gangen. Denn die Heiteretei kenn' ich, und es ist keine Brävere im ganzen Ort; aber von der weiß man nichts. Man weiß nicht, wer ihre Küh' und ihre Ziegen sind. Und wenn sie noch solche Augen hätt' wie die Heiteretei, wo die helle Guttat herausleucht't." "Die Schwarze," by contrast, has false eyes and is two-faced (2:295). She is not a phantasmagoric Doppelgänger like the Oriental princesses in *Die wahrhaftige Geschichte von den drei Wünschen*; such characters are not evident in Ludwig's writing after his initial pseudo-Romantic phase ended and he became one of Poetic Realism's leading champions. Nevertheless, her opaque background, her "strangeness" in the bucolic German village setting of *Die Heiteretei und ihr Widerspiel*, a physical "blackness," violence, and duplicity cast her as Annedorle's malevolent alter ego, and this shows the continued influence of Romanticism's gothic aspect in Ludwig's later adaptation of the Doppelgänger motif.

Such exoticism is generally lacking in Ludwig's most famous tale, the novel *Zwischen Himmel und Erde* (1856). This story of two brothers with completely contrasting personalities, rivals in love and in their work as slaters (though the virtuous Apollonius Nettenmair wishes only to live in harmony with his sibling Fritz), is the sole work in Ludwig's corpus to have attracted substantial critical attention. Understandably, the chief interest for most of the novel's analysts is generated by the relationship between polar opposites. Ludwig's bent for juxtaposing antithetical protagonists in order to attain the "Totaleindruck" (S1:266) that he made Poetic Realism's highest ideal reaches its climax here. Apollonius is gentle, self-effacing, selfless, chaste, temperate, reflective, and introverted, while Fritz is violent, egotistical, self-centered, dissolute, extravagant, heedless, and gregarious. One could continue to expand this list of binary oppositions to some length because the brothers represent the extreme ends of the psychological spectrum. However, precisely this extremity of contrasts creates a mirrorlike relationship between the two brothers. Some critics have perceived this circumstance, such as Jörg Schönert, who has noted that Apollonius's renewed ability to act responsibly and ethically in the world after a period of extreme self-doubt can be seen to function "spiegelbildlich zum sittlichen Verfall von Fritz" (159).

What allows this mirroring function to work is the assumption held by each brother that the Other is really his second self. They see in each other the reflections of their own personas, and though this is their tragic error,[6] this psychological nuance is what allows their truly antipodal personalities to be displayed to the reader. Two external factors bind them together: the father for whom they both work as slaters, and the woman, Christiane, to whom they are both attracted. We learn of their common interest in Christiane through one of Apollonius's flashbacks toward the outset of the novel, just before he reenters his hometown after a long sojourn in Cologne. His remembrance reveals at this early stage a great deal about the dynamics of his relationship and the two brothers' respective personalities. At a dance, Apollonius had been too shy to declare his love to Christiane. Fritz offers to be his go-between; under this ruse, he courts the young woman, and they marry.

Through the use of a shift in narrative perspective, Ludwig draws a parallel between Apollonius's return and his father's return from Cologne to work on the slate roof of the village's St. George Church thirty-one years earlier. At the outset of the old Herr Nettenmair's recall, there is a sudden shift to the memory of Apollonius under similar circumstances (3:8). This confusion of identities and events previews the development of more profound parallels in the personas of the father and his two sons. Old Herr Nettenmair imbued Apollonius with his work ethic and deeply felt sense of social, ethical responsibility, but Fritz inherited his temperamental need to dominate everyone and everything in his sphere of influence at all costs. The two sons personify the father's torn and tormented ego, that "divided self" (McInnes 704) Ludwig explored largely through the Doppelgänger and ego–alter ego motifs. This rent in the father's psyche is even reflected in the representation of the Nettenmair estate, described in great detail in the novel's opening pages (3:3–7).[7] The intensification of the split in the souls, words, and deeds of the two brothers drives the novel's plot. Fritz believes his authority as husband, father, and inheritor of the directing role in his father's business, that is, his ability to be dominant in all areas of his life, is threatened by his brother's return. This leads to his self-destruction; he alienates his family and nearly destroys the business (which suffered under his egotism even while Apollonius was in Cologne). Finally, in attempting to kill Apollonius by pushing him off St. George's tower, he falls to his own death. As they gradually discover the secret of Fritz's duplicity and suffer under his paranoid brutality,

Christiane and her children shift their affections to his brother. However, though his love for Christiane is mutual, though Apollonius becomes a hero after saving the town and its church from a fire, and though his own father also wants the two to wed after a period of mourning has passed following Fritz's funeral, Apollonius's feeling of guilt in connection with his brother's tragedy, his overwrought sense of morality and responsibility, preclude a nuptial bond.

Several critics have indicated that the brothers are actually united by their antithetical pathologies. For example, William Lillyman has argued that their projections are self-duplicating; each brother envisions the death of the other (76–77). Richard Brinkmann finds they possess something in common in their polarity, namely, an inability to perceive reality, a tendency to distort the real world because of their obstinacy (210). The novel itself often juxtaposes them, creating the mirroring quality, the imbrication of Double and Other so common to the Doppelgänger motif in Ludwig. They are both, for example, shown consistently on a precipice: Apollonius "between heaven and earth" and Fritz "between earth and hell." Despite the contrast in moral overtones here, Ludwig indicates *both* instances of precarious liminality stem from the brothers' respective delusions (3:68). As in *Die Heiteretei und ihr Widerspiel*, Ludwig uses these opposite yet parallel protagonists to attain the aesthetic totality and comprehensiveness in characterization in which he grounded his theory of Poetic Realism. As we will see in the next chapter, a similar ego–alter ego dialectic is at work in Meyer.

What is unique in *Zwischen Himmel and Erde* is the presence of a certain "mimetic desire" that enhances and complicates the ego–alter ego relationship. This concept was developed by René Girard to indicate a primary force in civilization, which is reflected in many canonic works of world literature. It signifies the attraction to an object triggered not by inherently pleasing or alluring features of the object itself, but simply by the fact that someone else, a rival, desires it. In the process of civilization, the clash of interests inevitably brings about discord. This leads to a scapegoating process; one contestant in the play of desires is constellated as the sole source of the ills suffered by the community through the lack of order engendered by the clash. His sacrifice unites the populace, and becomes thereby the forge of its civilization. In literature, a triangular relationship is often informed by mimetic desire. The erotic fascination exerted by one person on another is triggered solely because someone else has first found that object attractive. Such is the case in "Aus dem Regen in die Traufe"; Hannes has spent his entire life in the same house with Sannel, but he only begins to find her beguiling sexually when his apprentice expresses his admiration for her beauty

(2:314). However, this does not lead to the Double-engendering conflict implied by Girard's term, for the apprentice does not attempt to contest the tailor for Sannel's hand when Hannes makes his intentions clear.

To be sure, contestation is also apparently absent in the love triangle of *Zwischen Himmel und Erde*. Apollonius's passivity and lack of self-confidence preclude any contest for Christiane's affections. Fritz's initial interest in Christiane is stimulated solely by Apollonius's ecstatic praise: "Wie das Mädchen das Ziel war, nach dem alle Wege seines Denkens führten, so hielt es ihn, war er bei ihr angekommen, unentrinnbar fest. Er vergaß den Bruder so, daß er zuletzt eigentlich mit sich selbst sprach. Der Bruder schien all das Schöne und Gute an ihr, das der Held in unbewußter Beredsamkeit pries, erst wahrzunehmen" (3:13). Apollonius sees nothing devious in the circumstance that the brother who had volunteered to act as intermediary with Christiane ends up winning her love. The courtship between Fritz and Christiane takes place primarily while Apollonius is living in Cologne, under the tutelage of his commercially successful cousin, at the suggestion of his brother, who claims residence in the big city will teach his awkward sibling how to behave with women. Apollonius comes to assume and accept that Fritz was foremost in Christiane's mind from the outset of their triangular relationship.

However, Fritz's guilty conscience, as well as his inclination to judge Apollonius solely on the basis of his *own* character, turns his brother, in his own mind, into a rival for his wife. Girard argues that rivals in the triangular relationship become Doubles as they imitate each other in an ever heightened degree during the courtship process. The attempts by one contestant to distinguish himself from the other result in constant reciprocity, and this intensifies the Doppelgänger scenario: "This disconcerting return of the identical exactly where each believes he is generating difference defines this relationship of the doubles, and it has nothing to do with the *imaginaire*. Doubles are the final result and truth of mimetic desire, a truth seeking acknowledgment but repressed by the principal characters because of their mutual antagonism. The doubles themselves interpret the emergence of the doubles as 'hallucinatory'" (41). Ludwig's novel provides Girard's linkage of mimetic desire to the creation of Doubles an instance of dialectical reversal, for the emergence of the Doppelgänger occurs *precisely* in the "imaginaire" of Fritz Nettenmair. In the jealousy first instantiated by mimetic desire, he makes Apollonius his *assumed* rival and Double. His inability to judge his brother beyond the dictates of his own bad faith *create* a "hallucinatory" Double, but one that, in Fritz's mind, is real. The same process occurs in Apollonius, though his Fritz is a projection of his own selfless intentions and sense of responsibility. The process of *hallucinatory* doubling intensifies in a manner parallel to the narrative's delineation of the brothers' actual, "real" differences, and culminates in the tragedy played out on the tower of St. George Church.

Though Fritz's death brings little happiness in its train, as Apollonius's unnatural feelings of guilt do not allow him to fulfill the profound wish shared by Christiane, old Herr Nettenmair, and Apollonius himself for a marriage with his brother's widow, it does restore a balance and equilibrium to the family and the community. In this sense, the death represents a Girardian sacrifice, the act necessary to restore civilized order to a disturbed social nexus. Indeed, shortly before Fritz's violent end, when circumstances surrounding the accidental death of a slater in the nearby town of Brambach give old Herr Nettenmair good reason to believe the victim was Apollonius and his demise was perpetrated by Fritz, the father orders his son to commit suicide. When Apollonius turns up safe and sound in spite of Fritz's best efforts, the father commands the evil son's banishment to America.

Instead, Fritz determines to bring the conflict spawned by the dynamic of mimetic desire being played out in his own head to its logical conclusion; either one brother must plunge to his death from the church tower, allowing the other to gain sole possession of the desired object, or they must both die. This intention is evident in his first words to Apollonius after he climbs the stairs leading to the church's pinnacle in order to settle the matter: "Du sollst sie allein haben oder mit hinunter!" (3:165). Of course, it is Fritz himself whose death closes out the tumultuous, Double-engendering cycle of mimetic desire. To be sure, his demise does not represent the sort of sacrifice Girard singles out in his anthropological investigations as the means by which societies put an end to this violence when it threatens the commonweal. The true scapegoat is an "arbitrary victim" who will only retrospectively "appear responsible both for the violence that raged when it was alive and for the peace that is restored by its death" (165). Fritz Nettenmair does not fit this definition. Instead, he must be "sacrificed" by the narrative because the Girardian "mimetic crisis" (165) unravels strictly within the confines of his own psyche, with potentially catastrophic results for the external world. He is thus not an arbitrary victim, but his violent end predictably produces the same restorative results as the sacrifice of an innocent.

Ludwig did not create scapegoats of the sort found by Girard in his anthropological and literary studies, arbitrary victims of societies whose death is inscribed by a falsely all-encompassing guilt created only in retrospect. For particularly after the 1840s, Ludwig rejected the notion that external circumstances should be represented as responsible for personal tragedies. As Georg Kurscheidt has indicated, Ludwig's own "Anthropologie" maintained "daß der Mensch ein völlig autonomes Wesen sei, nicht Produkt, sondern Produzent seiner Umwelt" (238–39). This does not mean Ludwig intended that his protagonists be judged solely from the perspective of morality. For although the social milieu constellated in *Zwischen Himmel und Erde* is not to be held accountable for the ethically flawed behavior, the misdeeds committed by Fritz (such a direct connection would have constituted an etiology of the criminal of the sort favored by the Naturalism Ludwig detested), he is too tragic a figure to be unconditionally condemned. His culpability is clearly linked to unfortunate character traits, particularly the need to dominate, inherited from his father; in this sense, he is old Herr Nettenmair's own malevolent alter ego.

However, Ludwig's belief in individual responsibility, a belief enunciated in the novel's concluding paragraph when the narrator proclaims "Nicht der Himmel bringt das Glück; der Mensch bereitet sich sein Glück und spannt seinen Himmel selber in der eigenen Brust" (3:204), also means Fritz is not simply guilty "by reason of insanity," to use today's judicial parlance. Psychological and moral perspectives come into conflict here and create a contradiction in the novel, a contradiction Schönert sees as paradigmatic for Poetic Realism as a whole. While those affiliated with this movement believed that concrete reality as the psyche experienced it should be contemporary poetry's foundation, Poetic Realists such as Ludwig had to adjust this reality poetically when it didn't conform to an ideal totality ordered by the ethical domain's motive force, a totality that sublates all dissonances (167). But regardless of this aporia, evident in spite of Ludwig's best efforts to create a harmonious ethical universe in the novel, he makes it clear that no individual, public body, or extenuating circumstance should be regarded as responsible for Fritz's downfall.

If Fritz Nettenmair was to be shown as the sole agent of his own demise, then his defective internal mechanism had to be delineated in its broad circumference. In order to achieve such comprehensive characterization, indeed, in order to approximate the psychological and aesthetic totality Ludwig believed was no longer available to individual apprehension in real life (Kurscheidt 280–81), Ludwig drew on the Romantic Doppelgänger motif throughout the course of his career. At its beginning, Ludwig's Doubles resembled those of Hoffmann in their exoticism, though this similarity was calculated to deflate the idealism of Romantic aesthetics. At his career's height, Ludwig used the figure of the divided self to achieve in practice what he championed in theory, to attain what he saw as Poetic Realism's chief goal. This was the production of works of art mediated by creative fantasy, and "keine sogennante phantastische Welt, d. h. keine zusammenhangslose, im Gegenteil, eine, in der der Zusammenhang sichtbarer ist als in der wirklichen, nicht ein Stück Welt, sondern eine ganze, geschloßne, die alle ihre Bedingungen, alle ihre Folgen in sich selbst hat," and whose characters "als Totalitäten vor uns stehen" (S1:458).

3. The Oriental Alter Ego: C. F. Meyer's *Der Heilige*

In his seminal book *Orientalism*, Edward Said traces the evolution of this field as an academic discourse that places the Orient under the sign of an exotic but fundamentally negative alterity. This psychic distancing from the Orient is performed in order to pave the way for its colonialization by the West. Said notes that the Orient has almost always been for Europe "one of its deepest and most recurring images of the Other" (1). Just two pages later, he states his book "tries to show that European culture gained in strength and identity by setting itself off against the Orient as a sort of surrogate and even underground self" (3). Though both these assertions are consistent in indicating Europe's projection of itself as radically different from the Orient, the image of the Orient as surrogate self to Europe seems to contradict the hypothesis that the Orient served as a primary source for European visions of the Other.

Said's statements are not so much self-contradicting as they are illustrative of the deep-seated entanglement binding the motifs of the self and the Other in colonialist discourse on the Orient, particularly in the French and English literary works he discusses in his book. Of course, this entanglement is not restricted to literature dealing at some level with the Near, Middle, or Far East, those regions which (along with Africa) were most intensely subjected to English and French colonization in the nineteenth century. In the introduction, we took note of Paul Coates's plausible though somewhat overly global assertion that the acts of reading and writing themselves are largely generated by a Double-Other dialectic (Coates 1). Nevertheless, Said's book shows us how the insertion of the Orient into this space encompassing the existence of literary fiction can be elucidated to characterize not just the consciousness of individual writers and readers, but to reveal how an entire continent created, in some measure, its own self-image by generating protagonists who evolve highly ambiguous identities. European ambitions and ideals are transposed onto colonial subjects in such literature, while Western characters evolve what the reader is meant to perceive as Oriental attributes. In extreme instances of this tendency, such as the one we will examine, seemingly antithetical personas blend; the Oriental

"Other" becomes the Occidental narrator's alter ego, that is, not just his "Other" but his "other I."

Although Said's book justifiably focuses its literary analysis on works produced in the nineteenth and early twentieth centuries by the two great colonialist powers of that time, England and France, he shows that the peculiar mix of alterity and identity mediating Oriental motifs in the literature of this time was not restricted to English and French literature. For example, the "completion and confirmation" of the imaginative self through a "return" to the Orient as a site of both origin and difference is a fundamental theme in Goethe's poetic cycle *Westöstlicher Divan* (1819) (Said 167–68). This chapter will explore the treatment of the Orient (or, better, the Oriental) as it leads to the overlap of the ego and the alter ego in another seminal work of nineteenth-century German literature, Conrad Ferdinand Meyer's novella *Der Heilige* (1879). *Der Heilige* narrates the later life and death of a highly fictionalized and orientalized Thomas à Becket (he is transformed into the progeny of a Saxon father and an Arab mother) as described by the invented figure Hans Armbruster, a Swabian crossbow maker in King Henry II's court, where Becket serves as chancellor of England and, later, archbishop of Canterbury. Meyer's endowment of Becket with a "Saracen" heritage was not his own invention, but stemmed from his reading of Augustin Thierry's *Histoire de la conquête de l'Angleterre* (1825), which elucidates Becket's legendary background.[1]

The vital role of Orientalist thinking as a key element in Meyer's novella has been treated in previous Meyer scholarship. Indeed, the subtitle of one of the most recently published essays on the novella is "Orientalism in C. F. Meyer's *Der Heilige*." But though this essay, a chapter in Robert Holub's book on German Realism (152–73), demonstrates the way in which stereotypical views of the Orient and Orientals played a major role in shaping Meyer's narrative, it does not indicate that the dialectic of identity and difference underlying the relationship between Becket and the tale's narrator, Hans Armbruster, is itself the structural principle for Orientalism's manifestation in the novella. Holub's assertion—"Hans, whose career otherwise parallels Becket's in a remarkable and, as we noted above, somewhat artificial fashion, endeavors to distinguish himself from the saint with respect to Orientalism" (169)—will be amplified and corrected by this chapter. Previous secondary literature has attempted to underscore these characters' similarities or, in the case of Holub, their differences. The central hypothesis of this chapter holds that Becket is Hans's alter ego, a dialectic inversion of his own Being. Indeed, the parallels and the distinguishing features in the personas of Becket and Hans (and, as we will see, other figures as well) *together* constitute Orientalism as a central motif in *Der Heilige*.

The parallels in the careers and personalities of Hans and Becket—the network of associations allowing them to be seen, on a certain level, as ego and alter ego—are actually more profound than Holub's statement would suggest. To be sure, there is no inference that the two figures are marked by the sort of close physical resemblance suggested by the term "Doppelgänger" in its literal meaning. They do not share the external traits characteristic of Droste-Hülshoff's mirror and water images, cousins, and dream-conjured past selves. Ludwig's Hofmannesque couplings, his blood brothers, and even opposite sex pairings are more look-alikes than Hans and Becket. Thus, *Der Heilige*'s protagonists can only be regarded as ego and alter ego, and this by virtue of a remarkable confluence in their respective personal histories. Of course, on the surface, the temperamental and apparently rather naive Swabian seems to have little in common with the shrewd, calculating Englishman. But Kathleen Komar has pointed out parallel features in their lives. Both underwent formal religious education in their youth. Both spent time in, and became conversant with, the Islamic Orient. Both fail in their attempt to prevent catastrophe from befalling a young woman; Hans cannot rescue his first English employer's daughter, Hilde, from a rapacious Norman courtier, and Becket is unable to shield his own daughter, Gnade, from his sovereign's lust. They are motivated by morally commendable aims, but outward circumstances transform their designs into disastrous consequences. Employment at the court of King Henry is responsible both for their elevation and their ultimate downfall.

Gunter Hertling has shown how Meyer uses a bow ("Bogen") motif to evoke the mutual travels, histories, and destinies of Hans and Becket. Tamara Evans offers further, very precise parallels: both Hans and Becket are characterized by a manipulative smile, both are defrocked monks who had had themselves consecrated for opportunistic reasons, both are versed in the art of deception, both resided in Islamic Cordova. Both, of course, are bound in servitude to the same sovereign, though Hans displays, for the most part, a rather neutral attitude toward the king, with whom he has little in common. Evans even sees a parallel in Becket's political machinations to bring about Henry's downfall and Hans's ability through his story to unsettle profoundly the somewhat smug auditor to whom it is addressed in the present narrative frame, Canon Burkhard (74). And as even Holub notes, "the ambiguity of Becket's actions, motives, and statements parallels the epistemological ambiguity that riddles Hans's endeavor to relate his story" (166).

An examination of Meyer's subtle emphasis on the problem of rhetoric and narration in connection with the saint and his narrator further enhances their status as ego and alter ego. Parallels in their lives and personal characteristics establish a consistent background for the projection of such a dialectic, but this dialectic is only truly enacted in the novella when linguistic representation becomes, as it were, self-conscious. During the Romantic age, when the Doppelgänger theme gained both its name and its greatest popularity, the Double was quite literally a re-presentation of the original protagonist, usually an exact physical duplicate of this individual and often a material manifestation projected forth from the protagonist's psyche. Works of German Poetic Realism such as *Der Heilige*, while often alluding to their own fictive character, never flaunt their fabricated quality; this is one reason why they are considered "realistic." Thus, they avoid such resolutely Romantic devices as the transformation of a mental attribute into a corporeally discrete Double. Rather, when Poetic Realists wish to highlight their narration's status as a work of art, the evocation of the "other I" occurs in the space where aesthetic representation is deliberately made a theme within the fictive metatext. This is particularly evident in Storm, as we will see. In *Der Heilige*, the artifice of speech comes to the fore in the following exchange between narrator and auditor:

"Oft habe ich dabeigestanden, wann der Kanzler den König, dessen zur Jagd gesattelte Pferde schon im Schloßhofe wieherten und stampften, noch beim Überschreiten der Schwelle aufhielt, seine Rollen vor ihm entfaltete und den Unbändigen durch den Zwang seiner milden Worte nötigte, ihm Gehör zu schenken, und ich mußte mich wundern, wie er, den Stift in der einen und das Pergament in der andern Hand, Herrn Heinrichs hingeworfenen Bescheid wiederholte und entwickelte, denselben in eine schöne, geschmeidige Rede verwandelnd, daß es nur so strömte, wie flüssiges Gold."

"Auch deine Rede strömt, daß ich mich wundern muß," stichelte der greise Chorherr.

(13:37)

In a manner not unrelated to Romantic irony, Burkhard underscores the rhetorical, polished, and thus deceptive quality of linguistic representation by calling attention to the identity between the flowing character of Hans's framed narrative and the flowing speech Hans attributes to the central figure in his tale. In an often cited missive to Hermann Lingg dated 2 May 1880, Meyer noted that Becket's thoroughly diplomatic nature was directly tied to the experience of oppression he suffered as a Saxon or an Oriental (13:298). Holub correctly indicates that Hans the Swabian is similarly victimized; both Becket and Hans are subjected to the Norman court's prejudice (156). However, Hans's narrative gifts clearly stem from his immersion in the language and customs of Islamic Spain as well. In relating his sojourn there to Burkhard, he describes the seductive artistry and speech he experienced in Granada, which put his Christian faith to the test. It is there he discovered and learned to appreciate the gift of spinning ingenious fairy tales. There is both censure and praise in his remark that the Moors lie with greater sincerity, as a result of their powerful and vivid imagination, than the Christians. Early in this phase of Hans's narration, his auditor betrays a suspicion that he might be infected by the Oriental perspective (13:21–23), and Burkhard's taunting remark that Hans's speech is as flowing as the rhetoric Hans attributes to Becket shows this suspicion continues as the narration progresses. It is this suspicion, fueled by Hans's highly mannered speech, that leads Burkhard to unite narrator and narrated figure, to highlight their parallels under the sign of Orientalism.

The contiguity established between Hans and Becket within a common rhetorical style that bears the traces of an Oriental discourse is not restricted to one episode. In addition to the mutual possession of an "arabesque" fluency in European tongues (differentiations between which are almost absent in the novella), Becket and Hans are bonded by their command of the Arabic language itself. This brotherhood becomes most evident when Hans visits Becket while the chancellor is in mourning for his deceased daughter Gnade.

Becket had kept this daughter, the offspring of his relationship with an Arabic woman, hidden in one of his castles, but the king discovered and seduced her; it is suggested she succumbed to his advances partly due to her inherent Oriental deference to authority. When the king discovers a plot against her life, he orders Hans to lead her to safety in Normandy. As they flee the castle, an arrow meant for him fired by one of Becket's soldiers kills Gnade. The king assumes Becket will forgive him (an assumption again partly based on Becket's Oriental and thus "passively" accepting nature) and enlists Hans to send him a message. Naturally, Hans reenters Becket's Moorish castle with some trepidation. At the sight of Becket prostrate next to his daughter's coffin, Hans is moved with an inexplicable force (brought on by a memory of "das maurische Wesen in Granada") to recite, in Arabic, a verse from the Koran. When he hears the verse, the chancellor's demeanor undergoes a powerful transformation: "Es glitt eine Bewegung der Freude und Liebe darüber hin. Er wandte sich langsam zu dem, der ihn mit diesem Koranvers getröstet hatte" (13:65). Hans's reference to himself in the third person enhances his own temporary (but always latent) foreignness, his Oriental kinship to Becket in the brief moment of his recital and Becket's loving and joyful response. Though Becket's joy turns to loathing when he becomes aware of the king's seal on the letter Hans gives him, the scene establishes once again their affiliation on the linguistic plane.

In a chapter in his book on German Poetic Realism which treats *Der Heilige* as a paradigmatic example of this movement because of its precise yet often highly stylized and symbolic approach to detail, Walter Silz remarks that "nowhere else has Meyer interwoven his narrator so closely with his narrative" (98).[2] One might add that Meyer's precise attention to material details, which he invests with a symbolic content, itself plays a major role in establishing the kinship between Hans and Becket. This is especially true with regard to the novella's "Bogen" metaphor, used concretely in connection with Hans Armbruster's profession, but also symbolically to establish Hans's deep entwinement with Becket.[3]

In addition to evoking their fungible character denotatively and through symbols, Meyer conflates the identities of Hans and Becket by creating parallels in their rhetoric. In the course of describing the meeting at which Henry reveals to a reluctant Becket his wish to see Becket consecrated as the archbishop of Canterbury, Hans attempts to quote at great length the views expressed at that time by the chancellor on the deeply corrupt "body" of the church, which stands in inevitable contrast with its virtuous "soul." While citing Becket's views on the reasons why this circumstance makes it advisable to choose an openly vice-ridden, sinful abbot as primate, Hans is interrupted by an irritated Burkhard, who finds it impossible to believe that, even before his conversion, the future saint could make such a blasphemous suggestion; he asserts that such ideas must be those of Hans.

Hans's response, which continues the somewhat anti-Catholic Meyer's obvious barbs against the church's constitution and dogma, also admits to the conflation of his speech with that of Becket. He concedes Becket may not have used the exact words Hans attributed to him. Though his narrative is true to the spirit of Becket's speech, some of his own spirit may have slipped into his citations: "Daß aber etwas von dem Meinigen beifloß, ist nicht unmöglich, denn leider beten wir alle dieselbe Litanei, sobald auf die Sitten der Pfaffheit die Rede fällt" (13:83). The often described ambiguity in Hans's narrative partially stems from the auditor's, reader's, and Hans's own inability clearly to distinguish the narrating voice from Becket's. The "heathen" (at this point in the narrative) chancellor and the avowedly Christian Armbruster mingle their voices in condemnation of the church, thus strengthening the sense of their common outsider status, their alienation stemming partly from an acquaintance with an alternative, Oriental world.

Of course, Becket's attitude toward the church, and toward Christianity in general, changes radically upon his assumption of the archbishop's office. But this does not mean we are supposed to believe he has cast off his "Saracen" attributes; when Meyer describes his character in the letter to Lingg as "Orientalisch nachtragend, ich will nicht sagen: rachsüchtig, aber doch (gegen Laster u. Gewaltthat) feingrausam" (13:298), it appears Meyer intended Becket's abrupt adoption of an ascetic life, and the latter's campaign to rid England and its church of vice and corruption, to be seen as a calculated act to destroy the king (which, along with Becket's own martyrdom, is indeed its result), an act motivated by his "orientally vengeful" nature. But Becket's deeds have a positive result as well; they help to instill in the church and its pious Saxon followers a sense of renewal and hope.

Even in his role as instigator of a populist campaign for ecclesiastic purification, Becket may very well reflect Meyer's Orientalism. Said has noted that an extremely powerful paradigm operating in nineteenth-century Europe—initially employed by Romantics such as Schlegel and Novalis but most vitally manifest in the age of Flaubert (and thus Meyer)—was a belief in "the regeneration of Europe by Asia" (115). As a site of both origin and difference, the Orient was seen by Europe as an inspiration for reinvesting itself with a sense of volition and purpose. As a writer who, in his early years, was deeply steeped in the writings of German Romanticism[4]—and *Der Heilige* was one of Meyer's early novellas—Meyer may very well have intended his readers to see a link between Becket's capacity for inspiring regeneration, and the latter's alterity, his Oriental background.

As we noted, the German Romantics were also the first group of writers to exploit fully the motif of the Doppelgänger. Azade Seyhan has shown how the Orient served the German Romantics as a backdrop to scenes where a Western subject is transfigured through a dialectic interchange with an antithetical, Eastern character who is often only the evil aspect of the former's own self (75–82). This trend produced such texts as Achim von Arnim's *Isabella von Ägypten* (1811), where the exotic Oriental Other also functions as the title character's Doppelgänger, and the distinction between original and Double hangs precariously in the balance. The Oriental gypsy Isabella becomes cloned at the behest of Emperor Karl V by a Jewish magician, and her Double is also an (albeit soulless) Eastern Jewish figure, a golem (Seyhan 127–35). In Meyer's *Der Heilige*, Hans the narrator is a purely fictitious, somewhat orientalized Christian. His character is partly paralleled within the space of a historical framed narrative by Becket, who is historically genuine but fictively orientalized; his bogus ethnicity is half Moslem and half Christian.

Operating within the confines of Poetic Realism, Meyer would not create a text with a thoroughgoing, identity-confusing Doppelgänger motif of the sort present in Arnim's novella. But there are also circumstances internal to the narrative of *Der Heilige*, and thus unconnected to the constraints of the literary movement to which it belongs, that preserve (indeed radicalize) the distinctions in Hans's and Becket's personas, and thereby prevent the physical duplication evident in novellas such as *Isabella von Ägypten*. Said has noted that Western anti-Semitism and the particular matrix of racist attitudes toward the Islamic world prevalent in Orientalism are closely interrelated (27–28, 285–86). In the Middle Ages, which serves as the historical setting for Meyer's novella, hatred of Jews and Moslems in Europe was not so much based on racial stereotyping as it was on religious dogma. Jews were seen as the killers of Christ, and Arabs were regarded as the infidels who were occupying the Holy Land. Therefore, they were largely commingled in the eyes of Europeans as the despised Other, the often undifferentiated enemies of Christianity, whose extirpation (or conversion) could be regarded as furthering the Christian cause.

Hans begins his narrative with an extensive description of his personal history prior to his service at King Henry's court and his relationship with Becket. He is the scion of noble but deeply indebted parents, and the first act of his own life that he delineates is his confrontation with the Jewish usurer Manasse. His widowed mother had sent Hans to Manasse to request a delay in the payment of the debt her husband had incurred in mortgaging his property to the Jew. Manasse refuses this request, and two powerful sentiments drive Hans to murder him: "Da erfaßte mich plötzlich eine große Kümmernis und ein Erbarmen mit meinem siechen Mütterlein und auch mit dem blutigen Leiden unseres Heilandes, den die Juden grausam gemartert haben, und ich schlug den Manasse hart mit Fäusten, daß er starb" (13:18). Thus, the very first act mentioned by Hans in his autobiographical narrative is the murder of an Other, a Jew whose status would have been imbued with a matrix of alterity very similar to that which set the "Oriental" Moslem apart in the eyes of Christendom in the Middle Ages. Because his act is partly inspired by the same emotions that propelled the Crusaders (among whom his father had disappeared) in their contemporaneous wars against the Arabs, the deed can be regarded retrospectively as blocking any future absolute commingling of identities seen in such Romantic works as *Isabella von Ägypten*, where the Doppelgänger is as informed by Oriental alterity as is her original. Throughout the further course of *Der Heilige*, Hans will be pervaded by the consciousness that he is a pure Christian while (and when) he witnesses Becket's revelation of his Saracen-Oriental background. The murder of Manasse guarantees that Becket will function as Hans's Other as much as his second self.

In spite of the contrast between Hans's unmixed Christian heritage and Becket's partially Moslem ethnicity, the "foreign blood" he himself feels is flowing through his veins (13:86), there is a great deal of ambiguity attached to the question of which character is most authentically Christian. Hans's narration is not always reliable; as Evans has noted, Meyer often used the "Rahmenkonstruktion" device to place the veracity of his framed first-person narrative episodes into ironic question (63). In his missive to Lingg, Meyer indicated Hans's framed account was intended to provide a naive perspective of an extraordinary, singular ("einzig-artigen") personage (13:299), and in a letter to his sister Betsy dated 3 February 1877, he remarked that Becket's profound nature becomes distorted by another individual's outlook (13:284). Thus Hans's protestations of his unblemished Christianity to the suspicious Burkhard, as well as his suspicions regarding Becket's "heathen" nature, often have a hollow ring.

In his article on the ambiguity surrounding the issue of Becket's conversion, Lewis Tusken promotes the view that Becket accepts the archbishop's office in order "to challenge the Christian God. If He exists, and if He is just, Henry cannot continue to rule with His approval" (210). Though there is merit in this argument, since Hans's concrete descriptions of Becket's skepticism regarding the church and its teachings are too consistent to dismiss, Becket attains a genuinely Christ-like persona, which only emerges indirectly in Hans's discourse. Personally, Hans sees Becket as a heathen, but Becket's majestic sufferings inevitably remind one of Jesus' last travails.[5] At the level of speech, Becket most vividly assumes the identity of Christ in banishing Hans from his presence. Henry had ordered Hans to Canterbury after learning from him of the plot by Norman courtiers against the archbishop's life. Becket is indeed in great danger as Hans comes upon him surrounded by his clerics and presiding at a meal in a tableau reminiscent of Christ surrounded by his disciples at the Last Supper. Hans pleads with Becket to place himself under the king's protection, but his entreaties only move the primate to anger: "Da wandte sich plötzlich Herr Thomas gegen mich und schlug mich mit biblischen Worten: 'Hebe dich von hinnen, du Schalk und böser Knecht, denn du bist mir ärgerlich!'" (13:131).

The narrator, nominally pious in the presence of his clerical auditor, had embellished his tale with biblical quotations, but Becket's employment of (only slightly altered) citations from the Book of Matthew are unpremeditated, unplanned, and purely visceral. Thus the Oriental Becket is not only "perhaps the only truly Christian figure in the entire book," as Manfred and Evelyn Jacobson contend (71), but his spontaneous injection of Christ's words in a setting reminiscent of the Last Supper makes Becket, at this moment, into a Christ-like figure. This transformation is strengthened by our knowledge that the archbishop at the banquet table surrounded by his anxious clerics, like Christ at the Last Supper ringed by the apprehensive disciples, is about to suffer martyrdom. And given Christ's own Near Eastern heritage, Becket's Oriental background only adds to our sense that, however briefly, Meyer has symbolically intertwined the archbishop with the master he now serves.

Becket's refusal to take any action that might avert his murder, indeed his sly attempt to guarantee his own demise, anticipates the fictive Gustav Adolf's subtle and successful effort to sacrifice himself through assassination at the hands of his enemies in Meyer's novella *Gustav Adolfs Page* (1882). In Meyer's version of the great Protestant king and soldier's death during the Thirty Years' War, Gustav welcomes the seemingly repentant duke of Lauenburg back into his fold after their bitter break. The king knows Lauenburg has designs on his life, but nevertheless embraces him, an act imbued, in Meyer's description, with an aura of divine, Christ-like forgiveness (11:209). Lauenburg is also the Double of the tale's eponymous protagonist, Auguste (Gustel) Leubelfing. Gustel's physical resemblance to her male cousin August (along with the king's poor vision) allows the teenage girl to act in her cowardly relative's stead when the latter is called upon to serve as Gustav's page after two previous attendants are killed in battle. Her motives for taking on this dangerous, duplicitous role are ambiguous. Her veneration for the king, instilled from a childhood spent in Gustav's military camps, is mixed with a powerful erotic attraction to him.

Given the obvious similarities in appearance and name between the courageous girl and her cowardly cousin, one might regard August as Gustel's inwardly antithetical Doppelgänger. However, this term is not used in context with Gustel's connection to August. Instead, it is employed to evoke the Double-Other dialectic that inscribes the relationship between Gustel and her other male look-alike (and sound-alike), the evil duke. Like the duke—indeed, because her resemblance to him (particularly the circumstance that the duke's dropped glove perfectly fits her hand) threatens to reveal the truth of her identity—she becomes a refugee from the king. On horseback one evening after her flight, she glimpses her Double, and realizes he is the cause of her distress:

> Der Mond schien taghell und das Roß ging im Schritt. Bei klarerer Überlegung erkannte jetzt der Flüchtling im Dunkel jenes Ereignisses, das ihn von der Seite des Königs vertrieben hatte, mit den

scharfen Augen der Liebe und des Hasses seinen Doppelgänger. Es war der Lauenburger. Hatte er nicht gesehen, wie der Gebrandmarkte die Faust gegen die Gerechtigkeit des Königs geballt hatte? Besaß der Gestrafte nicht den Scheinklang seiner Stimme? War er selbst nicht Weibes genug, um in jenem fürchterlichen Augenblicke die Kleinheit der geballten fürstlichen Faust bemerkt zu haben?

(11:202-3)

Most critics have written disparagingly of Meyer's use of the Doppelgänger motif here. Even Freud, who was so profoundly inspired by its enactments in German Romanticism, felt it was forced and unfounded in this case.[6] Such disparagement, however, overlooks Meyer's masterful evocation of sexual ambiguity through his employment of the motif here, an ambiguity that lies at the story's core. Meyer consistently uses the masculine pronoun "er" to refer to Gustel, and her womanhood is highlighted in this passage only to make her insight into a putatively feminine attribute of the duke seem plausible. Indeed, Dennis McCort has argued that Gustel's perception of the duke as her Double is an act of unconscious sexual projection; in McCort's reading, Lauenburg becomes in Gustel's mind the "masked feminine self she abhors" (52). I would argue that Gustel hates not so much her womanhood as the limitations and the deceitfulness her gender imposes upon her, given her particular circumstances. She despises the effeminacy she observes in her cousin and the duke not for any perceived unnaturalness, but because they mirror, in reverse, her own sexually ambiguous situation. Becket, too, is marked by this androgynous quality, a quality tied, in typical nineteenth-century fashion, to his Oriental background. Indeed, this quality in Meyer's Becket is highlighted by an Oriental fairy tale Doppelgänger. Nevertheless, Meyer's use of the Double-Other dialectic to imbue the title characters of *Gustav Adolfs Page* and *Der Heilige* with hermaphroditic attributes is not simply indicative of subtle sexism and racism in nineteenth-century discourse, present though these elements may be. It is also another example of Poetic Realism's instantiation of the Doppelgänger motif to create psychically comprehensive, aesthetically balanced protagonists.

Der Heilige's fairy tale allegorically anticipates the events in the principal narrative. The fairy tale's protagonist, "Prinz Mondschein," serves as the Doppelgänger who highlights the archbishop's androgyny. They suffer similar fates, and possess almost identical attributes. Indeed, Becket's true (physical) Double is not Hans, but Mondschein. As is also often the case with Romantic Doppelgänger, their attributes and histories are so confluent that the suspicion arises that they are one and the same person. Mondschein's story is a tale set within *Der Heilige*'s larger tale, heard by Hans from the lips of a Moorish youth in Cordova. As the enthusiastic chronicler of florid narratives himself, Hans is naturally drawn to this young Moslem orator, though the latter's personal role in *Der Heilige* is too slight to suggest any other liaisons between him and the Swabian. Like Becket, Mondschein is an outsider who rises to the pinnacle of power and influence because his intelligence and perspicacity make a tremendous impact on a (for him) foreign ruler, the caliph of Cordova. Through Mondschein's statesmanship, the caliph becomes the most powerful Moorish king, much as Henry gained near omnipotence in his realm due to Becket's wise guidance. The prince shares Becket's somewhat feminine passivity and gentleness;[7] these qualities are reflected physically in their pale and delicate features (the source of Mondschein's name). Both of them earn the enmity of many jealous and suspicious courtiers.

At this point, the stories deviate somewhat, for Mondschein is given the hand of the caliph's sister, "Prinzessin Sonne," in marriage. Her death in childbirth inspires the jealous courtiers to hatch a conspiracy against the prince; he exposes them, but, like Becket, averse to violence, he requests their lives be spared. Nevertheless, the caliph beheads the conspirators, and sends the heads to Mondschein as a gift. This so horrifies the prince that he takes his daughter from her crib and steals away from Cordova at night, resulting in the same ruin for the Moorish king as Becket caused in turning his back on Henry. Even the tale's narrative framework is similar to Becket's; like Hans, the young Moorish narrator tells his tale with great passion. His insistence that he knows Mondschein is duly noted by Hans, who is among the crowd of listeners. Hans lends as little credibility to the Moor's tale as Burkhard does to Hans's own narrative (13:23).

Like Hans in his relationship to Becket, Becket's link to Mondschein is characterized by an interchange between identity and difference; the prince functions concomitantly as Becket's Double and as his Other. Though Hans expresses doubt as to the veracity of the Moor's tale (probably in order to establish his own credibility with the mistrustful canon), Hans cannot resist the temptation to tell the tale to Becket, hoping the chancellor will reveal whether he and Mondschein are the same person. Becket's response frustrates his inferred inquiry, for the chancellor's only gesture, after considering the matter with lowered eyes, is to lift his eyes to gaze at Hans and then slowly raise his finger to his lips (13:36). Later, Hans indicates belief in the tale, for in speculating on Gnade's possible ascension to the role of Henry's queen, he says to himself: "Ist sie doch zwiefach aus fürstlichem Geblüte!" (13:54). This clearly shows he believes her to be the daughter of Prince Mondschein and Princess Sonne, for nothing else could explain his conviction concerning her purely noble lineage.[8] Nevertheless, Hans's own unreliability as a narrator casts the identity of Mondschein and Becket into doubt. In addition, Becket's gesture commanding Hans to silence after the crossbow maker has told him Mondschein's story frustrates Hans's obvious wish to learn the truth about this possible congruence. This silent act ironically crosses the intratextual border of the novella. For it communicates to the reader the hopeless ambiguity of the narrative in its entirety, indicating that questions attempting to clear up its inconsistencies are better left unposed.

Even if we leave aside the thorny issue of the prince's possible identity with the chancellor (that is, the possibility that the two are really one person seen from different narrative perspectives) and regard the Mondschein episode strictly as the anticipation of the principal tale, we must take note of a circumstance that creates a radical difference between the two figures. Aside from the respective grievances leading to their betrayal of their rulers, the acts constituting this disloyalty are distinctly opposite in tone. In simply leaving Cordova, Mondschein retains the attribute of Oriental passivity in its truest sense; though he is revolted by the sack of heads presented him as a gift, he is too much the unresisting subject of an Oriental despot actually to engage in a confrontation. He is the Oriental vassal as Hegel envisioned him, lacking the will to "subjective freedom," for whom "no dialectic operates" because "the subject has not realized its antithesis and overcome it" (Seyhan 80).

This is decidedly not the case with Becket in his relationship to Henry. They truly *share* power after Becket becomes archbishop, though everything in their respective characterizations marks them as pure Others rather than as alter egos. Not only do their antithetical personal attributes imprint their affiliation with a dialectic,[9] but Becket's volition prompts him to act in a decisive manner against his polar opposite. To be sure, his oppositional deeds generally appear more reactive than active; he refuses Henry the kiss of reconciliation, rejects all attempts at compromise, and, finally, spurns the offer of royal protection that would have averted his martyrdom. But Becket really has no alternative to this manner of combat against Henry's rule, given the king's omnipotence, the loyalty of his Norman vassals, and their concomitant hatred toward the archbishop and his powerless Saxon followers. While it is true that Mondschein faces quite similar obstacles (though less opposition, since his most vicious enemies have been executed), he opts simply to depart.

Becket's reactional style is not a corollary of the "Oriental passivity" he seems to have exhibited when serving as the king's loyal chancellor, but a modus operandi necessitated by the forces at work in their dialectical relationship. Whether motivated by desire for revenge, Christian piety, or a combination of both,[10] Becket gives evidence of a subjective will absent in Mondschein's briefly delineated relationship with his sovereign. The results of their deeds are the same, as both Henry and the Cordovan king see their omnipotent rule undermined. Given Mondschein's "politische Weisheit" (13:23), we might speculate that he knew his departure would have this consequence. But in dealing with the problem of Orientalism and the related issue of identity and difference in the personas of Mondschein and Becket, actions and behavior play a determining role. Mondschein departs the king's court instead of directly condemning the king's atrocity, while Becket grasps the (albeit limited) power Henry has placed in his hands by excommunicating the king's strongest clerical ally, the Norman bishop of York, and having this excommunication proclaimed in all churches attended by Saxons. He creates his own loyal coterie of bishops and confronts the king and his Norman aristocrats at the Court of Windsor with a large band of Saxon adherents. In thus exercising his will and actively pitting himself against his nominal sovereign, Becket behaves in a manner contrary to Hegel's Orientalist vision and causes the reader to see him as not only Mondschein's Double, but his Other as well.

In his important letter to Lingg in May of 1880, Meyer lists six personality traits he attributes to Becket. We have already cited two of them, namely, the chancellor's "Oriental" vengefulness and diplomacy. The first quality Meyer connects to Becket's persona is simply "Orientalisches Blut" (13:298). If we combine Said's analysis of nineteenth-century European attitudes toward the Near East and its native occupants with Becket's personality as it manifests itself throughout most of the novella, then this "Oriental blood" was undoubtedly intended to signify a quiescent but dangerous lassitude, a superficial repose masking a preternatural and deadly awareness of the right moment to take revenge. Indeed, later in the letter to Lingg, Meyer asserts that Becket behaves passively due to his piety, intelligence, fatalism, and "aus der unbestimmten Ahnung, die Stunde der Rache werde kommen" (13: 299). Seen in this light, Becket's seeming transformation as archbishop into a man of decisive action, while it defies the Hegelian paradigm of Asian obeisance, still fits in harmoniously with stereotypes of the Oriental that were common in nineteenth-century Europe. In this regard, one could add that Becket as archbishop has no express wish to undertake direct initiatives against Henry, and his deeds contrary to the king's desires evince not so much individual ("Western") willfulness as a submission to God. As archbishiop, he believes he owes this new, higher "lord" the same absolute obedience rendered in his previous service as chancellor to Henry.

Given the almost uncontested dominance in the nineteenth century enjoyed by Orientalist thinking of the sort described by Said, which gave rise to a highly nuanced image of persons considered Oriental, it should come as no surprise that Meyer's version of Thierry's "Saracen" Becket is often true to racist type. Nevertheless, Meyer also noted that "Mein Becket ist ein edler Charakter, seine Buße eine echte" (13:300). In spite of his cunning and fatalism, Becket indeed emerges in *Der Heilige* as a sincere and noble (in the broad sense of this term) personage. These qualities run counter to contemporary perceptions concerning the Orient, and Meyer may therefore be said to defy stereotypes about the Oriental prevalent in his age. The seemingly antithetical traits in the fictional Becket are evidence not of inconsistency on Meyer's part, but of the ambiguity in European attitudes, which inspired nineteenth-century writers to treat the Oriental as both an "Other" and a "surrogate and even underground self" (Said 1, 3). As I have argued throughout the course of this chapter, the ambiguity Said perceived in Orientalist thinking manifested itself in *Der Heilige* through an undermining of boundaries between identity and difference; "Oriental" and "Occidental" figures are marked by *both* confluence and alterity in this work. It is not inaccurate to argue, as does Holub, that Meyer sustains and writes in the tradition of anti-Oriental European thought in his novella "by creating anew the division between them and us, between native and foreign, between self and other" (173). But we must add that in also mingling, dialectically mediating, and often conflating the deeds, attributes, rhetoric, and general histories of Becket, his narrator, his sovereign, and his prefigural Double, Meyer manages to erase these divisions at one and the same time.

In his discussion of *Der Heilige* in *Der Poetische Realismus*, Cowen situates Meyer's novella as a paradigmatic work of this movement through an emphasis on its puzzling, indeed contradictory character: "Die ganze Novelle besteht überhaupt aus einem Rätsel, das—will es ein Rätsel bleiben—ein Gleichgewicht der Alternativen, also eine gewisse Symmetrie voraussetzt: Die Symmetrie—verschiedene Elemente werden in eine Beziehung zueinander gesetzt—, mit anderen Worten: die poetisch verklärende Komposition der Realität—all dies dient gleichzeitig der Verrätselung" (257).

Cowen finds Meyer's exemplary status as a Poetic Realist lies in his adroit mixture of historical facts, culled from studies even more intensively pursued than is the case with other historically minded writers in the movement such as Keller and Storm, with carefully crafted details. This combination imbues Becket with his irresolvable contradictions—as both human and saint, Christian and Moslem, aesthete and ascetic. For Meyer, according to Cowen, the only valid mode of acceptable Realism is the one that acknowledges and evokes the individual's innately puzzling, contradictory qualities (Cowen 247–48, 258–62). This chapter has attempted to illustrate how Meyer's complex instantiation of Doppelgänger and ego–alter ego relationships enhances, indeed greatly expands, the paradoxical and antithetical nuances in the fictive Becket's persona, nuances detected by Cowen in this figure even when regarded as an entirely discrete character. Given the comprehensive quality these liaisons create in Becket as a narrated ego, we can say that Meyer's use of character dialectics in *Der Heilige* greatly aided him in approximating the aesthetic and psychological totality Ludwig and Schmidt, Poetic Realism's chief theorists, projected as literature's primary telos.[11]

4. Duplication, Fungibility, Dialectics, and the "Epic Naiveté" of Gottfried Keller's *Martin Salander*

In the introduction, I drew on the work of Hermann Kinder and Peter Uwe Hohendahl to underscore the utopian political dimension inherent in Poetic Realism's ideal of approximating totality in the work of art. The *Nachmärz* sociopolitical milieu was marked by deep class-based divisions, and Julian Schmidt equated representational totality with a projective harmony, with a comprehensiveness in literary works suggestive of an integrated, unified world. The conservative Schmidt's inclination toward epic narrative totality was shared by the great twentieth-century Marxist theorist Georg Lukács, though Lukács's voluminous writing on Realism strongly differentiates itself from that of Poetic Realism's chief spokesman in other respects. Albeit an admirer of Gottfried Keller, Lukács criticized Keller's last novel, *Martin Salander* (1886), because he felt narrative totality was lacking there. However, the underlying reason he and Poetic Realists such as Theodor Storm (whose aversion to *Martin Salander* will be examined in the next chapter) disliked the work may lie in its *reversal* of the utopian communal.

An evocation of such ideal communality may be seen at the outset of Keller's popular novella *Romeo und Julia auf dem Dorfe* (1856), where, prior to the dissolution of their friendship through the influence of the "Gründerjahre" capitalism Keller saw as corrosive to the bonds that had forged a unified and harmonious Swiss village society, the farmers Manz and Marti appear as Doubles. The Doppelgänger effect is achieved through a description of the two plowing friends approaching each other, then passing and drawing away, from a narratively distant third-person perspective. From this far-off vista, they seem identical, distinguished only by the way the wind blows the tips of their caps either forward or backward depending on the directions in which they respectively move (2:61–62). This technique is thus employed here to foreground the prelapsarian concordance, capable of seeming to blend their discrete identities, which marks their relationship.

Keller also drew on the Doppelgänger motif in *Martin Salander* to evoke an image of social, political, and spiritual totality, but the harmony represented is a negative one, characterized by amorality and the obliteration of historically grounded, shared community values. These facets of *Martin Salander* attracted the interest of one of Lukács's chief theoretical rivals, Theodor Adorno. Lukács, Adorno, and Adorno's sometime friend and collaborator, Walter Benjamin, all elaborated concepts of unity sometimes suggestive of Poetic Realism's aesthetic totality desideratum, though particularly Adorno was aware of the aporias and political dangers connected to such holistic narrative idealism. They were all interested in this element, or its subversion, in Keller's work, and I will therefore draw extensively on their critiques of the great Swiss writer in this chapter. Mainly by drawing on Adorno's negative dialectical reading of Keller's novel, I will attempt to show how Keller's peculiar, antisynthesizing adaptation of the Double dialectic in *Martin Salander* inverted Poetic Realism's priorities to create a holistic picture, indeed, but one of social *dis*integration.

In his essay "Über epische Naivetät" (1943), Adorno adumbrates the tension inherent in epic narration between the ever-the-same of the epic's mythic substratum and the telos of alterity propelling the narrative line itself. All epic is confronted by an inherent contradiction; its rational, communicative speech is inscribed by the universal fungibility and reductive tendencies constitutive of mythic order, while the epicist strives, above all, to resist the spell of identity. The desperate desire to escape this paradox is reflected both in the Homeric appeal to the muse to aid in conjuring the monstrous and in the attempt by Goethe and Stifter to create the simulacrum of originary, autochthonic bourgeois relations evoked by the noninterchangeable word. Epic naiveté is the technique by which the narrator attempts to break the spell of mythic identity. This naiveté is constituted by a rigid fixation on the object of narration that would block the power of such mythic identity, but this tenacious adherence to the concrete burdens the naive attitude with the appearance of obtuseness and ignorance. Nevertheless, in modern narrative, it is precisely epic naiveté that resists and calls into question the active forgetfulness of bourgeois reason. The comprehensive yet fixed character of epic naiveté overcomes the amnesia generated by the leveling process inherent in the protocols of the late capitalist era. Epic naiveté gives rise to seeming absurdity, inherent contradictions between form and representation, a lack of coherence, and even madness. But these characteristics, closely related to the allegoric element of the epic narrative, first make possible the epic's resistance to and negation of identitarian bourgeois-mythic rationality (*Noten zur Literatur* 1:50–60).

While identifying the apparent simplemindedness of epic naiveté, Adorno engages in a brief discussion of *Martin Salander*. He argues that Keller's last novel seems to betray a petit-bourgeois ignorance of the causes underlying the economic crises experienced by Switzerland as a consequence of rapid economic expansion in the second half of the nineteenth century by taking what appears at first glance to be a simple "So-schlecht-sind-heute-die-Menschen" attitude toward contemporary Swiss society. Seeming to miss the most salient features of this crisis, Keller's apparent ingenuousness is precisely what allows the emergence of a subversive remembrance: "Aber nur solche Naivetät wiederum erlaubt es, von den unheilschwangeren Anfängen der spätkapitalistischen Ära zu erzählen und der Anamnesis sie zuzueignen, anstatt bloß von ihnen zu berichten und sie kraft des Protokolls, das von Zeit einzig noch als einem Index weiß, mit trugvoller Gegenwärtigkeit ins Nichts dessen hinabzustoßen, woran keine Erinnerung mehr sich zu heften vermag" (*Noten zur Literatur* 1:54). Indeed, Adorno implies that Keller's seeming ignorance is merely a narrative strategy employed to facilitate the emergence of epic naiveté.

Despite its brevity, Adorno's critique of *Martin Salander* has been adapted in several contemporary critical discussions of this work. For example, Bernd Neumann cites Adorno's views on Keller's last novel in asserting that it envisions the end of the dialectic of the bourgeois Enlightenment, which has reached the terminal stages of its development. The "cruel" precision of Keller's description—for Adorno, constitutive of epic resistance to the mythic ratio's ever-the-same—reflects for Neumann the disillusion experienced by Keller, a disillusion Neumann appears to equate with the expiration of the bourgeois Enlightenment and its progressivist dialectics (300). Karol Szemkus cites Adorno's essay in defending Keller against the charge that his last novel was the conservative testament of a man unable to understand his own age, and his view of remembrance in Keller's work as "innere Zeitdauer, die dem Zeitablauf sich widersetzt" (90–91), closely corresponds to the theory of naive epic memory adumbrated by Adorno in his essay.

No attempt has been made heretofore, however, to explore the validity of Adorno's view of *Martin Salander* as a paradigm of naive epic resistance to bourgeois identitarian rationality and to its concomitant telos of a memory-obliterating interchangeability, or "Fungibilität," to borrow Adorno's term (*Noten zur Literatur* 1:55). In addressing this issue, this chapter will also delineate the probable underlying reason Adorno was drawn to this work; its motif of character duplication blocks the establishment of traditional narrative dialectics with their movement toward synthesis and closure. Instead, this doubling allows those protagonists not effectively nullified as individuated characters by what we might call a dialectic of identity and contrast to emerge as unique figures, informed by genuine alterity. Keller thus breaks the sway of mythic unity in a way that anticipates the telos of Adorno's later magnum opus, the *Negative Dialektik* (1966). In the preface to this work, Adorno describes his purport as follows: "Mit konsequenzlogischen Mitteln trachtet sie, anstelle des Einheitsprinzips und der Allherrschaft des übergeordneten Begriffs die Idee dessen zu rücken, was außerhalb des Banns solcher Einheit wäre" (8).

Had Keller adhered to a traditional delineation of antithetical, antagonistic characters locked in a conflict resolved at the conclusion of the narrative plot into an image of transcended struggle and harmonious closure, then his last novel could not have broken the spell of mythic unity, and thus could not have approximated the rupture Adorno sought to evoke in the *Negative Dialektik* and in his essay on epic naiveté. Indeed, through the Shakespeare criticism enunciated by the title figure of *Pankraz, der Schmoller* (1856), Keller indicated that hostile encounters between two fully diametrical individuals may have been rendered in an exemplary manner by the bard and show his omniscient grasp of theatrical personas, but that such complete and radical dramatic contrasts could not be found among the real-life individuals who populated the contemporary world. In this respect, Shakespeare was a "seductive false prophet" for the current generation of writers (2:40–41).[1] This perspective stands in radical contrast to that of Ludwig, who praised Shakespeare as worthy of emulation precisely for the delineation of extreme, polarized personality traits in his characters and for portraying the "Gesamtphysiognomie" of individual protagonists (S1: 64–69). As we have seen, such dialectics, which strive for totalized representation, the articulation of the complete range of human psychic attributes, were also favored by other Poetic Realists, inspiring the ego–alter ego juxtapositions explored in this book. At least at times, then, Keller's attitude toward characterization varied from that of his contemporaries.

Of course, it would be absurd to assert that there are no conflicts between diverse character types in *Martin Salander*. But through his sometimes subtle, sometimes overt technique of interchange and duplication, Keller achieves the sort of fixity, the concretization of attributes Adorno associated with epic naiveté, with the naive epicist's ability to subvert the mythic ever-the-same even while making it strongly manifest. An extended meditation on Adorno's discussion of *Martin Salander* as an exemplar of epic naiveté thus opens up a new way of critically examining the novel's structure as inscribed by duplication, fungibility, and a nontraditional dialectic.

As in his other novel, *Der grüne Heinrich* (first version, 1854; second version, 1879–80), Keller peoples *Martin Salander* with a large number of diverse character types. There have been a number of attempts to arrange them within specific categories. Margarete Merkel-Nipperdey has established the broadest, most traditionally dialectical system, dividing the protagonists into two antithetical groups, authentic and inauthentic. "Inauthentic" characters such as the swindler Louis Wohlwend, the superficial and greedy Weidelich twins, and the minor figures caught up in "Gründerjahre" scandals are driven and shaped by temporal concerns, informed by attributes generated by the age in which they live, and motivated by ambitions closely tied to their specific era. On the other hand, figures such as Salander's resilient and judicious wife Marie, his self-possessed son Arnold and his sympathetic, changeless, faithful friend Möni Wighart transcend and stand above time by virtue of a composure and order innate to their personalities and reflecting the eternal harmony ordering the universe. Through a dialectic that valorizes this latter set of characters (there are also two "ambivalent" protagonists, the twins' good-hearted but status-conscious mother Amalie and Martin himself), Merkel-Nipperdey believes Keller attempted to evoke the utopian image of a world inscribed by continuity, stability, and permanence.[2] Merkel-Nipperdey's view of the underlying telos propelling the narrative of *Martin Salander* thus stands in direct contrast to that of Adorno. The terminus of all traditional dialectics is stasis and unity, and by adopting such a model in her schematization of the characters in Keller's novel, it was perhaps inevitable that Merkel-Nipperdey would come to see this end point as Keller's ideal. Precisely because he rejected the "spell of such unity," Adorno adopted a technique he came to call *negative* dialectics, and he was attracted to *Martin Salander* by virtue of the anamnesis-inspiring naiveté, resistant to such unity, that he located in this work.

In his article on "The Place of 'Martin Salander' in Gottfried Keller's Evolution as a Prose Writer," J. M. Ritchie comes closer than Merkel-Nipperdey to identifying Keller's technique of duplication when he asserts that *Martin Salander* is a "rigidly planned novel in which a deliberate parallelism is pursued" (219–20). His article contains a small chart where the main characters are arranged analogically and antilogically. While taking note of the obvious parallelisms, such as the nearly identical relationships between the Weidelich twins and the Salander daughters, Ritchie emphasizes Keller's ability to almost duplicate scenes, and to imbue characters with the same attributes, while maintaining the scenes as completely discrete strands of the narrative and never bringing the analogous characters into contact with each other. For example, Martin surreptitiously drinks to his wife's health at their daughters' double wedding, but the act nevertheless attracts the attention of

Amalie Weidelich. In an entirely different episode narrated with much the same vocabulary and syntax, Martin drinks to the health of Wohlwend's sister-in-law Myrrha, for whom he is developing an infatuation, and this attracts Wohlwend's attention. Wohlwend's empty bombast is virtually repeated by Julian Weidelich, though they never meet. Thus, these duplications and parallelisms can take place while Keller maintains "no real unity of action" (220). Keller's skillful focus through parallelisms on specific personality attributes, patterns of syntax and rhetoric, and events during various and discrete moments within the narrative imbues his novel with the sort of density and concretion Adorno associated with epic naiveté.

Keller adheres to this focus while maintaining a fundamental *disunity* in the novel's episodic strands. In "Über epische Naivetät," Adorno asserts that the impulse to rupture the tissue of the narrative was characteristic of the greatest storytellers of the nineteenth century, and that this impulse drove them to paint and sketch, often in lieu of writing. Adorno implies that precisely this impulse, also evident in Homer's transformation of metaphor into action, is in some measure responsible for the distinction of the best nineteenth-century prose stylists, of whom only Stifter, Flaubert, Goethe, and Keller are mentioned by name (*Noten zur Literatur* 1:55). It would appear that the fragmentary, discontinuous character of the narrative in *Martin Salander*, the sort of discontinuity also generally valorized in Adorno's *Ästhetische Theorie* (first published in 1970) played a major, if unstated, role in drawing Adorno's critical attention to this novel.

Although Ritchie deserves credit for identifying Keller's use of discontinuous parallelisms in the narrative line of *Martin Salander*, it was Rudolf von Passavant who first articulated the significance of the novel's "motif of duplication." Keller's establishment of identical pairs causes the personalities of the individuals who constitute them to be mirrored, and thus their individuality is effectively canceled: "Die Zwillinge, die Söhne Kleinpeters und selbst Setti und Netti sind als verdoppelte, gespiegelte Personen ihrer individuellen Persönlichkeit beraubt. Wesen- und Charakterlosigkeit wird als Anlage zu unbesonnenem und unehrenhaftem Handeln verstanden" (97). The justification for Passavant's claim that Keller's doubling technique robs single characters bound into couples of any unique selfhood is particularly evident in the often discussed episode in which Martin, walking home after a disheartening political gathering, comes upon a local festivity where he sees his daughters dancing with the Weidelich twins. Throughout this lengthy scene, the respective pairs are almost never permitted to emerge into individuality. The words "Paar," "Pärchen," "Zwillinge," and "Töchter" all evoke their inescapable duality and duplication. Even when Keller must allow one of Salander's daughters to appear as a discrete entity by giving her speech, the interlocutor is referred to as "die ältere Tochter" rather than as Setti; she and a Weidelich son appear before Martin as "die Schwester mit dem ihrigen" and not as Setti and Isidor. Thus, even when referred to in the singular, Setti, Netti, Julian, and Isidor cannot escape an identification with the Other to whom they are bound (3:582–88).

The comic high point of the duplication of the twins comes when Setti and Netti tell their father how they tell the twins apart; Julian's left earlobe is somewhat rolled up, while Isidor's right earlobe resembles an egg noodle. With tongue in cheek, Arnold declares this circumstance to be of great scientific curiosity, indicative of an extinct species or the first hint of a new one. He advises his sisters to examine their own earlobes: "Wenn ihr Ähnliches aufweiset, so nehmt euch in acht, sonst wählen euch die Zwillinge zu ihren Frauen, um nach der Selektionstheorie eine neue Art von wickelohrigen Menschen zu stiften!" (3:588).

While there is an obviously lighthearted irony playing on the surface of Arnold's banter, the Darwinian principles to which Keller thereby subjects the two couples is deadly serious. For the twins represent deindividuated specimens of an atavistic barbarism only seemingly extinct. They will later display this trait, as married advocates, in their genuinely brutal disregard for their natural environment. They carry the seed within them, already shown in germination in earlier scenes depicting the twins' greed and cowardice as children, of a just-emerging class of completely remorseless and unscrupulous capitalists. Salander's daughters become their victims, undifferentiated and interchangeable because victimization and imprudence are the sole qualities they represent. Keller was not a naturalist, and while *Martin Salander* is imbued by an air of resignation, it is not propelled by the force of naturalistic Darwinian inevitability. Rather, the twins' subjection to Darwinian laws is simply the most extreme instance of Keller's attempt to make them appear as depersonalized and duplicated. By showing them to be interchangeable exemplars of an evolutionary pattern, Keller evokes a general depersonalization within an increasingly faceless (but no less rapaciously self-destructive) society, and this facelessness is the obverse of the loss of memory and genuine experience identified by Adorno in the era of late capitalism. In his brief discussion of *Martin Salander*, Adorno hints that Keller's act of narrative duplication first makes possible the representation of these twin losses: "In solcher Erinnerung an das, was eigentlich schon gar nicht mehr sich erinnern läßt, drückt dann freilich Kellers Beschreibung der beiden betrügerischen

Advokaten, die Zwillingsbrüder, Duplikate, sind, soviel von der Wahrheit aus, nämlich gerade von der erinnerungsfeindlichen Fungibilität, wie erst wieder einer Theorie möglich wäre, die noch den Verlust von Erfahrung aus der Erfahrung der Gesellschaft durchsichtig bestimmte" (*Noten zur Literatur* 1:54–55).

The reason Adorno feels Keller's description of the twins expresses a truth that can only remember something really lost to memory lies in his belief that temporality is simply indexed in the era of late capitalism, and thus dissolved into a deceptive contemporaneity which makes genuine remembrance impossible. He suggests the twins' interchangeability evokes a facelessness destructive of communal memory. Although Keller's epic naiveté, according to this view, cannot actually overcome the general loss of memory endemic to a society imbued by such fungibility, it can point toward a theory of this loss anchored in the experience of the society subjected to it. The precise attention to description and to concrete detail Adorno associates with epic naiveté as found in such works as *Martin Salander* creates a corrective for the loss of memory and a compensation for the untruth of all speech (*Noten zur Literatur* 1:54–55).

What is questionable in Adorno's terminology is the use of the term *epic* naiveté. Adorno's appreciation for the concrete narrative detail's ability to wrest remembrance from the mythic, rationalist ever-the-same was largely inspired by his reading of Walter Benjamin.[3] However, Benjamin associated *epic* memory with breadth, expansiveness, and communal collectivity, qualities lost in the modern age. Inspired by his reading of Lukács's *Die Theorie des Romans* (1916), he believed modern fragmentation effectively banished all possibility for epic recall. The sort of remembrance evoked through the relentlessly descriptive word, connected by Adorno to epic naiveté, is termed "Eingedenken" by Benjamin.[4] In light of Lukács's and Benjamin's critical differentiation between epic totality and the expansiveness of epic memory on the one hand, and the modern fragmentation of remembrance into shards of detail in discontinuous narratives on the other, Adorno's indiscriminate treatment of Homer's *Odyssey* and Keller's *Martin Salander* as related exemplars of epic naiveté itself appears naive. However, this appearance is false. Adorno's essay is part of the complex of material written in conjunction with the *Dialektik der Aufklärung* (1947), the product of a joint effort on the part of Adorno and Max Horkheimer. In this work, as Susan Buck-Morss has noted, Adorno and Horkheimer deliberately juxtaposed the mythic (Homeric) past with modern history in order to expose the identitarian character of time under the sign of Enlightenment dialectics and masked by "historical progress." Thus, "the archaic, the epic poem of the *Odyssey* was read as an expression of the most modern" (Buck-Morss 59). This is also the case in "Über epische Naivetät." Nevertheless, this synchronic approach somewhat weakens Adorno's attempt to situate *Martin Salander* in a precise historical frame of reference as an exemplary narrative of the "ominous" beginnings of the late capitalist era.

One should also recognize in Adorno's elucidation of epic naiveté a refutation of Lukács's valorization of Socialist Realism. In his essay "Erpreßte Versöhnung. Zu Georg Lukács: 'Wider den mißverstandenen Realismus'" (1958), Adorno strongly objects to what he regards as the mature Lukács's vulgar materialist theory of Socialist Realism with its ideal of a literature, which simply mirrors reality. Adorno notes in refuting Lukács's views: "Nur in der Kristallisation des eigenen Formgesetzes, nicht in der passiven Hinnahme der Objekte konvergiert Kunst mit dem Wirklichen" (*Noten zur Literatur* 2:164). Epic naiveté, with its resolute crystallization of the tiny detail and its concomitant refusal to conform passively to the empiricity of the external world, resists the sort of realism endorsed by Lukács. The apparent ingenuousness with which epic naiveté seems to ignore the real, or historically actual, allows it to adopt an independent principle of form, as Adorno also makes evident in his discussion of the contrasts between syntax, form, representation, and narrative development in the *Odyssey* toward the conclusion of "Über epische Naivetät" (56–57).

In spite of their more precise diachronic differentiation between the epic and the novel, both Lukács and Benjamin share with Adorno the ascription of a powerful epic quality to Keller's oeuvre. Lukács saw in Keller's comprehensive descriptions of his characters and in his complex unification of their internal and external features a form of "epische Großzügigkeit" (Lukács 48), although he felt precisely this sort of totality, Keller's "größte epische Stärke," is lost in *Martin Salander* (83). In a review, published in 1927, of Jonas Fränkel's edition of Keller's complete oeuvre, Benjamin also saw such a totality at work. But, typically for Benjamin (and contrary to Lukács, whose critical gaze generally overlooked the micrological),[5] the evocation of such comprehensiveness is seen to take place in the tiniest detail. Of Keller's prose, Benjamin says: "In ihr—und das ist die geheime Wissenschaft des Epikers, der allein das Glück mitteilbar macht—wiegt jede kleinste angeschaute Zelle Welt soviel wie der Rest aller Wirklichkeit" (2/1:288). As an example of Keller's concomitant delicacy in balancing the great and the small, he alludes to the episode in *Martin Salander* where the eponymous protagonist, dining with Louis Wohlwend and his family, is embarrassed by the man who twice ruined him financially. As was his habit, Salander begins to eat his soup as soon as he has it in his bowl. While he is lifting the spoon to his mouth, the hypocritical Wohlwend, having embraced a turgid form of Christianity from political and economic motives, orders his son to say a prayer. His timing is designed to disconcert Salander, and he succeeds (3:709–10). Of this passage, Benjamin notes: "Ein Löffel Suppe in der Hand des rechtschaffenen Mannes wiegt, wenn's darauf ankommt, das Tischgebet und Seelenheil im Munde des Gauners auf" (2/1:288).

Benjamin sees in the tiny detail of a spoonful of soup in Martin's honest hand the evocation of a powerful ethicism with more moral force than that possessed by Wohlwend's verbose but empty religiosity. It represents for Benjamin an instance of Keller's transmittal of normative, supratemporal codes of bourgeois-humane-ethical forms of existence (2/1:287), the sort of forms Keller saw threatened in the emerging era of late capitalism. For Adorno, Keller's failure to see the economic basis of this threat constitutes the surface naiveté inherent in *Martin Salander*. And while Benjamin saw in such descriptive moments as the arrested spoonful of soup on the way to Martin's mouth a comprehensive microcosmic reflection of real social relations, an epic fullness also discerned by Lukács in Keller's oeuvre *outside* of *Martin Salander*, Adorno perceived in the fixation on such details a rupturing of metaphysical, epistemological, and narrative unity. The relentless attention to descriptive details identified in *Martin Salander* by Benjamin and further adumbrated by Adorno both undermines the logic of identity and ruptures the evocation of a closed, comprehensive image of reality, the sort of totalitarian realism embraced by Lukács. "To be sure" ("freilich"), despite this antirealism, Adorno believes Keller's use of the motif of duplication expresses a genuine social truth, that the fungibility inherent in modern social structures is deadly to memory. Only such antirealistic aesthetic devices as epic naiveté can counter this memory-deadening tendency, in Adorno's view. For this reason, Adorno regards Keller's description of the Weidelich twins as an important accomplishment of an epic art that is realistic according to the laws of its own form. Such realistic art evokes a negative cognition, indicating the absence through loss of genuine experience.[6]

Though he does not make a reference to *Martin Salander*, Richard Brinkmann's discussion of nineteenth-century prose offers us a means perhaps better suited than that of Benjamin, Lukács, and Adorno to specifically examining the later nineteenth-century tendency motivating Keller's articulation, in this brief episode, of the complex interrelationship between totality, ethics, and the threat of change. In his seminal book *Wirklichkeit und Illusion*, Brinkmann notes that in the middle of the nineteenth century, German literature began to retreat from the pretension of trying to represent totalities ("Ganzheiten"). Thus what Adorno saw as a suprahistorical trend latent as a contradiction in all epics, and what Benjamin and Lukács saw as a phenomenon of the modern, postepic age, is seen by Brinkmann as an emergent trend specific to the era in which Keller was writing. Only *ethical* norms remain, and the nineteenth-century writer draws on these to create a sense of order in man's relationship to an increasingly disparate and contingent reality. I have argued in this book that Poetic Realism reacted to this contingency by valorizing the *projection* of a utopian totality in the work of art, and that this movement's writers drew on the Doppelgänger motif in order to achieve this projection. In Brinkmann's reading of the age, the privileging of the ethical over religious-metaphysical totalities leads to a new kind of piety: "Dieser ethische Anspruch, der sich zunächst immer noch an überkommene, konventionelle Ordnungen der Gesellschaft klammert, nimmt dabei mehr und mehr rein formalen Charakter an im Sinne der Aufforderung zu einer Art 'Wirklichkeitsfrömmigkeit,' das heißt zum schlichten Dienst an der gegebenen Wirklichkeit als einer aufgegebenen" (326).[7]

Keller's own "realistic piety" was inspired precisely by such a sense of mission. His adherence to what Brinkmann describes as outdated and conventional social arrangements and ethical norms was motivated by the disappearance of these codes in the emergent era of late capitalism, a reaction characterized by Adorno as apparently naive. But while Adorno indicates this supposed naiveté was caused by a petit-bourgeois ignorance of the economic conditions behind this disappearance, and Benjamin viewed it as a form of normative, atemporal ethicism, Brinkmann's analysis of this kind of writing identifies both its formal and its historical character. Salander's spoonful of soup indeed brims with an ethical suasion, but Brinkmann also allows us to see it as both an aesthetic manifestation of Keller's worldly piety, and as a metaphoric substitute for vanished social cohesion and totality. Because the projection of such cohesion and totality was Poetic Realism's highest aesthetic ideal, *Martin Salander* may be regarded as an indication of the movement's dissolution. Nevertheless, the novel's comprehensive representation of social disintegration approximates a certain negative totality. This is achieved by the deliberate conflation of the worldly-political and spiritual-religious realms.

Keller's opposition of a this-worldly religiosity to what he saw as hypocritical, narrow-minded church dogma is manifested consistently throughout his oeuvre. Nevertheless, the formal, structural aspect in his articulation of his particular theology is radically different in his two novels, *Der grüne Heinrich* and *Martin Salander*. A brief comparison of the religious dimension in these two works will help us further to understand why Adorno selected Keller's second novel over the first as a paradigm of epic naiveté. Gerhard Kaiser's analysis of the architectonic variation between these two works is useful as a starting point for this contrast. Heinrich's constant oscillation between a life governed by personal fantasy and external realities lends credence to Kaiser's articulation in *Der grüne Heinrich* of a "negative subject-object dialectic," generated by the antithesis between Heinrich's subjective perspective and the vast, unwieldy mass of experience he is unable to comprehend, and which thereby manifests itself as a fixed objectivity. In *Martin Salander*, the fragmentation of Keller's central thematics causes them to appear at the novel's surface or to disappear into its deep structure: "Die Subjekt-Objekt-Dialektik hat sich auseinandergelegt in amorphe Oberfläche und Tiefenstruktur" (1981:579–80). What emerges in a dialectical pattern in *Der grüne Heinrich* is evoked, in *Martin Salander*, in a discontinuous, even atomized fashion, through duplication and a concentrated descriptiveness, in other words, by what Adorno referred to as "epic naiveté." This contradistinction is nowhere more evident than in the religious element of the two novels.

Keller held conflicting views on religion, and this circumstance is reflected throughout his oeuvre by his concomitant embrace of the philosophy of the atheist Ludwig Feuerbach and his fascination with the theme of the divine. In *Der grüne Heinrich*, the two strands are brought together in a dialectical intertwining of contraposed characters and themes. One of the elements attracting Adorno's interest in *Martin Salander* was the fundamental interchangeability of the two twin brothers. Their fungible appearance and personality suggest the fundamental loss of memory endemic to late capitalist society, in which the objective world is stripped of its historical specificity through duplication and substitution. In *Der grüne Heinrich*, there is no such doubling of characters. Instead, figures with quite similar personalities but antithetical views, particularly concerning religion, are brought into a philosophical contiguity through Keller's instantiation of a dialectical attraction of opposites. The synthesis and ultimate culmination of this process occur in an episode entitled "Der gefrorne Christ" in the second version of Keller's novel. During the course of this chapter, the count, Dortchen, and Heinrich engage in a conversation on the verse of the Baroque poet and mystic Angelus Silesius. In the second version, the discussion takes place on the evening of the departure of the atheist Gilgus. The character of Gilgus does not appear in Keller's original version, but the narrator's comments in the first version on the dialectical affinity between passionate mystics and fanatic atheists anticipate his presence in the novel's revised form: "So werden auch stets ein recht herzlicher glühender Mystiker und ein rabiater Atheist besser miteinander auskommen und größeres Interesse aneinander haben als etwa ein dürrer orthodoxer Protestant und ein flacher Rationalist, weil jene beiden gegenseitig wohl fühlen, daß ein höherer spezifischer Wert in ihnen treibt und durchscheint" (1:726).

The "rabiater Atheist" is shaped into the figure of Gilgus in the later edition of *Der grüne Heinrich*. Here Keller puts the previously cited theory about the attraction between religious and philosophical opposites into practice by describing the close bond that forms between the atheist and the man of the cloth. Indeed, the first thing remarked upon by Heinrich after he mentions the chaplain's appearance with the volume of Silesius is the latter's regret at Gilgus's absence, and Heinrich senses after the chaplain begins to read from Silesius how extremities of view synthesize and become identical to one another; he hears Feuerbach in the words of the religiously devout Baroque poet (1:1064). Keller had earlier established a close kinship between another pair of religiously divergent characters—the count and the schoolmaster. Both are independent-minded and self-sufficient widowers, both are charged with the rearing of a single daughter, and both are admirable in terms of intellectual development and ethical sensibilities, though one is a pious Christian and one an atheist. Such a dialectic of reconciliation inevitably suggests a telos of synthesis and closure, and the effacement of alterity. The juxtaposition of opposites to evoke an overarching unity and to create a psychic totality with regard to characterization also approximates the ideals subtended by Poetic Realism's ego–alter ego dialectics. The equation here of seeming theological antitheses, while evoking a laudable image of transcendent, harmonious brotherhood, also inevitably creates a *positive* sense of identity, of the mythic-rational ever-the-same, and this is precisely what Adorno believed epic naiveté attempts, ideally, to *resist*.

Of course, these examples are not related to the negative subject-object dialectic in *Der grüne Heinrich* elucidated by Kaiser. According to Kaiser, the subjective ground of modern experience is constituted by alienation, the inability to feel comfortably, naturally situated in the world. Thus subjectivity becomes the objective condition of experience (1981:178) and "Das subjektiv Unbegriffene gerinnt zu starrer Objektivität" (1981:579). An instance of such dialectical coagulation can be seen in Heinrich's earliest attempts to come to grips with the concept of the divine. Heinrich's first sense of God is grounded in visual images—a weather vane and a tiger. The immediate catalyst for these concrete images is his mother's unsatisfying modernist representation of God as a "Geist," and they thus occur as a reaction to the abstraction of the mother's terminology (1:66–67). This kind of abstraction is lampooned as an unfortunate element in modern Swiss Reformed Church theology in *Martin Salander*, as we will see. But though the youthful Heinrich's reifications are an example of what Kaiser refers to as "negative subject-object dialectics," they have nothing in common with Adorno's "negative dialectics," which were conceived largely in order to *subvert* reification, the identification of a concept with an object. Nor is the epic naiveté adumbrated by Adorno to be equated with the "rigid objectification" (Kaiser) of concepts and experiences the subject is unable to comprehend. Instead, the naive epicist focuses his attention on the objective world as such, and thus blocks out the identitarian, universalizing concepts of the ratio, as when Homer fixes his narrative attention in the *Odyssey* on the rhythmic motion of the waves (*Noten zur Literatur* 1: 50–51). Heinrich's early representation of God can be seen as an imaginative child's recoiling from the impersonality of a recondite omnipotence. However childishly naive this reaction may appear, it does not constitute an example of what Adorno called epic naiveté.

Lee B. Jennings has noted regarding *Martin Salander* that soullessness "can be said to emerge as the chief social ill in this work" (1983:200). Such soullessness makes possible the creation of the parallelisms, duplications, and fungibility observed by Adorno and others in Keller's last novel. For only a measure of soul allows a person to emerge in his or her own distinct individuality. Protagonists empty on the inside, who are characterized by "'hollow-headedness'" (1983:200),[8] can be easily shown as interchangeable by an author, since only their external appearance is unique. Of course, the Weidelich twins, in whom Adorno discerns a duplication suggestive of a fungibility inherent in late capitalist society, are bereft of even this distinction. In *Martin Salander*, the fungibility ascribable to soullessness carries over to social institutions as well. For Keller portrays the Swiss Reformed Church as so abstracted in its theology and in its mission that it has become conflated with the state. Already in his novella *Das verlorene Lachen* (1874), Keller sought to evoke what he saw as the contourlessness and abstractness of Zwingli's faith in its contemporary configuration by saying of the work's main female protagonist, Justine: " . . . sie selbst hing der unbestimmten Zeitreligion an und war darin umso eifriger, je gestaltloser ihre Vorstellungen waren" (2:472).

However, what Keller saw as the duplicitousness, hunger for power, and hypocrisy of the modern Swiss Reformed Church are concentrated in *Das verlorene Lachen* in the solitary figure of an avaricious, self-deceiving minister. Neither this sort of relatively centralized focus[9] nor the theological dialectics found in *Der grüne Heinrich* structure the religious dimension of *Martin Salander*. Instead, the empty superficiality, the "soullessness" Keller detected in contemporary Swiss Reformed perspectives is manifested in the sometimes vaguely, sometimes directly delineated intertwining of church and state. Their essential fungibility comes to the fore at random moments of the narrative but is resonant throughout it, and this circumstance lends credence to Kaiser's assertion that the subject-object dialectic of *Der grüne Heinrich* dissolves in *Martin Salander* into an interplay between surface and deep structure. The complicity of church and state in this novel in the effacement of traditions that had provided a sense of purport and meaning to the lives of common people plays a major role in evoking the "unheilschwangeren Anfängen der spätkapitalistischen Ära" discerned by Adorno in its narrative (*Noten zur Literatur* 1:54).

The first conjunction of abstracted religion and contemporary politics is quite understated. Upset by the way a speaker resorts to patriotism to distort the issues surrounding an agricultural matter, Salander notes that even a Republican cannot profitably act contrary to the natural plan established by Providence ("die Vorsehung"). His sermon ("Predigt") is described by the narrator as inopportune, and the plan set forth by Salander's rival carries the day (3:580–81). In representing a politician's ability to gain acceptance for an absurd measure solely through a continuous resort to the words "Republik" and "republikanisch" (3:580), Keller mounts an obvious attack on the misguided nationalism of the "Gründerjahre." But by referring to Salander's speech, with its own appeal to an abstracted divinity, as a sermon, he also subtly creates an atmosphere at a surface lexical level that reflects and enhances the novel's deep structural entanglement of Swiss politics and the contemporary theology of the Swiss Reformed Church.

This conflation of the religious and the political becomes more overt during the course of the novel. When Martin discusses plans for the double wedding with his future sons-in-law, it is decided, in accordance with the "spirit of the times," that the ceremony and the sermon must be executed by "ein geistlicher Demokrat" (3:638). At the wedding, the minister reads a prayer simultaneously representing "den kirchlichen Sinn und die Rechte des freien Denkens" (3:643). In his toast to the couples at the banquet following the nuptials, the minister praises the conjunction of the two socioeconomic classes represented in the double wedding. He sees it as fully in accordance with the ideals of the age, in which church and state, "Gesamtvolk und Gott," constitute one democratic, harmonious, indivisible whole. Afterward, the "Pfarrer" refers to himself in conversation with Marie Salander as a "Volksredner" (3: 645–47). Martin feels uncomfortable with the minister's toast, but he nevertheless regards his wife's even stronger aversion as exaggerated. His choice of words in defending the minister is again calculated to evoke the duality of church and state, religion and politics, at a subtle, analogical level: "Es ist nur Manier! Jeder, der viel spricht, besonders in Politik, hat seine Manier" (3:649). Attending his first session as an elected member of the legislative assembly, Martin is one of the few representatives to take seriously the prayers and sacred oaths of this body. For though he is not inclined toward the church, he takes an affirmative attitude toward the liturgical character of the legislative precepts (3:659).

Martin's almost unconscious, automatic conflation of church and state, and their more overt entanglement on the part of the minister, create a consistent pattern in the novel despite the discontinuous manner in which the theme of this duality is invoked. In his discussion of *Martin Salander*, Adorno notes that the narrative word inscribed by epic naiveté takes an apologetic attitude toward the past (*Noten zur Literatur* 1:55). The veracity of this assertion can be seen in Keller's articulation of the nexus between religion and politics in his last novel. For the transformation of the secular (political) and the sacred (religious) facets of Swiss life from allied yet discrete spheres into an abstracted, self-understood, but unreflected interchangeability is shown to have damaging consequences and to lead to unforeseen aberrations.[10] Such results become evident in Wohlwend's hypocritical elucidation of a "Gottesstaat der Neuzeit" (3:712), and in Amalie Weidelich's desperate attempt to take comfort from the abstracted, impersonal quality of God as represented by contemporary Swiss Reformed theology and buttressed by her current sociopolitical status (3:738). Szemkus has shown how Keller manipulates various temporal elements in *Martin Salander* to reinvigorate the past implicitly and blend it into the present, while highlighting the uncertainty and confusion of the present, particularly at the novel's outset (91–94).

Amalie's somewhat absurd defense of her social equality in response to questions posed by Salander that do not even challenge her class status heightens this sense of a conservative nostalgia early in the novel (3:514–16). Her tragic fate toward the novel's conclusion is indicative of Keller's belief that the loss of old religious and social values destructively impacted his country. Amalie and her husband raised the twins in accordance with a firm belief in their own equality in the society at large, but without a strong religious or moral foundation. Indeed, she claims she doesn't even understand the modern, cultivated church services with their evocation of an abstract and recondite deity; though she is a true believer, she only attends these services in order to undergird the social and political prestige of her sons (3:726). There is a conscious entanglement of political, institutional corruption, social ambition, and a depersonalized theology in Keller's articulation of the circumstances leading to the Weidelichs' downfall. But this conjunction becomes most overt when Wohlwend is described as traveling around the country in order to drum up support for his theocracy. According to the terms of the constitution he designs for this ideal state, God's will and authority are enacted by theocratic synods consisting, in equal numbers, of clergy and laity. God himself, as president, is empowered to cast tie-breaking votes, which are made manifest through prayer. Wohlwend fails to gain enthusiasm for his idea, for he has no real religious conviction or understanding, and doesn't even care about the kind of theology upon which his theocracy would be founded (3:770–71). Nevertheless, the description of this plan represents the climax of Keller's evocation of the destructive fungibility of church and state in contemporary Switzerland.

As the religious dimension of *Martin Salander* makes evident, Adorno was correct to discern in Keller's last novel a thematics of duplication and fungibility evocative of an intellectually deadening sameness of experience, of the mythic-rational "Immergleiche" (*Noten zur Literatur* 1:50) as manifested in the emergent era of late capitalism. Keller's fixation on narrative details, such as Martin Salander's spoonful of soup, represents what Adorno sees as the attempt of epic naiveté to break this spell of the ever-the-same, to negate, through the precision of the descriptive word, the conceptual intentionality of a reflective reason whose hidden agenda is such identicality. Keller's use of character duplication gives the novel's duplicated protagonists a density, a static, concrete, arrested quality similar to that of the purely descriptive word. The practice marks a break with the synthesizing dialectics in the ego–alter ego juxtapositions evident in most of the works of Poetic Realism discussed in this book, including *Der grüne Heinrich*. This circumstance lends support to Adorno's suggestion that Keller's technique of character duplication, a form of epic naiveté, both reflects the sway of the ever-the-same and tries to undermine it. But the instrument of duplication and fungibility extends beyond simple character development; Keller's elucidation of a metaphoric equivalence between the religious and the political allows us to see the technique as a fundamental structural principle in the novel.

Nevertheless, it is Keller's establishment of duplication and fungibility as attributes of specific characters that sets into motion the sort of nontraditional dialectics Adorno himself valued. Keller had used binary groupings of characters to create a sense of balance—and stasis—in *Der grüne Heinrich*. We have mentioned the dialectical pairings of schoolmaster-count, Gilgus-chaplain, and Feuerbach-Angelus Silesius. When Heinrich is exposed to Frau Margret and her circle of friends, a group of Jews is matched against a group of pious Christian women, a nasty, sarcastic atheist is contrasted with a respectable and respectful nonbeliever, the poor and oppressed are set off against the up-and-coming, and Frau Margret's own serious, hardworking nature and sensuous piety are equipoised by her good-for-nothing, irreverent husband. This balance evokes a sense of synthesis, of movement toward dialectical unity. In *Martin Salander*, the motif of duplication allows those figures termed "authentic" by Merkel-Nipperdey to emerge in their alterity; if such characters as Marie Salander, Arnold Salander, and Möni Wighart emerge as "authentic," it is because they are truly unique. Marie is strongly individuated by her qualities of endurance and insightfulness, the mature Arnold is uniquely steadfast and resolute, and Möni Wighart is the only figure in the work whom one can regard as representative of faithful, reliable friendship.

We might combine the insights of Merkel-Nipperdey, Passavant, and Adorno to note that the "Motiv der Verdoppelung" (Passavant 97) instantiates a dialectic of identity and contrast in the novel, allowing the characters whose individuality is not effectively canceled through this process to emerge in their otherness. Their otherness is not simply a given, as in most novels; it is brought to the fore, highlighted, and made to stand out through the establishment of their clear contrast with those characters tainted by duplication and fungibility.[11] A bringing to the fore of the ideal of alterity, of what lies "outside the spell of unity" (*Negative Dialektik* 8) was the goal proposed by Adorno in his own negative dialectics. And it was in the evocation of the unique, the other, "das Verschiedene" (*Noten zur Literatur* 1:51) that Adorno saw the true social and aesthetic value of epic naiveté.

Do the nonsynthesizing dialectics in *Martin Salander*'s characterizations, with their underscoring of otherness in certain protagonists, indicate Keller rejected Poetic Realism's theoretical ideal of projecting a harmonious aesthetic totality? This question cannot be answered with a simple yes or no. Rather, as Christine Renz has argued, Keller felt the poetic image was indeed the only adequate means for representing such totality, but that this totality was concomitantly redemptive and negating (231). Its representation occurs in discontinuous moments, and the fragmentation resulting from such discontinuity underscores the artificiality inherent in these aesthetic "Erfüllungsmomenten" (372).

The motif of the Double in *Martin Salander* negates individuality in certain characters. However, precisely this negation in one set of protagonists allows, by way of contrast, the emergence of fulfilled, immanently integrated, and discrete personas in another. With regard to these latter characters, one may say *Martin Salander* does lead to the evocation of psychically comprehensive narrated egos through its "Verdoppelung" technique.

5. Guilt, Memory, and the Motif of the Double in Theodor Storm's *Aquis submersus* and *Ein Doppelgänger*

No writer associated with German Poetic Realism was more influenced by the Romantic Doppelgänger motif than Theodor Storm. Like other writers in the movement, Storm attempted to render the Double figure realistic while retaining its imaginative aspects. Critical studies of Storm are consistent in showing that Storm strove to adapt the Romantic Double to his own narrative purposes while resisting the Romantic fantastic elements associated with the motif. This resistance was not entirely successful. Andrew Webber has effectively demonstrated that Storm largely suppressed the supernatural elements of Romantic Doppelgänger tales while remaining greatly indebted to Romantic writers (particularly Hoffmann) in the creation of his own "double visions." According to Webber, Storm's attempt to contain and domesticate the uncanny features of the Doppelgänger motif was finally revoked with the phantom doubling of Hauke Haien and his ghostly night ride into oblivion in Storm's last novella, *Der Schimmelreiter* (1888). Though Eric Downing's essay "Repetition and Realism: The 'Ligeia' Impulse in Theodor Storm's *Viola tricolor*" focuses on the motif of doubling and duplication in the particular novella named in the title, he has also shown that the Romantic topos of substitution and doubling is evident throughout much of Storm's prose oeuvre despite his efforts to resist the Romantic by turning away from repetition and fantasy.

In spite of their well-informed discussions of Storm's attempt at overcoming the supernatural and the fantastic in his more quotidian adaptations of the Romantic Doppelgänger motif, both Webber and Downing largely ignore one of Storm's most celebrated formal techniques: the historical framed narrative.[1] And while there have been numerous studies of Storm's use of multiple temporal perspectives in his *Rahmennovellen*, and of the themes of memory and remembrance as integral components of his prose oeuvre,[2] none of these studies has examined in any more than a tangential manner the way in which the temporal-historical element in Storm's narrative framing strategy might relate to the motif of the Double in his work. Yet particularly in two of Storm's novellas, *Aquis submersus* (1876) and *Ein Doppelgänger* (1886), the Doppelgänger motif and the technique of the historical framed narrative intersect in a mutually influential manner.

Precisely this intersection suggests a new, fruitful means for examining two of the central dilemmas identified by Storm's critics in his work: the difficulty of establishing in the narratives a technique of fictive suprahistorical memory that can be seen to overcome the loss of real historical memory through the passing of time, and the related quest to come to grips with the problem of hereditarily or socially engendered personal guilt, the sort of guilt that burdens the individual not purely through his or her specific deeds, but also through the vagaries of history and fate. Storm's conjoining of the historical framed narrative to the motif of the Double represents the attempt both to engender an effective historical memory[3] and to deal with the problem of passively acquired guilt (or, as W. N. B. Mullan has termed it, "tragic guilt"). We will see that in the transition from *Aquis submersus* to *Ein Doppelgänger* a thematic shift occurs. Storm uses the historical framed narrative in the early novella to manipulate the motif of the Double in such a way that barriers to memory and its instantiation of a sense of tragic guilt are overcome. In the second tale, the temporally bifurcated narrative line is linked to the Doppelgänger motif in order to allow the reader to attain the sense that guilt and fate themselves have been transcended, expiated, and overcome.

More than any other critic who has written on *Aquis submersus*, Clifford Bernd has demonstrated that Storm deliberately, and through a plethora of techniques, subverts the establishment of what I term effective historical memory. The dialectical shuttling between the evocation of a memory capable of counteracting the destruction of remembrance through the passage of time, and a calling into question of the ability of memory to suspend this ravishment of historical recall, result largely from "the tension in the core of the narrative design between (1) the awareness that human happiness vanishes with the passing of years and (2) the reassuring feeling that the destructive effects of the passage of time can be overcome with memory" (Bernd 1966:11). Various commemorative techniques are employed throughout the novella to allow for the temporary establishment of a historical memory seemingly resistant to fleeting time, but these commemorative vehicles are shown, in steady succession, to be ineffective. These vehicles include the memoir-like recollections of the contemporary narrator, the actual handwritten memoir of the central protagonist, Johannes, discovered by the narrator (and which constitutes the historical framed narrative), the pictures painted by Johannes as well as the portraits of Gerhardus's ancestors in the Gerhardus family gallery, auxiliary paintings, and the evocation of popular tradition. As Bernd indicates, Storm calls the ability of these commemorative vehicles to generate an enduring historical memory into question at every turn. The contemporary narrator's discovery of the artist's memoir is only inspired by his sudden interest (after a youth spent ignoring it) in a Low German inscription attached to the house containing the manuscript: "Gleich so wie Rauch und Staub verschwindt, / Also sind auch die Menschenkind." Almost involuntarily ("Fast unwillkürlich"), he enters the house in search of accommodations for his young cousin (2:384). His powerful attraction to this particular inscription also tends subtly to undermine the reader's confidence in the veracity of his own precise, realistically delineated recollections. The memoir of the artist discovered by the narrator is strongly yellowed, indicating its own transience and unreliability as a permanent memorial.

The painting of Johannes's beloved, Katharina, has been tainted by a shadow, and other paintings are described as dimmed with dust, thus subverting their commemorative efficacy. Popular tradition, which has preserved the memory of the artist and his son through word of mouth, is shown to be spotty, inconsistent, and ignorant of their story in many particulars. The artist himself is shown at the novella's conclusion to have faded from historical memory, a victim of that transitoriness of all that is earthly which so obsessed Johannes's Baroque contemporaries. Thus Bernd's concluding commentary on the novella's theme (and final statement) concerning the futility of trying to create a steadfast commemorative of the past appears fully justified at first glance: "All that the audience hears is a stringent statement that succinctly lets them know that every endeavor to keep the past alive—either on the part of Storm, as an analysis of his creative process shows, or on the part of his fictional counterpart, as the language and context of the statement reveal—has come to nought" (Bernd 1966:52). Robert Holub has asserted that the novella's recollective narrative framework "contributes to the effect of realism" (138), but the very unreliability of this recollection contributes to our feeling that the narrative is a product of imagination rather than history. This is why the term "Poetic Realism" is justified in connection with such works.

Nevertheless, we have already seen that Storm had an aversion to the Romantic cult of the imagination. Perhaps this lends a certain irony to the fact that he employed a Romantic motif in *Aquis submersus* to counteract this dialectic cancellation of aids to a faithful recording of history: the figure of the Double. To be sure, the instantiation of this particular motif in *Aquis submersus* does not involve a complete external, physiological duplication stemming from the psychological schism of one protagonist, as is so often the case in the works of Romantic writers. Ralph Tymms has asserted that the literalness of the Doppelgänger motif is replaced in the period between the Romanticism of Hoffmann and the antirealist Expressionism of writers such as Georg Kaiser, and "is assigned a place in the symbolical literature that constantly reappears, to explain by means of a venerable ethical system of dualism the complex and disharmonious nature of man" (120). Questions of fate, personal responsibility, heredity, and "tragic" (because seemingly predestined) guilt in *Aquis submersus* so overdetermine the moral dimension of the novella that it might be an oversimplification to speak of an ethical "dualism" there. But precisely this moral quandary provides the primary thematic basis for Storm's adaptation of the Double motif.

On a structural level, Storm creates figures belonging to multiple time frames in *Aquis submersus*, so that the repetition of psychic and physical attributes occurs across the space of two distinct temporal periods. Thus Junker Wulf, Katharina's brother, is not consciously aware that he is the transsexual Doppelgänger of an ancestress. Because she, the original figure, is long dead, internal and external features are duplicated through heredity. It takes a painting to make Johannes aware that this ancestral doubling has occurred. Not long after this awareness dawns on him, the painting fills him with a sense of ominous horror. He clearly perceives in the painting of the Gerhardus family ancestress a presence that continues to have an impact on the realm of the living: "Da, unter dem Malen, fiel mein Auge auch auf jenes alte Frauenbildniß, das mir zur Seite hing und aus den weißen Schleiertüchern die stechend grauen Augen auf mich gerichtet hielt. Mich fröstelte, ich hätte nahezu den Stuhl verrücket" (2:407).

This physical reaction is so powerful that we have a vivid sense of the historical divide transcended and the memory-deadening passage of time momentarily revoked. Johannes's visceral response to the portrait of the *Ahnin* contrasts markedly with the description by the contemporary narrator of his youthful response to the portraits in the village church. He is strongly attracted to the paintings of the dead youth and this youth's supposed father, but he has no sense that they are reaching out to him beyond their painted representations and beyond the grave. Indeed, he so strongly senses the historical gap between them that his strongest desire is to bridge the gap himself by obtaining information about the figures in the paintings (2:381–82). The dramatically corporeal manner in which Johannes is impacted by the portrait of the ancestress suggests that the historical period separating viewer and viewed has been bridged without the need for such an investigation. Of course, one could argue that Johannes, as an artist, is much more open to the sheer material suggestiveness of a portrait than an inexperienced youth. But Storm's terminology suggests much more is at stake; while the portrait of the dead boy merely spoke ("sprach") to the contemporary narrator (2:381), the piercing ("stechend") gray eyes of the ancestress actually arrest Johannes with her gaze (2:407).

The use of the linguistic term "sprach" suggests the need for semiotic interpretation; the narrator must decode a signifier to arrive at what it signifies, and this is what inspires him with the urge to do some research. There is a much purer visuality governing Johannes's experience of the ancestress's portrait, a material presence equaled only in his experience of Katharina's picture at the novella's conclusion. But this latter deceptive shock of recognition causes "the old time" ("die alte Zeit") to rise before his inner eye (2:452) while, in his reaction to the *Ahnin*'s representation, all perception of temporal distance is obliterated and a moment of sensual synchronicity occurs. Such synchronicity evokes, on a temporal level, the sense of aesthetic totality that we have found to be Poetic Realism's highest ideal. The synchronic cut anticipates the evocation of the *Ahnin*'s duplication in figures contemporary to Johannes: namely, Junker Wulf and Bas' Ursel. Downing has shown that the use of a painting either to anticipate (and even engender) the repetition of one figure in another (as in *Viola tricolor*, 1872–73), or as a preternatural presence itself doubled by living characters (as in *Waldwinkel*, 1874, and *Im Schloß*, 1861), is not uncommon in Storm's oeuvre (Downing 279–80). A similar effect is achieved by a magic mirror in Storm's Romantically influenced fairy tale, *Der Spiegel des Cyprianus* (1865); the Doppelgänger created by this mirror presage future events and, indeed, future lives. What is unique in *Aquis submersus* is the linkage of portraiture to repetition-doubling within the space of a historical framed narrative which takes place in the forgotten past. Bernd has shown that the superfluity of commemorative vehicles in the novella, and the resonance of their futility, are greatly enhanced through temporal bifurcation in the narrative line. Since they are dialectically canceled as aids to an effective historical memory, the use of a Doppelgänger motif first brought to bear through the related motif of the almost living portrait can now begin to be seen as a way to overcome the nullification of remembrance.

Before we examine how the motif of the Double is brought into play in *Aquis submersus* in the figure of Junker Wulf, it is necessary to examine a controversy that has sprung up around this issue. Citing the work of Frederic E. Coenen, Bernd notes "popular tradition" relates that the only child of the *Ahnin* died without offspring; she had been cursed by the *Ahnin* for having fallen in love with a man not of her social caste, and this curse led to her death by drowning (2:407–08). This does not jibe with Johannes's conviction that Wulf is the Double, through heredity, of the *Ahnin* (2:402). Bernd believes this inconsistency was created as a deliberate tactic by Storm to cast doubt on the reliability of popular tradition as a commemorative medium (Bernd 1966:42–43). Also noting that the childlessness of the *Ahnin*'s daughter means Wulf could not possibly be their descendant, Mullan asserts "that this inconsistency is merely a slip on Storm's part and that C. A. Bernd attaches too much significance to it when he argues that it is a deliberate device" (234–35). Though one can only speculate, there may be some truth to both points of view. Bernd demonstrates conclusively that Storm intended to show that popular tradition in the tale is one among a host of unreliable mnemonic devices, and despite Storm's frequent engagement in ironic dissembling through the evocation of false resemblances in *Aquis submersus*,[4] the theme of the inheritance by a later generation of its ancestors' physical, psychological, and moral characteristics is so powerful and pervasive in this novella that it is difficult to believe he was deliberately creating a delusive familial chain here. His inconsistency may have consisted in evoking the unreliability of the *Volksmund* in so subtle a manner that the popular perspective could be conflated with Storm's authorial intent.[5]

Johannes's sense that the *Ahnin*'s malevolent nature has been inherited and duplicated in the person of Wulf is brought forth in his first description of her portrait. Gazing at the gallery of pictures representing the Gerhardus family, he notices that Katharina's countenance resembles the combined physiognomy of her parents. This leads him to puzzle over the harsh, small-eyed visage of her brother. He senses these traits must have been passed on from somewhere in the past, and his suspicions are almost immediately confirmed when he casts his gaze upon the portrait of the ancestress, the wife of a Gerhardus who had lived about one hundred years before. The shock of recognition, his sense that Wulf's features constitute a transsexual repetition of those of his ancestor, leads Johannes to fear this long-dead personage as much as her Doppelgänger: "Wie räthselhafte Wege gehet die Natur! Ein saeculum und drüber rinnt es heimlich wie unter einer Decke im Blute der Geschlechter fort; dann, längst vergessen, taucht es plötzlich wieder auf, den Lebenden zum Unheil. Nicht vor dem Sohn des edlen Gerhardus; vor dieser hier und ihres Blutes nachgeborenem Sprößling soll ich Katharinen schützen" (2:402).

Though as yet unaware of it, Johannes is beginning to confront the circumstance that hereditary iteration is dangerous and even tragic when such an echo across the abyss of history is the *only* means, given the failure of all commemorative media, to overcome the ravages to memory of passing time. Storm's novella gives an interesting twist to George Santayana's oft-misquoted line that "those who cannot remember the past are condemned to fulfil it." In Storm's world, the difficulty of remembering the past cannot be overcome through any active human endeavor. Thus, the past will fulfill itself, will make itself a "presence," through the agency of doubling and repetition. The popular legend of a curse leading to a death by drowning will repeat itself in the reality of the death by drowning of the son born, without the knowledge of the father, to Katharina and Johannes. While the *Ahnin* was the agent of the legendary curse, her Double, Wulf, is the agent of the real one. For in setting his dogs on Johannes, he literally forces him into Katharina's arms, leading to the conception of their ill-fated child. Wulf thereupon forces their tragic separation. As Johannes leaves Katharina's bedchamber, he perceives a bony hand behind the windows next to the tower containing this chamber. It is lifted as though in curse: "Sie drohete nach mir mit aufgehobenem Finger und schien mir farblos und knöchern gleich der Hand des Todes. Doch war's nur wie im Husch, daß solches über meine Augen ging; dachte zwar erstlich des Märleins von der wiedergehenden Urahne; redete mir dann aber ein, es seien nur meine eigenen aufgestörten Sinne, die solch Spiel mir vorgegaukelt hätten" (2:420).

Johannes had actually viewed the hand of Bas' Ursel, but in the moment she is perceived as the ancestress's Doppelgänger, the past once again manifests itself in the form of effective historical memory, a memory effective more because than in spite of the distortional power of the imagination. Gerhard Kaiser has said of Storm, and in connection with *Aquis submersus*: "Er braucht Geschichte und erfundene fremde Geschichten als Attrappen und Kulissen eines Lebensgefühls, in denen es sich offenbart und versteckt. Geschichte ist bis auf die Stimmung ausgequetscht" (1979:433). It might be more accurate to say that Storm must use the "window dressing and backdrop" of an imaginative Doppelgänger scenario to bring the historical past, seemingly consigned to oblivion, into a vivid, memorable manifestation.

At this point, the question arises as to why all other forms of commemorative media, all other means of overcoming the ravages of time and making history "present" through an effective historical memory, are doomed to failure. The Baroque setting of the historical framed narrative, and Bernd's critical study of this novella, lead us to believe the transience of all that is earthly, or all that is human, is responsible for the difficulty of remembering the past. The diachronic flow of events, people, and objects, which consigns them to metamorphosis, evanescence, and oblivion, renders their originary manifestation an impossibility after a certain amount of time has passed. The motto on the door of the house where the contemporary narrator discovers Johannes's manuscript is repeated at the commencement of the second volume of that manuscript in the original Low German: "Geliek as Rook un Stoof verswindt, / Also sind ock de Minschenkind" (2:431).

This repetition is similar in technique to Storm's use of the Doppelgänger motif. Just as the *Ahnin* is first shown transposed into a portrait in Johannes's narrative and then manifests her originary presence in the bony hand of Bas' Ursel (at least in the mind of Johannes, to whom she temporarily becomes fully materially present), so the motto is first encountered in translation and then rendered in the actual, physically present dialect in which it was written. This doubling of the motto, along with the contemporary narrator's final paragraph on Johannes's disappearance from human memory (he is not even mentioned in the city's chronicle [2:455]), strengthens the sense that doubling and repetition are instantiated because they are the only means of bridging the hermeneutic gap between past and present. Walter Brecht has spoken of the "ungeheure Kluft" evoked by Storm "zwischen dem vergangenen Inhalt der angeblichen Chronik oder Handschrift und dem gegenwärtigen Erzähler, ihm selbst," even as Storm emphasizes the continuity of time and history's ability through a puzzling and merely portended atavism to become "tageswirksam" in the present (447, 452). According to Brecht, this oscillation between the past and present in Storm's work demonstrates the uncertainty of life, Storm's belief that man always walks at the edge of an abyss (458).

Although Brecht is certainly correct in his assessment of Storm's complex stance on history and temporality, it seems certain that neither human transience nor the simple ability of the past to intrude upon the present are at the root of Storm's evocation of an abyssal uncertainty in *Aquis submersus*. Most critics are in agreement that the question of guilt forms the central problematic of the novella.[6] This question of guilt, and not just the obliterative tendency of passing time, also bears heavily on the issue of why commemorative media are shown to be ineffective in this work. When Brecht speaks of the presence in Storm's oeuvre of "Individual-, Familien-, Sitten- und Kulturgeschichte als rätselvoller, mehr geahnter Atavismus" (452) in his 1925 article on Storm's treatment of history, he adumbrates, as a literary technique, a phenomenon Freud would identify thirteen years later as a pathology in his study *Der Mann Moses und die monotheistische Religion*, a pathology he termed "Die Wiederkehr des Verdrängten." Although Freud primarily developed this concept to illustrate how events experienced in the first five years of life and then repressed will later manifest themselves in the neurotic symptoms of adults (16:201–9, 233–36), he notes this phenomenon may have an atavistic dimension: "Eine neue Komplikation tritt aber hinzu, wenn wir auf die Wahrscheinlichkeit aufmerksam werden, daß im psychischen Leben des Individuums nicht nur selbsterlebte, sondern auch bei der Geburt mitgebrachte Inhalte wirksam sein mögen, Stücke von phylogenetischer Herkunft, eine archaische Erbschaft" (16:204–5). When Johannes, as he glances for the first time at the portrait of the *Ahnin*, resolves to protect Katharina, not from Gerhardus's son but from the scion born of her blood, of blood coursing surreptitiously through other generations (2:402), he is identifying, in its atavistic dimension, the return of the repressed.

Of course, the central figure inscribed by the nexus of guilt motivating the narration of Storm's novella is not Wulf but Johannes himself. In urging Katharina not to leave him so that she may look after their child when he finds her, after many years of separation, in the "Priesterkoppel," he brings about the neglect that will lead to their son's drowning. There is an atmosphere of fatedness connected to the tragedy; the tale of the witch and her consanguinity suggests once more that certain families are doomed and damned. Johannes's feet seem, without his volition, to carry him to the site where the event takes place (2:445), and the motif of repetition and doubling indicates that the *Ahnin*'s curse will be fulfilled. For we have already seen a pattern whereby the representational (the painting of the *Ahnin*, the translation of the motto in the contemporary narrative frame) is remanifested as an originary presence (the *Ahnin*'s hand in the hand of Bas' Ursel; the appearance, in the second manuscript of the historical framed narrative, of the motto in its actual Low German script). So, too, the *Ahnin*'s curse, only a legendary rumor in connection with the tale of her drowned daughter, becomes a material reality with the drowning of her descendant's son.

However, as Mullan has noted, "Johannes is not, and does not consider himself to be, simply the luckless victim of an external fate. He too bears a responsibility for the catastrophe and he acknowledges it in full, both when he paints the initials C. P. A. S. below the portrait of his dead child and later when he writes his manuscript" (237).[7] In other words, Johannes's sense of guilt helps inspire both the painting of his son and the composition of the manuscript. Nevertheless, both of these acts constitute a form of repetition and doubling that turns the pattern we have just noted on its head. For whereas the portrait and the curse are transformed through the shifting of the purely representational (art and narrativized popular tradition) into that form of "actuality" we have come to term "Poetic Realism," Johannes's writing and painting repeat and duplicate the "realistic" in the media of absolute representationality. Of course, one must place terms connoting the authentic in quotation marks, for all of these elements belong to the metatext *Aquis submersus*, that is, to *Aquis submersus* as a fictive textual totality. But the dynamic of this metatext is itself constituted by a narrative flow from the representational to the material-factual and back. Through a guilt inscribed by both fate and personal responsibility, Johannes is trapped in the interstice of this never-to-be-sublated dialectic. Its infinite quality is engendered by the historical framed narrative; the discovery of Johannes's pictures and his manuscript by the contemporary narrator, and this narrator's subsequent attempt to discover the reality behind Johannes's textual ("C. P. A. S.") and pictorial representations, show Johannes to be endlessly caught up in this dialectic. For hermeneutic investigation, from one generation to the next, will not allow the dead to rest in peace.

This circumstance, as much as the atmosphere of transience in the novella, is responsible for the feeling of abyssal uncertainty it evokes. And though the Doppelgänger motif informs *Aquis submersus* with a sense of atavism strong enough to counteract the transience by engendering a synchronicity constitutive of effective historical memory, aesthetic totality, and psychological comprehensiveness, the revelation written, through doubling and repetition, into this memory, is only the condition of instability itself. Johannes would expiate his guilt through the painting of his dead son, but the painting only replicates it. The discovery of this painting by the contemporary narrator, the desire this discovery instills in him to understand the artwork, and the fact that the artwork is now available to posterity for examination and interpretation—these circumstances indicate that the hermeneutic process will make the replication of this guilt an endless act. Only posterity's indifference, a real possibility given the consignment of Johannes's person and his greatest painting to an apparent disappearance from the pages of history at the novella's conclusion (2:455), could save him from this fate. But of course, a complete "submersion" into the obliterative "waters" of time seems an equally undesirable alternative.

Like *Aquis submersus*, the novella *Ein Doppelgänger* is structurally constituted by the intersection of the motif of the Double with a historical framed narrative. As in the earlier novella, the theme of guilt is of overriding importance here. But we will see that the closure inscribed into the narrative of the later work allows the main character's burden of guilt to be overcome. As several critics have noted, Storm was greatly influenced in the composition of *Ein Doppelgänger* by the most famous novella associated with Poetic Realism to intertwine a complex treatment of guilt with the motif of the Double, Droste-Hülshoff's *Die Judenbuche*. Ingrid Schuster has observed that, like Droste-Hülshoff's Friedrich Mergel, John Hansen's inferior social status is what leads to the mise-en-scène of a Double. The sublation (only partial in *Die Judenbuche*) of the Doppelgänger figure evident at the conclusion of both works is due largely to another similarity identified by Schuster: "Im Tode werden die Doppelgänger eins: der Selbstmörder Johannes Niemand wird als der Mörder Friedrich Mergel erkannt; John Hansens Schuld und Sühne finden ihr Ende" (169). Building on Schuster's analysis, Gunter Grimm finds the expiation of guilt as an ethical dilemma to be the central problem of *Die Judenbuche*, while Storm turns the social question into the main theme of *Ein Doppelgänger* (333–34). Heinz Rölleke's intertextual reading of the two tales has uncovered other similarities with respect to character attributes and plot development. For example, both John Hansen and Friedrich Mergel come under the influence of malevolent characters (Simon and Hansen's criminal accomplice Wenzel). These evil figures help inspire the impressionable young men who stand under their influence to commit crimes by taking advantage of their charges' poverty and wounded pride (1992:250). John and Friedrich bear a physical resemblance, as they wear long hair which hangs, unkempt, around faces marked by suffering and deprivation (1992:253). Rölleke assumes Storm's reading of *Die Judenbuche* played a major, albeit probably unconscious, role in the composition of *Ein Doppelgänger* (1992:255).

We can add that neither Droste-Hülshoff nor Storm allows the reader to feel that a miserable social standing actually absolves their respective protagonists of their guilt in killing another human being. Thus, guilt and penance constitute the fundamental moral nexus of the two works. What most profoundly distinguishes them on a structural level is Storm's employment of a historical framed narrative. Droste-Hülshoff's tale is told from the viewpoint of a straightforward retrospective third-person narrative voice, while the story of John Hansen is related by a protagonist who has vague memories of Hansen from his childhood (when he was known to the narrator as John Glückstadt, the appellation Hansen had been given as the result of his incarceration in a prison in a thusly named town). During a stay at the dwelling of a forester whom he had met at the outset of the story in an inn, and whose wife he learns to be Hansen's daughter, the narrator's recollections of Hansen's life suddenly come flooding back to him. Of course, Hansen and Glückstadt are the same person, while Friedrich Mergel and Johannes Niemand are, apparently, cousins. The ambiguity of their relationship, a deliberate obfuscation on the part of Droste-Hülshoff, prevents a definitive resolution of the issue of guilt in the text; this lack of closure forces the reader to draw his or her own conclusions.

Of course, such an ambiguity cannot obtain in *Ein Doppelgänger*. Because Glückstadt and Hansen constitute one physical entity, there is no mystery regarding the identity of Hanna's murderer; her husband is fully responsible. Tymms has asserted that Storm's novella "returns to the romantic conception that the two sides to a morbidly divided character are spiritual Doubles" (86), but in Romantic tales one typically encounters two physically separated beings who resemble each other in all or most corporeal particulars. This is the case not only in such Romantic works as Jean Paul's *Siebenkäs* and Chamisso's *Peter Schlemihl* (where the Double is a shadow separated from its owner), but in Keller's *Martin Salander*, which appeared in the same year as *Ein Doppelgänger*. However, what unites *Martin Salander*'s twins, Julian and Isidor Weidelich, spiritually is an absolute *lack* of soul, an almost pathological *absence* of social consciousness and moral empathy. In the previous chapter, we noted that Theodor Adorno believed the circumstance that these twins are duplicates of each other points to a loss of genuine, distinct, personal experience in the modern age. This loss, which leads to a virtual interchangeability of individual personas, is in turn deadly to remembrance. Thus, Adorno sees in Keller's novel a possible starting point for the articulation of a theory of this loss of genuine experience in contemporary society and the obliteration of memory to which this loss leads.

In light of Adorno's reading of *Martin Salander*, it is relevant to Storm's treatment of memory and temporality in his contemporaneous novella *Ein Doppelgänger* that he intensely disliked Keller's novel. Keller and Storm maintained a lively correspondence in the 1870s and 1880s, and they were generally supportive of each other's work. But in a letter to Keller dated 12 January 1887, Storm did not attempt to conceal his distaste for Keller's novel: "Ihren 'Salander' habe ich in drei Fortsetzungen vor Mai in der Familie gelesen, und ich leugne nicht, etwas verschnupft worden zu sein, und nicht nur die bei mir saßen, auch von meinen Korrespondenzfreunden kamen verwunderte Fragen" (Goldammer 1960:171). Peter Por has asserted that Storm's antipathy toward Keller's last novel led to the dissolution of their friendship (427).[8] As a sensitive reader, Storm may very well have discerned in *Martin Salander*'s twins the obliteration of social memory through a soullessness so profound that its rescue appears impossible. Although in *Aquis submersus* personal and social memory also face the threat of effacement, Storm attempted to counter this looming loss through the evocation of a numinous historical presence generated through motifs of doubling and repetition.

In *Ein Doppelgänger* as well, the Doppelgänger motif establishes an effective historical memory, for its articulation conjures up the brutal social realities faced by the chief protagonist, and victim of this doubling, in the period constituting the historical framed narrative: John Hansen's fellow villagers *condemn* him to be John Glückstadt. Keller's use of a similar motif to show the *decline* of historical remembrance may very well have led, or at least contributed, to Storm's revulsion toward *Martin Salander* and to his own discomfort at the title he ultimately gave his own novella. He only decided to call it *Ein Doppelgänger* after much hesitation—the working title was *Der Brunnen* (Grimm 332)—and he admitted to feeling that the final appellation he gave the work was "etwas geschraubt" (Storm, cited in Grimm 333).[9] Storm's final choice of his title therefore shows how important he believed it was that the reader see two distinct personas in the figure of John Hansen, that John Glückstadt be perceived as a genuinely discrete alter ego, as Hansen's demonic Double.

Why is Storm so intent on having the reader regard John Glückstadt as the Doppelgänger of John Hansen? The answer is not simply tied to the evocation of a troubled social order. In addition, only when we regard Hansen and Glückstadt as Doubles can we see Christine's father through *her* eyes. For as Tymms notes, Christine "remembers him as two separate men—one her father, whom she loved, and the other his terrifying double, who supplanted him for a time" (86). Of course, this memory is false; John Hansen was but one man. Only the traumas of her childhood cause Christine to remember him as divided into distinct halves. Overcoming these traumas means learning to see Hansen as but a single being, and Christine can only begin to learn this way of regarding her father when remembrance brings about the return of the repressed. And once again, this engendering of an effective memory is a function of the historical framed narrative.

Before we examine how Storm constructed the temporal frame of the narrative in a manner allowing Christine, at the novella's conclusion, to read her father correctly, it is worth exploring how her traumatic childhood led her to perceive him as two men. Certainly, the narrator's recollections show us Hansen's mood swings were so extreme that he acted like two distinct beings. At one moment, he appears to be a loving father and husband. The next moment, provoked by the taunts of his wife, he turns violent and abusive. Hanna becomes particularly derisive when Hansen is out of work and upbraids her for never having learned the art of washing fine clothes. She suggests there is another means by which they could earn money: "Wir können Wolle spinnen; das hast du ja sechs Jahre lang getrieben und kannst es mich selber lehren!" (3:552). This mocking reference to his incarceration for a deed (a robbery without fatal consequences) his fellow villagers will not forgive generates what his daughter must perceive as Hansen's metamorphosis into his alter ego. Known as John Glückstadt to the villagers, he is desperate to be able to exist as John Hansen within his family circle. When his wife momentarily revokes this possibility by turning him, once again, into Glückstadt the convict, he assumes this identity in a setting where he cannot endure it. After expressing his outrage that she, of all people, could say such a thing, he gives her a powerful shove, causing her head to collide violently against a setscrew protruding from their oven. The child had removed the brass knob from the oven, causing the setscrew to be exposed. After a brief scene during which immediate and profound remorse changes Glückstadt back into the despairing husband John Hansen, Hanna expires. All of this is witnessed by Christine (3:551–53). Though her immediate reaction to the chain of events is subdued, and even passive (3:553–55), her internal shock and horror is no doubt magnified by a sense of indirect responsibility for her mother's death. The intensity of Christine's grief, the repression of which is already evident in her understated response to what she has seen, must be in large part responsible for her psychic doubling of her father.

As is typical in novellas where a tale set in the past is framed at its outset and its conclusion by a contemporary setting, the amount of narrative space devoted to characters and events in the present is relatively slight in *Ein Doppelgänger*. Before the narrator, inspired by his newly made acquaintance with Hansen's daughter, begins through his sudden recollective powers to spin out the father's story, the adult Christine makes only a couple of brief appearances. The narrator had been invited to the forester's house because of "die Art Ihres Sprechens," as the forester tells him, a style of speaking that strikes the forester "als gehe es mich ganz nahe an" (3:519–20). We had just learned that the forester's father was a poet, and that the forester himself had memorized much of Uhland's verse in his youth (3:518). But when the narrator is introduced to Christine, he describes himself as "ein schlichter Advokat." He thereupon mentions his name, which causes her to look at him in surprise (3:522). When the narrator and Christine discover that they grew up in the same village, her ambivalent feelings about John Hansen become immediately evident. Because the narrator cannot remember his name, her eyes grow moist and she exclaims: "Sie hätten ihn kennen müssen," but soon thereafter she describes him as a depraved "Schreckbild" while her mother was still alive (3:526, 527).

Having learned the narrator and his wife have conversed about their hometown, the forester admonishes the narrator not to speak of her father, out of a fear that his wife's image of her beloved father will converge with the image of John Glückstadt, the horrific Double occupying an equally powerful space in her psyche: "ihr Vater, den sie kindlich verehrt, würde mit jenem Schreckbild zusammenfallen, das ihre Phantasie ihr immer wieder vorbringt und das leider keine bloße Phantasie war" (3:529). Of course, precisely this convergence must take place through the return of the repressed past of Christine's life with her father, and this unification of John Hansen with his imaginary Doppelgänger can only be generated by the effective historical memory produced by the historical framed narrative. Certainly, no better agent can be found for delving into the complex web of guilt and innocence, truth and fiction surrounding the names John Hansen—John Glückstadt, and thus for recollecting the past, than a lawyer who is also reminiscent of a poet. For Christine's lived experiences must be fictively and yet truthfully reiterated in order that the distortive repression to which they are subject in her psyche can be lifted. Whether in literature or in the actual experience of an analysand, the return to the "primal scene" always entails an imaginative element.[10] This is inevitable, indeed necessary, for only thus can the repressed past be engaged with "poetic justice." Though he only recreates her memory of her father through secondhand knowledge and imagination, the lawyer-poet narrator is precisely the right figure to bring Christine's past back to her. His narration will allow her to overcome the psychic doubling that occludes her image of her father. In other words, the narrator's imaginative recounting of the story of John Hansen will allow Christine to surmount the real but distorted phantoms of her past.

Of course, the ultimate sublation of the Doppelgänger must be prefigured in the narrator's historical account of Christine's father, before she herself can make this psychic transition. The contemporary frame at the outset of the novella shows her to be so deeply possessed by the idea that her father consisted of two men, a loving, caring parent and his brutal, reckless Doppelgänger, that the latter figure must be exorcised in the historical framed narrative before she herself may come to see her father as one, albeit troubled and inwardly divided, man. One of the few figures who show sympathy and compassion for Hansen's plight in the course of the narrative is the village's mayor, and it is left to him to banish the figure of John Glückstadt by extirpating his name. This occurs in the last lines of the historical framed narrative, just before the contemporary narrator awakens from the reverie that led him to recall or invent the story of Christine's father, in the course of a conversation between the mayor and an old woman who represents the popular view that Hansen stands eternally condemned by his past guilt: "'Wahrhaftig,' sagte die Alte ganz erstaunt, 'Sie haben noch immer Ihre sonderbaren Meinungen von diesem John Glückstadt!' 'John Hansen,' berichtigte der Bürgermeister ernsthaft" (3:574).

Upon the conclusion of the historical framed narrative, when the narrator becomes once again aware of his actual, present-day surroundings, he is able, by recalling a childhood episode, to solve another problem vital to Christine's ability to surmount her psychic doubling of her father: namely, the mystery of Hansen's disappearance. His unexplained vanishing had naturally made Hansen into a phantom in the mind of his daughter, for a phantom will be all that is left to a child when its parent becomes permanently absent without even the closure of death or comprehensible separation. Such a phantom, rather than a present, materially concrete father, may easily give rise to a Doppelgänger. In this sense, the novella does indeed return to the Romantic concept of the Doppelgänger as a projection of a subjective consciousness, but, in this case, the consciousness produces the Double of another rather than of itself. When she learns her father had died by falling down a well, looking for potatoes at night with which to feed her, Christine will be able to envision her father as a single being, John Hansen, the loving parent who lost his life trying to provide for her. And indeed it is love, or at least sympathy, that generates the reverie itself. After the narrator relates to the forester all he had recollected and experienced in his own spirit, the forester calls his tale "Poesie." This prompts the narrator to reply: "Nennen Sie es immer Poesie; Sie könnten es auch Liebe oder Anteil nennen, die ich rasch an meinen Wirten genommen hätte" (3:577). Perhaps it would be most accurate to say that the spirit of love, of fellow feeling, generates in the lawyer a reverie based on memory but poetic enough to evoke the love of a father for his daughter and thus to dispel that father's phantom Double from her head, thereby allowing her a sense of closure with regard to the troubling complex of guilt plaguing her own childhood memories.[11]

Curiously, as he takes leave of Christine and the forester, the narrator quietly calls out: "Leb wohl, John Glückstadts Tochter!" Though the name of the Doppelgänger had been exorcised from the historical framed narrative at its conclusion, the appellation is still fixed in the narrator's consciousness. But when he goes on to reflect that only the first syllable of this name, signifying happiness ("Glück"), has remained to her (3:578), one senses this dissolution of the term denoting Hansen's ominous alter ego, and its resulting transformation into a positive signifier, represent the ultimate banishment of the phantom Double. The name appears two more times at the novella's conclusion: when the forester recounts his wife's placement of a garland of roses on the frame of the "Bild des John Glückstadt" in his first letter to the narrator, and when the narrator announces his upcoming second visit "zu John Glückstadts Tochter und zu meinem wackeren Oberförster" (3:579). But since by now the forester has already told the narrator's tale to his wife with purely positive results, the character of a phantom Double adherent to the name has been eviscerated, and the name itself rendered harmless.

The banishment of John Glückstadt as a haunting Doppelgänger from the mind of his daughter, a banishment made doubly efficacious through its being rendered both within the historical framed narrative and in the contemporary setting that frames it, brings in its train (if we read intertextually) the detoxification of two iterative motifs employed in *Aquis submersus*: pictorial representation and hereditary continuity. While in *Aquis submersus* the portraits of the *Ahnin* and the dead child, respectively, instantiate the motifs of a demonic Double and a guilt never to be expiated, the descriptions of Christine's photograph of her father in *Ein Doppelgänger* are precisely intended to show the resolution of both these specters. Shortly before his departure from the house of the forester, the narrator sees the faded photograph, the frame of which is covered by a garland of everlastings just picked by Christine. The narrator describes it as follows: "Es war John Glückstadt nicht; es war John Hansen, wie er im Herzen seiner Tochter fortlebte, für den sie gestern ihren frischen dauerhaften Kranz gepflückt hatte; mit diesem John hatte der Doppelgängerische Schatten noch nichts zu schaffen." Upon seeing it, the narrator feels the urge to tell Christine to banish the phantom in her mind, for he knows it is one with her father (3:576–77).

The actual occurrence of this exorcism is indicated by the second description of the picture, in the letter sent by the forester to the narrator telling of his wife's reaction to the latter's tale. The picture now has a full garland of roses, and Christine now has "nicht nur den Vater, sondern einen ganzen Menschen" (3:578–79). In substituting roses for everlastings as a setting for Hansen's photograph, Christine moves from the commemoration of her father *as Hansen* to a full resurrection of this man as a complete and fully unified human being. The two descriptions of the picture thus show, in successive stages, the obliteration of the demonic Double and the emergence of a totalized, undivided individual whose now fully realized humanity, while not absolving him of guilt, shows it to be a universal, and thus pardonable, condition.

The Double as Other pattern, and the related, sometimes concomitant motif of an ego's imbrication with an alter ego, are juxtapositions typical in Poetic Realism; we have seen them in the works of Droste-Hülshoff, Ludwig, and Meyer as well. Unusual in *Ein Doppelgänger* is the circumstance that Hansen and Glückstadt are, empirically, one person. More importantly, the completion of the narrated ego through the *obliteration* of the Double represents the fullest possible synthesis in Poetic Realism's ego–alter ego dialectics. Like most of the other Poetic Realists we have examined, Storm adopted and adapted this motif to create an aesthetically and psychologically comprehensive protagonist, whose persona thereby emerges in its totality. By "poeticizing" the historical "reality" of Hansen-Glückstadt's life through recollection by his daughter under the poet-lawyer's guidance, Storm allows Glückstadt as the Double-Other of Hansen to become fully integrated into Hansen's one imaginatively projected Being. Uniquely, then, Double and Other, ego and alter ego, become sublated and disappear, and a complete but single psyche emerges at the novella's conclusion.

At the end of his letter to the narrator, the forester tells him that his arrival will coincide with the presence of his and Christine's son. Christine's love and affection for her then absent son had been evident in the first half of the novella's contemporary frame, prior to the historical framed narrative (3:522, 524). But after the narrator's tale is delineated and then transmitted to her by her husband, Christine's maternal love takes on a new dimension. As the forester puts it in the letter: "seine Mutter ist schier verliebt in ihn und studiert sein Antlitz, um darin immer einen neuen Zug aus dem ihres Vaters aufzufinden" (3:579). Having commemorated John Hansen as her father, and having subsequently resurrected him as a fully integrated human being, Christine now seeks his hereditary iteration in the physiognomy of her son. A curse in Storm's earlier story, repetition through lineage becomes a desideratum in this one.[12] In *Aquis submersus*, a historical framed narrative intersects with the motif of the Double to sustain memory, but only a memory that recalls humanity's abyssal, permanent guilt, instability, and uncertainty. *Ein Doppelgänger* uses this same intersection to celebrate our ability to overcome the demons of the past and to look to the future as rife with possibilities of renewal.

6. The Alter Ego as Narration's Motive Force: Wilhelm Raabe

Storm's historical framed narrative in *Ein Doppelgänger* is used to redeem a long-dead figure by bringing his shadow side to light through a sort of psychoanalytic recollection. An erudite and reliable poet-lawyer allows John Hansen's daughter to remember him in his totality. By skillfully bringing to the surface Christine's memory of John Glückstadt, the admirable narrator banishes this Doppelgänger from existence as the chief (albeit subconscious) torment in her life. Storm thus makes his narrator a heroic pre-Freudian psychoanalyst, somewhat self-doubting but seemingly omnipotent in his ability to illuminate and thus detoxify a disturbing primal scene. A significant constituent feature that allows Storm's contemporary, Wilhelm Raabe, to be viewed as the writer who closes the book on German Poetic Realism is his profound subversion of narrative omniscience. Narrators such as Meyer's Hans Armbruster may be coarse and somewhat droll, or modest and skeptical like Storm's lawyer-poet, but the reader may depend upon the ultimate accuracy of their historical memory. This memory creates narratives that are, in the final analysis, cogent and coherent. This is not necessarily the case with Raabe. In an essay on the dissolution of Poetic Realism in Raabe's late novel *Die Akten des Vogelsangs* (1896), Eberhard Geisler has noted that Poetic Realists saw as one of their chief tasks the delineation of life's underlying unity. This book's chief thesis maintains that Poetic Realists reworked the Romantic Doppelgänger motif in the service of evoking this ideal aesthetic and psychological unity and comprehensiveness, a totality Poetic Realists found harder than the Romantics to sustain because they set greater theoretical limitations on the poetic imagination's dialectical predilections. While Raabe admired Poetic Realism's ideals, he gave up in his later work the illusion of such dynamic, all-encompassing synthesis. Instead, Raabe came to underscore life's ultimate fragmentary character, and subtly undermined Poetic Realism's ideal of reconciliation (Geisler 365–80), the sort of reconciliation evident in *Ein Doppelgänger* between an orphaned daughter and her dead father, and brought about by the narrator's banishment of the latter's malevolent alter ego. In Raabe, on the contrary, alter egos are the *product* of unreliable narrators, a concomitant world view that sees life as fragmentary and incapable of synthesis, and occluded historical memory. In Raabe's oeuvre, alter egos are most often manifested when a narrator stumbles in recollecting the past.

The distinction between Raabe and other Poetic Realists such as Storm regarding the way in which the ego–alter ego juxtaposition and narrative memory are imbricated is particularly evident when one compares Storm's *Ein Doppelgänger* to Raabe's novel *Stopfkuchen, Eine See- und Mordgeschichte* (1891). Eckhardt Meyer-Krentler has already undertaken such a comparison, for he believes the frameworks of both tales are so similar that Raabe's novel may be read as a caricature of Storm's novella. Meyer-Krentler's intertextual reading of *Stopfkuchen* and his articulation of Raabe's apparent antagonism toward Storm have recently been called into question (Goldammer 1993). However, regardless of the issue of Storm's direct influence on *Stopfkuchen*'s composition, there are obvious parallels between *Ein Doppelgänger* and Raabe's novel. Both works are written in a first-person narrative form. The two narrators both seek to puzzle out a mysterious murder ostensibly committed in the distant past by two deceased fathers of now happily married daughters. These two fathers were concomitantly loving and brutal, socially stigmatized, and fiercely protective. The narrator must sublate the two fathers' dark sides (their evil alter egos) in order to allow their daughters peace of mind with respect to their childhood. The process of narrative healing is enacted largely through conversations between the narrators and their male hosts, that is, the daughters' husbands. But while Storm's lawyer-poet is the true hero and arbiter of his tale, Raabe's Eduard is completely at the mercy of the novel's title character for the revelation of redemptive truth. Eduard's childhood friend Stopfkuchen (Heinrich Schaumann) is the tale's most discerning judge of character, and Eduard is merely the vehicle by means of which he chooses to reveal the truth about his wife's father.

Poetic Realism's delineation of life's underlying coherence and totality and Raabe's ultimate subversion of these representational desiderata—the contradicting tendencies that allow Geisler to situate Raabe at the point of the movement's dissolution—are evident in the antithetical modes in which the Doppelgänger and ego–alter ego motifs are manifested in *Ein Doppelgänger* and *Stopfkuchen*. As Meyer-Krentler has indicated, the narrator in Storm's novella dissolves Christine's conflicted and tormenting paternal visions and causes them to be replaced with a unified, harmonious image of her father. Precisely the opposite is the case in *Stopfkuchen* when Schaumann reveals to Eduard that the friendly, seemingly harmless postman Störzer, who plays a major role in the narrator's fondest childhood reminiscences, actually committed the murder of the bully Kienbaum popularly attributed to Tine Schaumann's father. To Eduard's positive image of his "harmless youthful acquaintance Störzer" is added a "Doppelgänger, Kienbaum's murderer." Raabe reverses Storm's idealizing and harmonizing tendency: "Gegen die Eindeutigkeit von Eduards schöner Erinnerung setzt Stopfkuchen eine irritierende Bildermischung." Rather than dissolving a "Doppelgänger-Schreckbild" like Storm's narrator, Heinrich Schaumann engenders one (Meyer-Krentler 200–201). As is the case with many other of Raabe's first-person narrators, Eduard's memory is unreliable and incomplete. Eduard and other narrating egos usually need the assistance of more dynamic and worldly wise narrated Others. Indeed, these other, narrated characters with their alternative perspectives often function as conflicted alter egos to the narrators themselves.

Meyer-Krentler suggests that the Doppelgänger relationship between a highly fallible narrator and a narrated character whose testimony is less dubious because his personality is marked by greater vitality, self-assurance, and zest for material (that is, nonbookish) life is exemplified by the bond between Eduard and Schaumann (201–2). However, the term "Doppelgänger" only properly characterizes a textual liaison (whether between a self and a discrete "Other," a self and his or her water, mirror, dream, or artistic image, present self and past or future self, a genuinely "split" self, or between the self and his or her imaginative projection) marked by physical identity, or at least close resemblance. Thus, the link between Eduard and Schaumann can be more accurately described as a juxtaposition of ego and alter ego not marked by the Double motif, with the exception of one episode discussed later. This sort of link between the first-person chronicler and his chronicled alter ego is also evident in the two other novels belonging to Raabe's so-called Braunschweig trilogy, *Alte Nester, Zwei Bücher Lebensgeschichten* (1879) and *Die Akten des Vogelsangs*.[1] The tendency both culminates and is reversed in Raabe's last work, the novel fragment *Altershausen* (written in 1899–1902, but first published in 1911). For this reason, I have chosen these works from Raabe's enormous output as this chapter's primary focus.

Nevertheless, a brief look at Raabe's first work, *Die Chronik der Sperlingsgasse* (1856), is also in order, for this work provides a rare instance of Raabe's actual employment of the term "Doppelgänger."[2] Almost from the moment his works began to attract critical attention, reviewers and literary scholars have highlighted (and sometimes exaggerated) the influence on Raabe by Romanticism's two most celebrated instigators of the Doppelgänger motif, Jean Paul and E. T. A. Hoffmann.[3] Particularly in his early work, literary historians in the first part of the twentieth century noted the presence of Romantic perspectives and structuring devices such as the Double. For example, in Raabe's early historical novel *Der heilige Born* (1861)—dismissed by one of Raabe's most prominent critical biographers, Hermann Pongs, as freighted with too much "Kinderromantik" (150)—the mad vicar Festus, tortured by a virtually split personality, was found by the early Raabe scholar Hermann Junge to possess striking affinities to the Doppelgänger-afflicted mad monk Medardus in Hoffmann's *Die Elixiere des Teufels* (Junge 20).[4] Thus, it is not surprising that a direct allusion to the figure of the Doppelgänger takes place in Raabe's first work.

The narrator of *Die Chronik der Sperlingsgasse*, Johannes Wachholder, is like the other narrators we will encounter in the Braunschweig trilogy and in *Altershausen*: studious, reflective, somewhat timid and undaring, and vaguely dissatisfied with his lot in life. As with the later first-person narrators in Raabe's novels, his thoughtful and yet restive nature is ideal both for lending him insights into Germany's troubled socioeconomic panorama in the second half of the nineteenth century and for allowing him to sense his own incompleteness as a person, a lack that can only be filled by an alter ego. Wachholder is a reader of Jean Paul's *Siebenkäs*—he makes a reference to this work in which the term "Doppelgänger" was first minted early in *Die Chronik der Sperlingsgasse* (1:81)—so it is natural that he draws on this motif while he engages in his most common activity as narrating ego, namely, sitting at his window and contemplating the world. The Double he evokes in Raabe's first work through narrative detachment by referring to himself in the third person anticipates a parallel conjuration in Raabe's last work. For, like Professor Friedrich Feyerabend in *Altershausen*, Wachholder refers to himself as an Other so that his youthful self may emerge as his Double: "Lange hat der Musensohn in tiefe Gedanken versunken dagesessen; jetzt springt er plötzlich auf und dreht mir das Gesicht zu—das bin ich wieder: Johannes Wachholder, ein Student der Philosophie in der großen Haupt- und Universitätsstadt. Sehr aufgeregt scheint der Doppelgänger meiner Jugend zu sein" (1:21).

In the later novels, the narrators' youthful selves will tend to be conjured when they take trips to their boyhood and/or student homes. Wachholder's Double is purely the product of memory, and is not attached to the physical site he currently inhabits. Thus detached from its natural physical setting, his junior alter ego is of an even more spectral and tentative nature than those conjured in the Braunschweig trilogy and in *Altershausen*. This may explain why here, but not in the later works, Raabe employs the Romantic term "Doppelgänger." As Charlotte L. Goedsche notes throughout the course of her study on narrative structure in Raabe's first novel, only Wachholder himself holds the *Chronik*'s two primary time layers—past and present—within the context of a single thematic unity. In the later works, the narrators' physically palpable alter egos will allow this thematic unity to be preserved. If, as Goedsche suggests, the student who constitutes Wachholder's Doppelgänger in this passage seems quite distant from the first-person narrator (Goedsche 125), this is due to the twofold nature of this distance, physical as well as temporal. Wachholder's student and contemporary lives both unfold in Berlin, but in different places within the giant metropolis. In later works, the physical distance between narrating ego and narrated Other will be obviated through the narrators' return to the "Heimat," making their juvenile selves less a product of detached memory and thus less Romantically spectral. The dehaunting of the narrative will be further enhanced by the presence of a second set of concrete alter egos, namely, the narrators' boyhood friends. However, a spectral haunting will be reinstated in the last novel of the Braunschweig trilogy.

Shortly after his vision of himself as a student, Wachholder takes stock of his own current psychologizing tendencies. His shadow self— the youth of his past—had made a declaration of love in his imaginative memory to Marie, the young woman whom in reality he had been too shy to court and who, ignorant of Wachholder's love for her, marries the painter Franz Ralff. The elder Wachholder realizes his Doppelgänger's proclamation of an adoration never effectively expressed and requited is another instance of his mental self-flagellation, which protects him until he is ready to emerge a serious and insightful man (1:22). Walter Schedlinsky has argued that the distance Wachholder perceives toward his younger second self reflects the narrator's realization that his doubts about his own identity are temporary, and that he has established a more stable personality in his role as friend to Marie and Franz. Schedlinsky believes Wachholder's view of himself as a failure is tied to the societal prejudices he has internalized (66).

The trouble with this interpretation is that Wachholder projects his youthful Double as someone who *overcomes* his limits and is able to express his love directly to Marie, rather than confirming his earlier self-perceived shortcomings. Wachholder's Double is thus a poor choice to defend a thesis that is in itself, however, quite intriguing in its view of role playing in Raabe's novels: "Der ungeliebte Doppelgänger wird zum Paradigma der Nichtidentität des Subjekts mit seinem vergesellschafteten Sein" (Schedlinsky 445). Raabe's narrators do indeed tend to feel a vague dissatisfaction with their socialized selves. Nevertheless, they sense these selves to be so thoroughly entwined with their identity that their utopian self-images, as with Wachholder's wished-for student persona, tend to reflect an ideal projection of their Being. These projections stand *above* their actual selves, which are normally integrated into society in a manner the narrators find dissatisfying. The true narrative tensions existing between Wachholder and his student Doppelgänger are grounded in Wachholder's own ambivalent attitude toward his past and toward human striving in general. Stanley Radcliffe has noted that Wachholder tends to regard the personal ambition of his youth in the same light as all mortal endeavor; both are marked by ultimate vanity. Nevertheless, his entire tale is imbued with an idyllic tone, and lacks any trace of bitterness (Radcliffe 58). Wachholder's ambiguous feelings toward his younger Doppelgänger—feelings informed by sentimental nostalgia, idealized projections, and yet insights into the folly of his real and imagined past—are responsible for what Schedlinsky accurately terms the "nonidentity of the subject" with his earlier self. Contrary to Schedlinsky's argument, however, Wachholder has very fond feelings toward the shadowy image he visualizes in communion with Marie, but he realizes this dreamlike projection is as evanescent as his authentic juvenile undertakings.

Another factor in Wachholder's equivocal attitude toward his wish-fulfilling past life shadow is tied to his constant narrative oscillation between the universal and the particular. On one level, the two dimensions intertwine; Wachholder's personal disappointments are macrocosmically substantiated by the disappointing social state of affairs after the failed promises of the revolutionary events in 1848. The fragmentation of personal life mirrors Germany's own continued fragmentation. What modifies the negative tone produced by this disillusion are the moments when the narrator feels at one with the world and senses the harmony and continuity of life. Poetic Realism's chief theorists, Ludwig and Schmidt, believed the projection of such congruous totality in the face of the revolution's disappointments should be German literature's chief goal. This projected unity is nowhere more evident than at the novel's conclusion, when Wachholder's overwhelming sense of fellow feeling allows him to perceive a physical proximity to his beloved adopted daughter Elise (the offspring of the deceased Marie and Franz) and her husband, though they are in Italy. Opening his window one last time, he apprehends a predictable continuity in the thoughts and dreams of all social types: the young girl, the pondering scholar, the king, the infirm (1:171). This nostalgic identification with the Other on a universal scale—a utopian narrative embrace of the sort Fredric Jameson would term an act of the "political unconscious"[5]— confirms Wachholder's love for an idealized Doppelgänger actually enmeshed in life rather than detached from it. It also anticipates first-person narrative identification in the Braunschweig trilogy novels with figures with their own discrete identities, but who are also projections of the narrators' own most deeply embedded yearnings and desires. Seen in this light, Raabe's use of character dialectics usually adhered to Poetic Realism's goal of psychological totality in characterization.

The narrator in *Alte Nester*, the first novel in the Braunschweig trilogy, shares some of Wachholder's attributes. Therefore, the suppressed ideals he projects into an alter ego whose relationship to life is less ambivalent and hesitant than his own may be expected to match those of his predecessor in Raabe's pantheon of narrating protagonists. Friedrich Langreuter is a bachelor who lives largely aloof from society, mostly spending his time in scholarly pursuits. A life devoted to research was actually his boyhood dream, but its fulfillment causes him to lead a life of somewhat dissatisfying detachment. His isolation as a man contrasts with a boyhood spent largely in the company of four close friends: Irene von Everstein, the daughter of a count at whose estate Langreuter and his mother live after the latter's husband is murdered in the count's service, Eva and Ewald Sixtus, children of the count's forester, and a somewhat older boy named Just Everstein, scion of a relatively impoverished branch of the count's family.

While this coterie was still quite young, Just Everstein was a most detached and studious individual. His distracted bookishness lent him an air of eccentricity amusing to his friends and the local peasants, but causing his guardian, the querulous but well-intentioned Jule, to assume he will end in poverty when he reaches maturity, at which time he must replace her in running his estate, Steinhof. However, it is Langreuter who retreats to an ivory tower existence, while Just Everstein, forced to give up Steinhof and undergo the rigors of pioneer life in America due to the machinations of a swindler, becomes wise in the ways of the world. His scholarly inclinations were partly inspired by Langreuter and he is somewhat able to indulge his didactic bent as a schoolteacher for his community in rural Wisconsin. Nevertheless, the self-reliance he develops through struggling with harsh conditions as a pioneer is what makes it possible for him to return to the site of his youth, purchase the Steinhof, bring Jule back to the estate, and make it profitable by growing hay. He persuades Irene, widowed and living in poverty in Berlin, to accept lodging at his estate. Ewald Sixtus returns to Germany after accumulating enough money as an engineer in Ireland to buy Werden castle, the count's old estate. He visits Langreuter in Berlin and persuades the scholar to accompany him back to their childhood village. Eva remained in the village living with her father, so the concluding part of the narrative mirrors the novel's commencement in that we observe all the erstwhile playmates joined together once more at the scene of their youth. They live their lives apart only in the novel's long middle section.

In the last third of *Alte Nester*, Just becomes the dynamic focal point. He buys the Werden castle when Ewald—who purchased it hoping to win the love and obedience of Irene, at once his childhood sweetheart and fierce competitor—discovers repairs to the utterly plundered and dilapidated estate are beyond his means. Not only does Just engage to marry Eva, but he deliberately acts to bring about the union of Irene and Ewald. Always standing outside these events is the novel's narrator, who believes his contribution to the lives of his companions lies in their chronicling. He relates Just's slow development from impractical adolescent dreamer to a wise and competent adult. Nevertheless, *Alte Nester* has little in common with novels belonging to the *Bildungsroman* genre; Raabe not only indulges in the "Heimkehr" motif (common to the Braunschweig novels and *Altershausen*) in order to mirror the novel's first and third sections, but creates synchronous cuts through Langreuter's narrative memory[6] during the course of the second section, the contemporary events of which are largely played out in Berlin. These cuts are especially significant in establishing Langreuter's Doppelgänger-informed relationship to his own youthful self. When he realizes during a conversation with Everstein how accomplished the eccentric has become, Langreuter feels suddenly transported back to the old Steinhof cherry trees. However, the new dynamics of his relationship with Everstein cause him to imagine the trees are grimacing at him (14:121). At the deathbed of Irene's child in the company of Just, the widowed Irene, and her French governess (also a figure from their youth), Langreuter returns twice in his mind to the "old nests," the intertwined branches in which the children played (14:129–30). Unlike Wachholder's relationship to his student Double in *Die Chronik der Sperlingsgasse*, Langreuter's bond to his childhood self is mediated not by any personal growth and transformation. Instead, it is solely the result of his chronic chronicling, the need to relive his history in order to understand and narrate the past and the present.

Langreuter's lack of a distinct, mature identity, and his proclivity to delineate life in its synchronic totality rather than actually living and experiencing events in their diachronically developing immediacy leads to a constant re-visioning of his past self. As Uwe Heldt has noted: "Während Just seine Identität, seine Idylle im 'Wechsel der Erscheinungen' einfach lebt, kann Langreuter sich dieses Leben nur im Bild vorstellen" (95–96). Although Eduard Klopfenstein's comment that in

Raabe's first-person narratives "Die Ich-Person spielt eine Doppelrolle als erzählendes und handelndes Ich, was zum vornherein die Erzähl- und die Handlungsschicht einander näherbringt" (141) is true of all the novels in the Braunschweig trilogy, Langreuter must be characterized as the narrating ego least involved in the novels' actual plot dynamics. Standing mostly outside the action even while it is being played out, he appears to himself on especially dreary days like a character in a bad novel (14:150). His encounters with his past life, his enactment of the childhood Doppelgänger through self-remembrance, are the products of such doubts, his ambiguous feelings about his present and historical identity, his feelings about himself as "narrating" *and* "acting ego." As Fritz Martini puts it, he is a narrator "der in sein Ich versponnen ist" (723).

This self-entrapment consistently reproduces the encounter with a youthful Double. Just as Jacques Lacan's infant must repeatedly gaze at himself in the mirror in order to develop a coherent—albeit imaginary—sense of his own discrete ego (the inchoate activity at the heart of the French psychoanalyst's famous "mirror-stage"),[7] Langreuter must often peer into the looking glass of his early self to reattain his identity as "Fritz" or "Frédéric," the two childhood monikers reattached to him by the French governess before he returns to Steinhof (14:134). He comes to find it unpleasant to think of himself as "Doktor der Philosophie Friedrich Langreuter" (14:147), and usually does so in his bouts of self-contempt. Only as pure "Fritz" would he extricate himself from the ego entanglement described by Martini, but the Lacanian gaze by which he would regain his unconflicted identity only leads deeper into his solipsistic snare.

To prevent his chronicle from turning into a bad novel like his life, he must rely on his *alter* ego, Just Everstein. Ewald Sixtus was his closest male friend in childhood (his deepest sense of kinship was with Eva), but, in Ewald's presence in the ruins of Werden castle after their return, he can only relive childhood memories as pure repetition, as a haunted recurrence of the same (14:208). When Just begins to move decisively to take charge of the situation, Langreuter senses life's dynamic possibilities, how much substantive change and transformation are a part of its rhythm. To be sure, describing himself sitting (like Wachholder in *Die Chronik der Sperlingsgasse*) at his window in Berlin once he has returned to his adult routine, he remarks on the regularity and repetition of life, guided by fate (14:243). However, the novel closes with a more kinetic view of destiny by reprising the narrator's most vivid image of Just during their shared youth, on a rock where "der Vetter Just—den Kopf in den Händen und die Arme auf die Kniee stützend und so in das Blaue hineinstarrend—einst saß und wartete auf *menschliche Schicksale*" (14:269, Raabe's emphasis). This last description of Just repeats the first one; he is initially portrayed sitting on the same rock, standing up, yawning, grinning, and stretching, a picture of amiable aimlessness, whose acts are sketched out in the present tense to lend the ur-scene an air of immediacy. Nevertheless, Langreuter already alludes in this episode to the potential capacity for deeds latent within his friend, and he foreshadows both his ultimate view of Just and the dynamics that will drive their symbiotic relationship in the following sentence: "So einer, der etwas selber erlebt und erfahren hat, ist immer klüger als derjenige, welchem er nachher davon erzählt" (14:46).

Thus, Just Everstein represents for Langreuter the performer of deeds, while he sees himself as their chronicler. Just comes to transcend Ewald in his eyes as the paradigmatic liver of the *vita activa*, the worthiness of which allows the narrator to resign himself to a *vita contemplativa*.[8] When he is not vicariously living life through the sage of Steinhof as his admiring biographer, he views life as a never-ending return of the same. It is this dissatisfying mode that pushes him to reexperience his past and mentally repeat his life as "Fritz," as his youthful Doppelgänger. This is a natural consequence of those moments when he sees life governed by an implacable, and, more importantly, unchanging destiny. He then seems wrapped up in the solipsistic ego pithily described by Martini. However, when he narratively enters into the spirit of an *alter* ego, a man who waits for, and efficaciously *shapes*, human destiny, he seems most content to be Dr. Friedrich Langreuter, scholar and historian. His symbiotic bond with Just Everstein allows him to push past his personal aporias. Through inward union with this Other, his narrative attains the ambience of a holistic closure somewhat rare in his own creator's prose.

There is a certain symmetry in the relationship between Langreuter and Just Everstein on the one hand, and *Stopfkuchen*'s Eduard and Heinrich Schaumann on the other. To be sure, Eduard had enough inherent energy to move to South Africa, marry and raise a family, and amass a tidy fortune. In his ability to reap success abroad and afford a yearned-for "Heimkehr," he resembles Just more than Langreuter. Unlike Just, Schaumann attains financial stability at home, inheriting his father-in-law's estate and making it prosper. However, both he and his dynamic predecessor in the trilogy transcend a youth marked by apathy and good-natured ridicule by others. Just's awkwardness and disinclination to pursue productive, practical work at an early age is reflected by his thin, gangly physique, while Schaumann's enormous girth is the product of his childhood gluttony and a certain physical apathy. Both transform themselves in adult life into larger than life figures who exercise a powerful fascination—and indeed control—over their respective narrators through a remarkable omniscience regarding the ways of the human and natural world, and an ability to accomplish all they wish. At least during the narration's contemporary frame, Eduard is like Fritz Langreuter, a somewhat self-doubting narrator whose life is devoted solely to chronicling; this circumstance is reflected in Eduard's self-imposed isolation from his fellow passengers and the crew on the ship sailing back to Africa after his stay in Germany is over. Like Langreuter, Eduard feels the continuous need to revisit his childhood self through memory. And like Langreuter but even more so, Eduard is dependent on his more worldly wise and masterly Other to transcend ambiguity and create a successful narrative.

The degree to which Stopfkuchen becomes an alter ego for his narrator, someone antithetical to himself but with whom he must identify, is evident when Eduard is back in his quarters following Schaumann's climactic revelation of Kienbaum's murderer: "So wahrscheinlich bald nach Mitternacht hatte ich mich ganz in des Dicken Stelle, das heißt seine Haut versetzt, das heißt war in dieselbe hineinversetzt worden." He imagines himself attaining Stopfkuchen's girth and—as Stopfkuchen—telling the narrator (Eduard himself) the story of his success through consumptive tropes, as though he has won his wife and estate by eating and adding them to his person. This enactment of himself as Stopfkuchen's Doppelgänger, and thus the possessor of his wisdom, allows Eduard finally to sense that there is a genuine reason ("Grund") behind all things (18:197). Identification with the alter ego counteracts the self-doubts about his chronicling, which persistently impede his narrative undertaking; he tends to see himself as unable to write for his contemporary fatherland (18:8), and (through an insult by Tine Schaumann he realizes is unintended) as a writer of trivial adventure histories (18:109). As Michael Limlei puts it, Eduard becomes Stopfkuchen's "apostle," imitating his behavior, assuming his physical and spatial identity, and adopting his life philosophy (347).

This wholesale immersion into Stopfkuchen's Being doesn't resolve all of Eduard's ambiguous feelings about himself and his capacities as narrator, but it does enable him ultimately to complete his story. By mentally becoming Stopfkuchen's Double, he at once overcomes a certain humbling fear of and awe at his friend and his own inner self-skepticism. Horst Denkler has written of Raabe's fear of his fellow humans. This fear is transmitted to his protagonists, who live in dread of humanity's dark deeds and words, but also come to be horrified at the "'Canaille' in sich" (Denkler 58). Eduard is no self-loather, but he does sense his limits, and his faith in the predictable, innate goodness and innocence of those he knows well is deeply shaken by the knowledge that his childhood friend Störzer was Kienbaum's murderer (18:195–96). In *Stopfkuchen*, Raabe enacts the Doppelgänger motif as the inward imbrication of narrating ego and omniscient narrated Other in order to represent the temporary transcendence of these fears. This transcendence acts to enable narration itself, and the characters' imbrication allows a comprehensive psychological totality to emerge.[9]

Nancy Kaiser has indicated that the common thread running through the Braunschweig trilogy novels is the primary focus on "the problematic aspects of perceiving one's social environment and the related question of the possibility of structuring and living a justifiable individual existence" (2). In both *Alte Nester* and *Stopfkuchen*, the first-person narrators must virtually subsume the identity of their tales' principal protagonists, fashioning themselves through inward contemplation into the egos of these alter egos, in order both to apprehend correctly the environment they chronicle and to justify their existence as narrators. The ego–alter ego juxtapositions in these works are thus concomitant to the dynamization and rendering whole and total of the narrating self and the narration itself. The possibility for such activity is problematized in the final work of the trilogy, *Die Akten des Vogelsangs*, by the inability—or unwillingness—of the primary narrated Other to transcend his youthful lack of rootedness and his unproductive tendencies. In this, Velten Andres is radically distinct from his counterparts in the trilogy's first two novels, Just Everstein and Heinrich Schaumann. Jeffrey Sammons has titled the chapter on *Die Akten des Vogelsangs* in his seminal book on Raabe "The Split Self" (1987:300–15), and the term adequately indicates the unbridgeable gap between Velten Andres and his narrator, Karl Krumhardt. Velten Andres never assumes the status of a larger than life, worldly wise, fully realized, and wholly successful personality characteristic of his predecessors in the trilogy, attributes that allowed the immanent sublation of narrating ego within narrated Other.[10] Nevertheless, as the concept of a "split self" suggests, a single, albeit fractured identity is evoked by the novel. In this sense, it is possible to speak of an ego–alter ego relationship between Velten Andres and Karl Krumhardt in the last work of the trilogy.

Like Eduard, Krumhardt is comfortably situated and, at least outwardly, well integrated into society at large. He, too, is a family man, and makes a nice income as a jurist and government bureaucrat. However, his success comes at a cost; he must suppress his transcendent idealism and yearning for a return to the communal ambience that had nurtured him and his playmates, Velten and Helene Trotzendorff, during their relatively idyllic youth in the Vogelsang. Karl must push his utopian inclinations aside and resignedly accept pastoral Vogelsang's displacement by big-city commodification, impersonality, and vulgarity. Helene marries a wealthy American after having returned to the New World and fulfilled an adolescent wish to once again live in comfort in the land of her early childhood. She had resided in the United States until her father's unwise business practices forced her, in the company of her mother, to return in poverty to the latter's own original home in the Vogelsang. However, Helene comes to see the Vogelsang as her lost paradise. Only Velten clings to his spirituality and concomitant renunciation of modern, materialistic values throughout the entire course of the chronicle. He restlessly travels the world trying to find a life-style compatible with his ideals, and vainly tries to dissuade Helene in the United States from entering a life of morally desolate materialism. Rather than see his childhood home swallowed up by the growing soulless city springing up around it, he burns all the cherished possessions of his youth and auctions off what remains of the house. He returns to Berlin to die in the little dwelling where he had found some kindred spirits—the family des Beaux and his landlady, the widow Feucht—during his student days.

It is a letter from Helene Mungo (the name of her late husband) announcing Velten's death at the very outset of the novel that inspires Karl to chronicle their young lives in the Vogelsang. Constant returns to the present-day narrative framework within which Karl is writing make it clear he is inspired to memorialize the past not just through shock and sadness at his friend's death, but by a deeply felt desire to reimmerse himself in Velten's powerfully visionary persona. Only thus can he reactualize the long dormant idealism in his own soul. As Sammons puts it: "Velten incarnates an unused but also unappeased potential in Krumhardt's self" (1987:313), and only by integrating his narrating ego with the narrated Other can he temporarily unify this "split self." As with the other two novels in the trilogy, then, the narrator's ambivalence, self-doubts, and sense of lack instantiate the ego–alter ego dialectic and drive the narrative. Karl asserts near the novel's close: "Die Akten des Vogelsangs bilden ein Ganzes, von dem ich und mein Haus ebensowenig zu trennen sind wie die eiserne Bettstelle bei der Frau Fechtmeisterin Feucht und die Reichtümer der armen Mistreß Mungo" (19:404). Above everything, the chronicle of the Vogelsang is the chronicle of Velten Andres's life, and it is Velten in particular from whom Karl Krumhardt, inwardly, cannot bear the thought of separation.

Raabe uses the following lines from Chamisso's poem "An meinen alten Freund Peter Schlemihl" (1834) as the epigraph for his novel: "Die wir dem Schatten Wesen sonst verliehen, / Sehn Wesen jetzt als Schatten sich verziehen" (19:212). On an evening when Karl is particularly filled with cares, disappointment, and weariness while writing the chronicles, he is visited by Velten's ghost, who asks him if he is sick of the game ("Spiel"). Inspired by the proximity of his friend's spirit, "dem stolz-ruhigen Schatten gegenüber, der so wesenhaft Velten Andres in meinem Dasein hieß," he decisively responds *"Nein!"* (19:345, Raabe's emphasis). Juxtaposing the novel's epigraph with these lines uttered in the presence of Velten's shadow, Nancy Kaiser asserts: "The motto thus depicts Krumhardt's difficulties in compiling his *Akten*, in maintaining his orientation" (8). Given the fact that Velten's spiritual presence persuades the narrator to continue the "game"—a term that signifies both his writing and his bourgeois life, for he is vexed on this evening both by familial and official duties as well as by the piled-up documents he would gather into a coherent history—in spite of his fatigue and despondence, we might conclude it is precisely his friend's shadow, that so "substantive" element in Krumhardt's own Being, that *provides* his orientation and *allows* the narration to continue.

To be sure, Krumhardt—and Raabe—know the imaginative presence of an expired Other as a link to the past is radically evanescent; this is why Velten is conjured as a shadow. But if shadows are fleeting in Raabe's works, they are also omnipresent. To cite just a few examples: the title figure in the story *Else von der Tanne* (1865) is warned by an old woman not to fall over her shadow, for a fall is a fall into one's shadow, and one might not rearise (9/1:182). The old woman's prophecy of a fateful shadow fulfills itself in Else's murder. The narrator of the historical novel *Unseres Herrgotts Kanzlei* (1862) refers to the figures who populate the tale as faint "Schattenbilder" (4:172). In *Pfisters Mühle* (1884), the shadows cast by the narrator (typically, a scholar) and his wife possess a double signification; they indicate the happy pair's fundamental compatibility, but also foreground the impending demise of the mill named in the story's title, as well as the end of the natural, harmonious way of life it symbolizes (16:118–20). Stopfkuchen finds it acceptable to be fat "im Schatten" (18:54), and Eduard thereupon comments on the enormous sheltering shadow Schaumann casts for his wife: "Sie war nicht eingehutzelt unter seinem Regimente in dem Schatten, dem beträchtlichen Schatten, den er warf" (18:55). *Alte Nester*'s Langreuter, sitting in melancholy reflection in a room in the Werden castle where he and his playmates frolicked long ago, imaginatively observes "die Schatten an den Wänden bald heiter, bald traurig vorbeigleiten" (14:209).

Shadows in Raabe may be fleeting and transitory, but they provide his most substantive metaphoric link to the past. In *Else von der Tanne* and *Pfisters Mühle*, they also constitute a prophetic link to the future. As with Stopfkuchen's protective shadow and the deceased Velten's motivational shadow, they nurture and inspire. In *Die Akten des Vogelsangs*, Raabe draws on Chamisso's Romantic shadow motif in reconstellating the Romantic Doppelgänger thematic. The novel may illustrate how the passage of time turns substance into shadow, but when Velten's spirit enters into Karl and prompts him to push on with his chronicle, we observe a shadow-producing substance, namely, the narrative itself.[11] Only if we consider the many facets of Raabe's shadow motif, as well as the *dialectical* implications of the shadow-substance dichotomy in the Chamisso verse, can we understand the significance of Raabe's comment on the epigraph in his letter of 8 November 1895—cited by Nancy Kaiser to sustain her interpretation of the motto (8)—to Paul Gerber: "Auf der Buchausgabe werden Sie ein Wort aus dem Peter Schlemihl finden, welches vierzig Jahre nach der 'Chronik der Sperlingsgasse' nicht ohne Grund am Schlusse einer so langen litterarischen Lebensarbeit steht" (19:468). In the *Chronik*, it should be noted, Wachholder refers to his artistically inspirational youthful reincarnation not only as a "Doppelgänger," but also as his "Schattenbild" (1:21). Raabe's shadows envelop narrating egos and narrated Others in a synchronic embrace from the beginning of his long career almost to its conclusion.

To be sure, Karl's relationship with Velten is highly conflicted. When the jurist insists to his deceased friend's shadow he is *not* tired of the "game" and will press ahead with his care-plagued middle-class life as well as with his chronicling, he also reflects his ongoing attempt to shore up and defend his own personal values and, indeed, his very identity against Velten. In his article on the narrative structure of the *Akten*, Wolfgang Preisendanz has cogently argued that Karl's return to the past through his writing is the attempt to ground this identity by means of a conversation with himself. His remembrance of things past is an effort to arrive at self-understanding. Karl struggles with his own life's history in wrestling with Velten's shadowy presence, a battle that demands a great sacrifice: the suppression of the narrator's own idealism, antibourgeois inclinations, and latent individual needs. He must constantly invoke his property, position, family, and secure social status, and convince himself of their decisive merits, in order to keep his friend's influence, which is articulated in their inner dialogue, at bay (1981:210–24).

Nevertheless, the struggle with Velten would not be as painful and costly as Preisendanz describes it if Velten did not personify a powerful element in Karl's psyche. If Karl's examination of his own youthful self in his memorial forays into his childhood history seems less vivid and substantial than is the case with the narrating egos in *Alte Nester* and *Stopfkuchen*, this is due to the circumstance that the narrated Other is far more powerful as a haunting presence in his *contemporary* Being than is the case with Just Everstein and Heinrich Schaumann. Unlike the other two principal nonnarrating protagonists in the trilogy, Velten is dead, so his specter can most effectively infiltrate and incorporate the stifled elements in Karl's spirit, thereby becoming his alter ego. Karl asks halfway through this narrative: "Was trübt das Auge mehr als der Blick in verblichenen Sonnen- und Jugendglanz?" (19:317), but it is Velten's forceful nowtime presence in his Being that at once inspires and occludes, drives and troubles, his gaze into his juvenile past.

More than any other critic, Irmgard Roebling has pointed out the complex filiation between Romantic Doppelgänger novels and *Die Akten des Vogelsangs*. This extends even to Raabe's onomastics; she sees "Velten" as borrowed from the "Doppelheldengespann Walt und Vult" in Jean Paul's *Flegeljahre* (1804–5) (Roebling 111). Roebling finds that while Romanticism's Doppelgänger reflect this movement's notion of an all-encompassing and autonomous ego, Raabe's books mirror the later nineteenth century's sense that the ego no longer constitutes a universal middle point, and that the unity of the ego has dissolved. Velten represents for Roebling the lost and yearned for maternal component in Karl's ego. While this is quite debatable—there seems nothing even remotely maternal in Velten's persona[12]—her view that the deceased childhood friend is for the narrator the "willed Other" or the Lacanian "other desiring" (Roebling 111) is very cogent, as is her remark that Velten and Karl personify "die systematische Aufspaltung eines Gesamtsubjekts in widerstreitende Rollen" (103). Although Romanticism's embrace of Fichte's sovereign and omnipotent superego stands in stark contrast to Poetic Realism's putative enunciation of the decayed ego, the systematic division described by Roebling tends to apply equally to the Doppelgänger enactments and other ego–alter ego juxtapositions of both movements.

Any similar inclination to view the narrated Other in Raabe's last work, the novel fragment *Altershausen*, as a Lacanian desired Other (the idealized, often Double-inscribed holistic psyche projected by an ego that perceives itself as fragmented) is problematized by the circumstance that *Altershausen*'s chief third-person protagonist is handicapped by severe mental retardation, the result of hitting his head when he fell out of a tree as a child. Raabe's last narrating ego, Professor Dr. Friedrich ("Fritz") Feyerabend, therefore resembles his first, Johannes Wachholder, in his attempt to heal the split self through recourse to an imaginative mirror image: a Doppelgänger stemming from a creative re-vision of his own youthful Being. However, unlike Wachholder and in common with the Braunschweig trilogy's narrators, Feyerabend feels (before he actually returns to his birthplace Altershausen and learns the truth about his best friend's condition) driven to reestablish childhood links to a primary male Other. As with these earlier narrators, this compulsion stems from a sense of vague dissatisfaction with his staid and stale professional persona. But unlike Just Everstein, Heinrich Schaumann, and Velten Andres, Ludchen Bock possesses no evident transcendent qualities. He is neither larger than life in physique, worldly wisdom, and success like Just and Stopfkuchen, nor is he a great idealist and renouncer of coarse material life in the manner of Andres. He is, instead, an old man with the behavior and mental capacities of a prepubescent boy, as when Feyerabend last knew him. Feyerabend's return to Altershausen is motivated by a "homesickness" for youth and for life, and by the need to know Ludchen Bock's perspectives on these overarching matters (20:289). He is, of course, shocked to discover Ludchen is incapable of such reflection; Ludchen cannot look back and wax philosophical about their shared boyhood because he has never ceased to live it. Ludchen cannot mediate for Feyerabend between his own psyche and the external world like the alter egos in the Braunschweig trilogy. Instead, he can only constitute a looking glass, seemingly held in front of his childhood friend when they converse, into the past, since Ludchen is a figure frozen in time, a time when narrating ego and narrated Other were both boys. This looking glass thus functions as a mirror, a mirror that frames the professor's own youthful Doppelgänger.

Given Raabe's tendency to imbue his chief third-person protagonists, at least in the Braunschweig trilogy, with highly desirable attributes, indeed, with an almost metaphysically unerring competence, it is not surprising that certain critics have viewed Ludchen Bock in a beatific light. Gerhart Mayer has spoken of this child-man's profound and unconstrained joy in existing, which stems from a naive and loving faith in life (219). Martini is even more extreme in finding Ludchen possesses a reallife superiority over his youthful playmate, since he never became conscious of the sort of "detached ego" from which Feyerabend suffers, and lives in a timeless dream world (735). More recent critics have tended to view this eternal child from a diametrically opposite perspective. Ulrich Adolphs sees Feyerabend as attempting to define his identity through the act of writing. Ludchen is incapable of such creative self-definition; from this perspective, he is silent ("stumm"), defined solely through the corporeal, specifically, his obsession with the absolute chronological regularity of his meal times. His silence reifys for Feyerabend the latter's fear of a block in writing, the inability to create the ego through this medium of artistic self-reflection. Ludchen's alleged superiority is thus untenable (101–2). Theo Buck refers to Raabe's correspondence to argue in far stronger terms than Adolphs that Ludchen is a tragic figure, a completely debilitated imbecile who cannot help his childhood friend in Feyerabend's search for a harmonious existence (32–34).

Raabe's balanced presentation of Ludchen's persona allows both points of view enough viability that they cancel each other out; he is neither a German version of the Russian "holy fool" nor simply a hopeless, anxiety-producing imbecile. His uncomplicated ego does allow him to experience moments of childish bliss, but he is easily intimidated by, and suffers terribly at the hands of, Altershausen's bullies. In the final analysis, Ludchen is rather neutral, trapped by and immobilized in the past like a fly in amber. His psychic simplicity renders him a limpid reflecting surface, which allows Feyerabend's own past to emerge before him. Hermann Helmers cites *Die Chronik der Sperlingsgasse* in noting remembrance in Raabe's narrators leads to the conjuncture of present existence and images from the past. This causes a split in the ego; former and present selves become imbricated, and "Der Erzähler wird zum Doppelgänger seiner selbst" (321). This could also apply to *Altershausen*; Raabe's last work shares with his first the lack of a coherent, physically discrete alter ego, so that the Doppelgänger motif is enacted solipsistically, ultimately without the projection into a desired Other. Ludchen Bock is the reflecting medium through which Feyerabend's youthful Double begins to reemerge.

Altershausen alternates between a first- and third-person narrative frame, and this circumstance both problematizes and enriches the novel's figuration of a split self. The novel begins with the description of an elderly gentleman resting in bed after a night spent with family, friends, colleagues, and patients in celebration of his seventieth birthday. Only after several paragraphs does the narrator reveal the old man himself is the "Ich" who is writing the memoirs (20:203–4). Subsequently, the third-person stance predominates. Feyerabend seems to become merely the chief protagonist, distant from the narrating voice itself.

However, the novel sustains a constant tension between narrating ego and narrated Other, and "Feyerabend" himself is its exponent. The narrator hopes to transcend the past, but repetition—with Ludchen's caretaker Minchen Ahrens (who follows the same daily routine all her adult life) as its muse—provides the tale's temporal foundation. The predominant tone of an insurmountable cyclicality created an aporia allowing no real diachronic progression; this is why Raabe could not complete the work.[13] By means of interaction with—and self-reflection through—the timeless child Ludchen Bock, and by conversing with a woman, Minchen, whose existence is governed by eternal iteration, Professor Geheimrat Dr. Friedrich Feyerabend becomes at certain moments his own childhood self, Fritz, a quarrelsome schoolboy in need of upbraiding. Minchen's confused form of address thus imbricates the distinguished privy counselor and his youthful Double: "Aber Kinder! Jungens! . . . Herr Geheimer Rat!" This conflation of his contemporary self with a juvenile Doppelgänger depresses Feyerabend (20:303–4). The cause of his despondency might lie in the episode's confirmation of his critically celebrated self-as-nutcracker dream's ultimate message; the present repeats the past, and the adult man (or nutcracker) is only superficially something other than the Double of what he was as a boy. One can only be consoled by the thought that life continues ever anew, and contains some pleasurable moments (20:287–98).

Eduard Beaucamp has noted that remembrance is so powerful a movens in Raabe's prose that the past continuously remanifests itself, constantly pushing for its own "reproduction" (101). We have seen that the Doppelgänger motif, and the dialectic juxtaposition of narrating ego and narrated alter ego, were seminal elements in this iterative process. In works previous to *Altershausen*, youthful Doubles, alter egos, and shadows linked the past, the present, and even the future. Indeed, these motifs acted to generate narration itself. Enveloped by Altershausen's material reality, Feyerabend also senses he has become his own shadow (20:276). Ludchen's ghostly presence at Feyerabend's side during a brief pause in a minister's speech at the professor's birthday celebration (20:219–20) inspires his return home, and readers of *Die Akten des Vogelsangs* might expect him, like the ghost Velten Andres next to Karl Krumhardt's armchair (19:344–45), to inspire an exhaustive chronicle.

However, the presence of ghosts and shadows, Feyerabend's actual meeting with Ludchen, and the enactments of the professor's own youthful Doppelgänger through dreaming and in conversation with his childhood friends do not revitalize the past and invigorate the present with vivid memory, as they did in earlier novels, where dynamic narrated Others spurred the narrating egos to create comprehensive memoirs. Instead, the process of remembering vanished time led Raabe and his narrator in *Altershausen* to regard chronology as governed by a rather depressing cyclicality. When narrative memory and the conjuration of the youthful selves it generates cause an author to see personal history not as a seminally inspiring creative force, but as leading, mentally, to the eternal recurrence of the same, then he or she will regard literary art as no longer worthy of pursuit. This change in perspective overtook Raabe as he was writing *Altershausen*, and brought his career to an end. It also signaled the definitive conclusion of Poetic Realism.[14] For it indicated that the attainment of this movement's telos of representing life as a complex, manifold but integrated, unified totality had become overwhelmingly problematic.

Conclusion

Many literary historians regard the diachronic development of national literatures as informed by a consistent fluctuation between epochs of romanticism and realism. In romantic periods, according to this view, artists tend to let their fantasy roam free and are not terribly interested in representing the world objectively, "as it is." In realistic ages, the artist attempts to hold a mirror up to the external world, exposing all the imperfections and deficiencies of ordinary, everyday life. Most historians agree that when a nation's political circumstances are fortuitous, readers and writers favor diverting literature imbued with highly imaginative constructs, whereas economic decline or episodes of war and pestilence tend to produce sober, realistic narratives.

With regard to Germany in the nineteenth century, almost all historians believe that the failure of the Napoleonic Wars to bring about democracy and unification led to the end of Romanticism. What emerged in its stead was the hard-edged, politically flavored realism of "Young Germany" writers. The misery attendant to the 1848 revolution these writers helped inspire further enhanced the realistic trend, but inclined politically disillusioned writers to create somewhat poeticized images of totality in their work. In Julian Schmidt's aesthetics, this holism was intended to project a utopian political communalism. Unified, integrated, holistic art, in his view, would help pave the way for a nation blessed with these attributes. This perspective has been clearly delineated by many scholars. Some have alluded to the conflicted affinity that emerged as a result of these desiderata, most significantly enunciated by Schmidt and Ludwig, between Romanticism and Poetic Realism. I have attempted to show that this contemporaneous attraction to and rejection of Romanticism on the part of Poetic Realists is most evident in the *Nachmärz* generation's adaptation of the Romantic Double motif.

The Romantics drew on subjective idealism's notion of a self-replicating ego to create their Doppelgänger. The protagonist's ego is constricted by bourgeois confinements, but his or her Double is a capricious and often supernaturally endowed persona capable of transcending such limitations through ironic humor and the power of imaginative, artistic thought. Already in Droste-Hülshoff, one can see the Double transformed from the site of contestation between the everyday and the artistic to a construct resonant with social and sexual conflict.

Her Doppelgänger are spawned primarily through the repression of the feminine and the erotic by predominant patriarchal values. Ludwig's adaptations of the Doppelgänger motif reflect his valuation of literature characterized by aesthetic and psychological totality, the creation of which was, indeed, Poetic Realism's most defining goal. Meyer's ego–alter ego juxtapositions point to the concomitant conflict and union of self and Other on a universal scale, as evident in the relationship between "Occidental" and "Oriental." Keller's Doubles are twins who are *not* imbued by the psychic synthesis of an ego–alter ego dialectic; the totality they evoke is one of an absolute loss of communal values, and, indeed, of historical memory. In the two novellas of Storm we examined, Doppelgänger also foreground the problematic of historical and personal memory, but show the potential for its restoration as well. This restoration leads to the overcoming of the split persona, so that the evisceration of the alter ego enables the emergence of spiritual unity. The relationship between Raabe's narrating egos and narrated alter egos not only allows the evocation of a synthesizing dialectic in the psychological realm, but generates narration itself. A central focus of this narration is the memorial evocation of the narrator's youthful self, his nostalgically constellated childhood Double. An admired alter ego from the past inspires the narrating ego to chronicle their lives.

My central thesis is that Poetic Realists drew on the Romantic Doppelgänger motif to achieve their movement's central desideratum: the narrative projection of psychological and aesthetic comprehensiveness. Raabe's increasing view of empirical reality as so hopelessly fragmented that even this projected totality was in vain therefore clearly indicates Poetic Realism's end as a discrete literary period. Nevertheless, writers continued, and will continue, to employ the Double figure and to enact other ego–alter ego juxtapositions as a means for exploring the split between the conscious and subconscious mind, for examining the deep divisions always latent within even the (apparently) most harmonious individual human psyches.

Notes

Introduction

1. Among the works that provide a relatively comprehensive treatment of the Double as a feature of world literature (albeit mostly confined to the Occident), I particularly recommend the book-length studies of Coates (*The Double and the Other*), Keppler (*The Literature of the Second Self*), Robert Rogers (*A Psychoanalytic Study of the Double*), and Tymms (*Doubles in Literary Psychology*), as well as the anthology edited by Crook (*Fearful Symmetry*). Frenzel's lexicon *Motive der Weltliteratur* gives a concise overview of the motif (94–114).

2. See, for example, Claude Lecouteux's article on Doubles and dream phantoms in German literature of the Middle Ages. In this essay, "alter ego" is used as a term equivalent to "double," "Doppelgänger," and the early Germanic term "hamr." A. Didier Graeffe's essay, "Goethe's Faust: Ego and Alter Ego," treats Mephistopheles as a "projection" of Faust's inchoate moral turpitude. In Graeffe's view, Mephistopheles thus frees Faust to pursue an active life. Such an imaginative projection inevitably suggests a Romantic Doppelgänger of the sort inspired by Fichte's subjective superego constructs. In *A Psychoanalytic Study of the Double in Literature*, Robert Rogers also tends to use the terms "Double" and "alter ego" interchangeably. In *Double, Alter ego und Schatten-Ich*, Dieter Wellershoff calls Madame Bovary an alter ego of Flaubert, and not his Double (10), but refers to the chief male protagonist of one of his own works as "ein Double oder ein Alter ego des Autors" (20). These examples suggest that most writers who treat the subject of a "second self" make no concrete methodological distinction between the terms "Double" and "alter ego."

3. Keppler, *Literature of the Second Self*, defends his substitute expression "second self" by arguing "it suggests twofoldness without implying duplication" (3). However, some element of duplication seems inherent in the notion of a second self.

4. Krauss, *Doppelgängermotiv*, has succinctly summarized the role played by subjective idealism in the German Romantics' dualistic world view; when the outside world opposes its ambition, the ego becomes divided into ideal-real, and endless-finite poles. This process leads to the enactment of the Doppelgänger motif: "Nimmt das Gefühl dieser Ichspaltung aus der Welt der Vorstellung Gestalt an, kristallisiert es sich in der Welt des Visuellen, dann entsteht das Doppelgängertum als die vergegenständlichte Gegenüberstellung des Ich zu sich selbst" (7).

5. These debates have been well summarized by Cowen, *Der Poetische Realismus*, 9–29.

6. Cowen (ibid., 15–16) notes the term "Poetischer Realismus" was first used by Schelling, but indicates in his discussion concerning debates about the term that most critics agree Ludwig, not the Romantic Schelling, gave the age its name. Cowen also points out that the theoretical essays in which Ludwig articulated his notion of Poetic Realism first began appearing in published form in the 1870s (133). In *German Poetic Realism*, Bernd credited René Wellek with showing that Schelling had no real impact on the period, and that "the credit for coining the formula specifically designed to characterize that literary movement, therefore, should return to Ludwig" (102). In his recent book *Poetic Realism in Scandinavia and Central Europe*, however, Bernd's research into the Scandinavian roots of the movement lead him to conclude that the Swedish professor of aesthetics Per Daniel Atterbom was the first to use "Poetisk Realism" to designate this period (80–84). The person who introduced "Poetischer Realismus" in Germany for this purpose was Carl August Hagberg. He wrote an essay using the term in 1838 at the behest of Friedrich and Heinrich Brockhaus for their journal, *Blätter für literarische Unterhaltung*. The Leipzig publishers urged Hagberg to write his now forgotten essay on the Swedish literary scene after their inspiring visit to Uppsala, home to both Atterbom and the man who issued the first "manifesto" for Poetic Realism, the librarian Johan Erik Rydqvist (118–20).

7. See particularly Preisendanz's study *Humor als dichterische Einbildungskraft: Studien zur Erzählkunst des poetischen Realismus*.

8. The concept of a transcendent superego was, of course, conceived by Fichte. For a summary of his role in the development of the Romantic Doppelgänger figure, see Krauss, *Doppelgängermotiv*, esp. 20–24 and 47–55.

9. See particularly Werner Hahl's essay "Gesellschaftlicher Konservatismus und literarischer Realismus. Das Modell einer deutschen Sozialverfassung in den Dorfgeschichten," in Bucher, ed., *Realismus und Gründerzeit*, 1:48–93.

10. Jürgen Hein's *Dorfgeschichte* provides concise overviews of these many diverse typologies.

11. On Schmidt's rejection of Auerbach as a Poetic Realist, see Bernd, *German Poetic Realism*, 23.

12. For a discussion of this influence, particularly in its sociopolitical dimensions, see Eisele, *Realismus und Ideologie*, 104–10.

13. See, for example, Kurt Schreinert's introduction in the historical-critical edition of the novel, esp. vi–viii.

14. The Fichtean aspect of this scene is also discussed by Krauss, *Doppelgängermotiv*, 54–55.

Chapter 1

1. The most articulate explication of German Poetic Realism as restricted to Schmidt and his mid-nineteenth-century followers is provided by Bernd, *German Poetic Realism*.

2. See Gaier, "'Concurrenzstücke,'" 135.
3. See esp. Silz, *Realism and Reality*, 36–51.
4. This tendency is evident, for example, in Staiger, *Droste-Hülshoff*, and Schneider, *Realismus und Restauration*.
5. Among the best recent examples are the articles by Howe, "Breaking into Parnassus," and Pickar, "Covert Misogyny."
6. Heselhaus, *Droste-Hülshoff: Werk und Leben*, even speculates here that the dream is specifically designed to refute Novalis (74).
7. The inscription of Ledwina's dream by Thanatos is also suggested by Peucker's reading of this work, though she sees a tendency toward Romanticism in the dream's implied link of death to a poetic knowledge of the self at its origin. See Peucker, "Droste-Hülshoff's Ophelia," 386–89.
8. See Hallamore, "The Reflected Self," 64–66.
9. Haller, "'Das Spiegelbild,'" sees the split as one between good and evil (255–56).
10. See esp. 331 and 334 of Nollendorfs' article "'... kein Zeugniß ablegen.'"
11. Cf. also Lietina-Ray, "Das Recht," 107–9, who provides several other plausible reasons why we should not assume the corpse's scar automatically reveals the suicide to be Friedrich.
12. The nuances in his name have been articulated by Alan P. Cottrell's "The Significance of the Name 'Johannes.'"

Chapter 2

1. Droste-Hülshoff's status as a Poetic Realist is enhanced by the judgment of Ludwig's most important English language scholar, William McClain, who believes *Die Judenbuche* is "an outstanding example" of Poetic Realism. See *Between Real and Ideal*, 51.
2. Ludwig's explication of Poetic Realism as a process of stylization, purification, and typification is well summarized by Steinmetz, "Die Rolle des Lesers," 226.
3. I am completely in agreement with McClain, one of the few critics to analyze *Die wahrhaftige Geschichte von den drei Wünschen*, who finds fault with "the cluttered style and the poor articulation of the story as a whole." See *Between Real and Ideal*, 28–29.
4. As Puknus notes, love in many of Hoffmann's tales can be regarded as the "andächtige Verklärung des anderen" ("Dualismus," 61), which also presupposes the successful integration of the Other's disparate character traits, including those embodied in a Double.
5. Consider, for example, Ludwig's juxtaposition of two secondary figures in the *Geschichte*'s quotidian realm; the decisive, firm brunette Madame Flötenspiel, half Juno and half Venus, and the abstract, blond, saturnine Dame Müller (1:119).

6. As Lillyman, *Otto Ludwig's "Zwischen Himmel und Erde,"* has noted: "Each incorrectly assumes, on almost all occasions, that the other is exactly the same as he himself is, that the other will act in almost any given situation exactly the same as he himself will" (52–53).

7. For a discussion of the manner in which this estate as described in the novel's opening mirrors the family's psychic rift, see Osterkamp, *Arbeit und Identität*, 160–61, and Brinkmann, *Wirklichkeit und Illusion*, 145–216. Brinkmann indicates that even the narrator reflects this fissure, as he shuttles in these opening pages from attention to empirical details to an omniscient, all-encompassing perspective driven by Ludwig's interest in sustaining an aesthetic totality (160).

Chapter 3

1. For a discussion of how Meyer adapted Thierry's book and other historical materials on Becket and Henry II, see Hardaway's "C. F. Meyer's *Der Heilige*."

2. On *Der Heilige* as an exemplary work of German Poetic Realism, see esp. 107–9 in Silz's book *Realism and Reality*.

3. See Hertling, "C. F. Meyer's *Der Heilige*," 140, 143–44.

4. The deep impression the German Romantics made on Meyer is stressed by Burkhard throughout the course of her monograph *Conrad Ferdinand Meyer*.

5. For a detailed analysis of these parallels, see Silz, *Realism and Reality*, 104–5.

6. For a summary of critical reactions to Meyer's use of the Double figure in this episode of *Gustav Adolfs Page*, see McCort, *States of Unconsciousness*, 117, n. 26.

7. The characterization of the Middle East's native inhabitants as passive and feminized in nineteenth-century discourse is one of the central themes in Said's *Orientalism*.

8. See Onderdelinden, *Rahmenerzählungen*, 112.

9. Guthke, *Wege zur Literatur*, has described with particular aptness Meyer's overarching dialectical procedure, especially with regard to characterization, and cites *Der Heilige* as Meyer's most paradigmatic work in this regard (187).

10. For Nietzsche, as is well known, Christian piety and a desire for revenge stemming from social resentment are inextricably intertwined, and this circumstance has inspired Wetzel's interesting Nietzschean interpretation of Meyer's novella, "Der allzumenschliche Heilige."

11. This helps explain Schmidt's generous praise of the work, and his belief that Meyer belonged to Poetic Realism's "innermost circle," despite contemporary condemnation of *Der Heilige* from a moral perspective, and despite the fact that Schmidt had not read the novella in its entirety when he wrote a laudatory review of the work. Meyer was quite grateful for Schmidt's commendation. See Cowen, *Der Poetische Realismus*, 251–52.

Chapter 4

1. Cowen, *Der Poetische Realismus*, has shown that Pankraz's views are fully in accord with those of his creator (68–69).
2. See esp. 103–4 and 133–38 of Merkel-Nipperdey's *Gottfried Kellers "Martin Salander."*
3. Benjamin's influence on Adorno has been elucidated by many critics. For a particularly comprehensive treatment of Adorno's reception of Benjamin, see Buck-Morss's book on Adorno, *The Origin of Negative Dialectics*.
4. See Benjamin's essay "Der Erzähler" in his *Gesammelte Schriften*, 2/2: 438–65. The role played by Lukács in inspiring Benjamin's theory of the epic, particularly in the realm of epic memory, is discussed in Wohlfarth, "Messianic Structure," esp. 149.
5. Ernst Bloch has expressed this contrast between the critical perspectives of Lukács and Benjamin as follows: "A sense for the peripheral: Benjamin had what Lukács so drastically lacked: a unique gaze for the significant detail, for what lies alongside, for those fresh elements which, in thinking and in the world, arise from here, for the individual things ('Einzelsein') which intrude in an unaccustomed and nonschematic way, things which do not fit in with the usual lot and therefore deserve particular, incisive attention" ("Recollections of Walter Benjamin," 340).
6. See *Noten zur Literatur*, 1:54–55. In his essay "Balzac-Lektüre," in *Noten zur Literatur*, 2:19–41, Adorno notes that the modern epic narrative must describe the world with an exaggerated precision due to this loss. Epic realism is thus a "Realismus aus Realitätsverlust" (30). Adorno sees in the use of a wealth of descriptive detail in the epic narrative of nineteenth-century realists like Balzac and Keller a compensatory mechanism, an epistemological technique employed to make up for the loss of genuine experience and a sense of nonalienated reality in the external world.
7. This sort of secular piety has been termed "Weltfrömmigkeit" in connection with Keller's oeuvre by one of his more important contemporary commentators. See Wenger, *Auseinandersetzung*, 77–142.
8. Jennings uses this term in paraphrasing Marie Salander's reaction to a comment made by Martin concerning Isidor Weidelich.
9. The minister's disingenuousness seems to contrast with the simple and sincere piety of the impoverished Ursula and her daughter Agatchen. However, their respective professions of faith are not really antithetical, because there is also an empty, mechanical dogmatism underlying the religious persuasion of the two women. See esp. 2:521–22.
10. Wenger, *Auseinandersetzung*, views this entanglement in *Martin Salander* as Keller's engagement with the "Verweltlichung" of the spiritual, in which contemporary Swiss Reformed Church theology was regarded by Keller as partly culpable. Wenger points out that the notes and poems for the planned conclusion to the novel also take up this theme of secularization. See esp. 53, 95, 127, 179–80.

11. Even Merkel-Nipperdey's "ambivalent" characters (*Gottfried Kellers "Martin Salander,"* 135–36) fit into this taxonomy, for they are *partially* doubled; the Weidelichs are duplicated in many particulars by the Kleinpeter family (see 3:663–71), and Wohlwend unquestionably represents Martin Salander's dark side. See Passavant, *Zeitdarstellung*, 50–53, for a discussion of their spiritual affinity and somewhat parallel careers. The only main character who doesn't seem to belong in this schematization is Myrrha, but she is really much more a projection of Martin's fantasies than a protagonist in her own right.

Chapter 5

1. Though Webber's comment on Haien's ghostly emanation in the contemporary narrative frame of *Der Schimmelreiter* provides an interesting exception to this tendency: "By succumbing to an act of superstition in his sacrificial death, the enlightened Haien recreates himself as a phantom double, outliving the end he thought to find by his plunge into the abyss. His metamorphosis lets the uncanny spirit emerge from the narrative picture into the framework which should contain it. Here, the uncanny is accorded a real 'presence' in spite of the Realistic frame-hold" ("The Uncanny Rides Again," 873).

2. Among the most notable of the many works treating the themes of temporality, memory, history, and historical framing in Storm's oeuvre are those by Laage (*Theodor Storm: Studien*, 1–19), Bernd (*Theodor Storm's Craft of Fiction*), Pastor (*Die Sprache der Erinnerung*), and Brecht ("Storm und die Geschichte").

3. This term should not be confused with Hans-Georg Gadamer's famous concept of an "effective historical consciousness" ("wirkungsgeschichtliches Bewußtsein"). As Weinsheimer has noted: "Wirkungsgeschichtliches Bewußtsein, the awareness that one's own understanding is affected by history, is consciousness that one has a horizon and understands within a particular situation" (*Gadamer's Hermeneutics*, 184). I intend the term "effective historical memory" to signify something quite distinct from this: namely, the notion of an ideal narrative-fictive memory able to transcend the hermeneutic limitations suggested by Gadamer's term.

4. This technique is the focus of Duroche's article "Like and Look Alike: Symmetry and Irony in Theodor Storm's *Aquis submersus*."

5. In relating the tale of the curse to Johannes, Katharina merely uses the terms "So heißt's auch" and "soll es gewesen sein" to indicate that the tale stems from popular oral narrative. But she believes the *Ahnin* would have cursed her as well (2:407), and this conviction foreshadows her tragic fate.

6. The critical treatment of this dimension of *Aquis submersus* has been nicely summarized by Mullan, "Tragic Guilt," 226–30. Nuber has recently argued that the guilt problematic has been overemphasized by Storm scholars. See "Ein Bilderrätsel," esp. 227–28.

7. Of course, I would have to disagree with Mullan's assertion that "the motifs of the curse and the ghost are employed purely for their atmospheric value" ("Tragic Guilt," 237).

8. Laage has disputed this view by noting Keller's own dissatisfaction with *Martin Salander*. Laage argues that personal difficulties in Keller's life were responsible for putting an end to his correspondence with Storm (" 'Der Storm-Keller Briefwechsel,' " 12).

9. This phrase was used in a letter to his son-in-law dated 19 May 1887, thus around four months after his letter to Keller. See Grimm, "Theodor Storm: *Ein Doppelgänger*," 333.

10. Lukacher's *Primal Scenes* provides a thorough treatment of this phenomenon in both literature and psychoanalysis.

11. Terence John Rogers's study *Techniques of Solipsism* focuses on what the author sees as the solitary, isolated character of life inherent both in the themes of Storm's novellas and in the narrative perspectives themselves. His interpretation of the exchange between the narrator and the forester at the conclusion of *Ein Doppelgänger* is, therefore, virtually opposite to mine: "For all its commitment, for all its hard and glowing realism, this story rests on a factual foundation which has been established, not through the sober collation of facts or reports or experiences, nor through the privileged assertions of a 'fictional' narrator, but explicitly through the unbridled movements of a single consciousness in trance. Inevitably, the facts lose some of their quality of being steadily and implacably 'there'; the structure they constitute is balanced finely on a pinpoint of fantasy and within an ace of being broken up in uncertainty" (98).

12. Storm's complex, ambivalent views on patrimony, his subtle blending of the themes of lineage and temporality, and his portrayal in certain works of a redemption of the past through an heir are explored by Körber in her essay on the temporal element of Storm's novellas, "Zeitablauf und Zeitwahrnehmung in den Novellen Theodor Storms."

Chapter 6

1. Geppert's recent comprehensive study of European Realism maintains this movement is immanently defined by narrators whose relationship to the figures about whom they write can be characterized as a search to identify with the Other. The "Erfahrung bzw. Vorstellung des 'Fremden' im Ich als dem anderen" is the attempt to create a "Konsens" (609) balancing the ideal and the real, aesthetically (indeed romantically) tinged natural harmony and the need to come to grips with the alienating economic realities in industrialized society. Out of the oscillation between the narrator's self-representations and his projections into alter egos, this balancing act is sustained, and a "pragmatic" Realism emerges. With regard to Raabe, Geppert believes this trend is particularly evident in the Braunschweig trilogy (*Der realistische Weg*, 268–69, 591–655).

2. Raabe uses the term for comical effect in the story *Keltische Knochen* (1864–65) when describing two scholars of similar appearance who argue over the ethnicity of the ancient bones named in the title. The squabbling scientists remind the narrator of the two rabbits he witnessed a magician

produce from one: "Ein ganz ähnliches Experiment schien mit dem Prosektor Zuckriegel vorgenommen worden zu sein—er war zum zweitenmal in der Gaststube beim Seeauer vorhanden und—zankte sich bereits aufs heftigste mit seinem Doppelgänger" (9/1:212).

3. For an overview of the critical discussions of this influence, see esp. Sammons, *Shifting Fortunes*, 4–6.

4. Bertschik has noted Hoffmann's *Der Sandmann*, with its famous Doppelgänger constellations, also strongly influenced the composition of *Der heilige Born* (*Maulwurfsarchäologie*, 182–86).

5. See Jameson's thusly titled book.

6. Di Maio has shown how multiple perspectives in Raabe's Braunschweig novels—an alternation between first- and third-person narrating voices, along with Romantic irony and an adroit use of citations—also help overcome limitations imposed by linear, sequential narration, and allow the representation of chronological simultaneity. See *The Multiple Perspective: Wilhelm Raabe's Third-Person Narratives of the Braunschweig Period*.

7. See Lacan's essay "Le stade du miroir comme formateur de la fonction du Je telle qu'elle nous est révélée dans l'expérience psychanalytique" in *Écrits*, 93–100.

8. Originally, the *vita contemplativa* was privileged by philosophers over the *vita activa*, which was associated with turmoil. In the modern age, particularly in the thought of Marx and Nietzsche, greater value was attributed to "active life." This hierarchic reversal, occurring as it did in Raabe's time and, largely, in the writings of his fellow Germans, may have influenced the attitudes evident in *Alte Nester*. For an overview of the evolving historical relationship between the two concepts, see Arendt, *The Human Condition*, 12–17.

9. This should not be taken to signify that Eduard's empathetic identification with Stopfkuchen allows him to perfectly narrate his friend's thoughts. For as Geppert has noted, Eduard lends his voice to an "Other" who always "means" something somewhat different than what Eduard actually "says" (*Der realistische Weg*, 626).

10. This circumstance allows Geppert to assert that in *Die Akten des Vogelsangs*, unlike the other two novels in the trilogy, this sublation lacks a positive valence: "Auch die Formel vom 'Ich als dem anderen' erhält jetzt einen zuletzt ganz negativen Inhalt" (638).

11. Raabe introduces a direct shadow into substance metaphor into *Im alten Eisen* (1887), when Peter Uhusen describes how the fame of his long-lost boyhood friend, Albin Brokenkorb, allowed this celebrated scholar to appear concretely before his mind's eye: "Was eine Wirklichkeit war, wurde zu einem Namen, einem Klang und blieb lange Jahre weiter nichts als das. Dann aber wird bei Gelegenheit solch ein Klang wieder zu—zu einem Schatten, auf den man sehen kann, auf den man hinsieht, und der, je länger man auf ihn hinsieht, desto mehr Knochen, Blut und Fleisch bekommt" (16:399).

12. Geppert, however, is correct to note that Velten grows up in, and constantly seeks to find his way back to, "the world of the mothers" (*Der realis-*

tische Weg, 642), a world characterized by preindustrial, harmonious, and holistic values.

13. This is the thesis of Oehlenschläger's article, "Erzählverfahren und Zeiterfahrung: Überlegungen zu Wilhelm Raabes *Altershausen*," and it is more compelling than most Raabe scholarship in its explanation of Raabe's inability to complete this work.

14. Cf. Bernd, who argues that Raabe's narrative "polyperspectivism" after *Der Hungerpastor* (1862–63), as well as the sociological bent in Theodor Fontane's prose, are the clearest signals of Poetic Realism's demise (*Poetic Realism in Scandinavia and Central Europe*, 203–4 and 215–23).

Works Cited

Adolphs, Ulrich. "Schreibakt als Suche nach Identität: Wilhelm Raabes 'Altershausen.'" *Jahrbuch der Raabe-Gesellschaft* (1985): 92–106.
Adorno, Theodor W. *Negative Dialektik*. Frankfurt a.M.: Suhrkamp, 1966.
———. *Noten zur Literatur*. 4 vols. Frankfurt a.M.: Suhrkamp, 1974–80.
Arendt, Hannah. *The Human Condition*. Chicago: University of Chicago Press, 1958.
Beaucamp, Eduard. *Literatur als Selbstdarstellung: Wilhelm Raabe und die Möglichkeiten eines deutschen Realismus*. Bonn: Bouvier, 1968.
Benjamin, Walter. *Gesammelte Schriften*. Vol. 2. Edited by Rolf Tiedemann and Hermann Schweppenhäuser. Frankfurt a.M.: Suhrkamp, 1977.
Bernd, Clifford Albrecht. *German Poetic Realism*. Boston: Twayne, 1981.
———. *Poetic Realism in Scandinavia and Central Europe, 1820–1895*. Columbia, S.C.: Camden House, 1995.
———. *Theodor Storm's Craft of Fiction: The Torment of a Narrator*. University of North Carolina Studies in the Germanic Languages and Literatures, no. 55. 2nd ed. Chapel Hill: University of North Carolina Press, 1966.
Bertschik, Julia. *Maulwurfsarchäologie: Zum Verhältnis von Geschichte und Anthropologie in Wilhelm Raabes historischen Erzähltexten*. Tübingen: Niemeyer, 1995.
Bloch, Ernst. "Recollections of Walter Benjamin." Translated by Michael W. Jennings. In *On Walter Benjamin: Critical Essays and Recollections*, edited by Gary Smith, 338–45. Cambridge, Mass.: MIT Press, 1988.
Brecht, Walter. "Storm und die Geschichte." *Deutsche Vierteljahrsschrift* 3 (1925): 444–62.
Brinkmann, Richard. *Wirklichkeit und Illusion: Studien über Gehalt und Grenzen des Begriffs Realismus für die erzählende Dichtung des neunzehnten Jahrhunderts*. 2nd ed. Tübingen: Niemeyer, 1966.
Bucher, Max, et al., eds. *Realismus und Gründerzeit: Manifeste und Dokumente zur deutschen Literatur 1848–1880*. 2 vols. Stuttgart: Metzler, 1975–76.
Buck, Theo. "Am Rande des inneren Monologs: Zur Erzählkonstruktion von Raabes 'Altershausen.'" *Jahrbuch der Raabe-Gesellschaft* (1987): 24–45.
Buck-Morss, Susan. *The Origin of Negative Dialectics: Theodor W. Adorno, Walter Benjamin, and the Frankfurt Institute*. New York: Free Press, 1977.
Burkhard, Marianne. *Conrad Ferdinand Meyer*. Boston: Twayne, 1978.
Coates, Paul. *The Double and the Other: Identity as Ideology in Post-Romantic Fiction*. New York: St. Martin's, 1988.
Cottrell, Alan P. "The Significance of the Name 'Johannes' in *Die Judenbuche*." *Seminar* 6 (1970): 207–15.
Cowen, Roy C. *Der Poetische Realismus: Kommentar zu einer Epoche*. Munich: Winkler, 1985.

Crook, Eugene J., ed. *Fearful Symmetry: Doubles and Doubling in Literature and Film. Selected Papers from the Fifth Annual Florida State University Conference on Literature and Film*. Tallahassee: University Presses of Florida, 1981.

Denkler, Horst. *Neues über Wilhelm Raabe: Zehn Annäherungsversuche an einen verkannten Schriftsteller*. Tübingen: Niemeyer, 1988.

Di Maio, Irene S. *The Multiple Perspective: Wilhelm Raabe's Third-Person Narratives of the Braunschweig Period*. Amsterdam: Benjamins, 1981.

Downing, Eric. "Repetition and Realism: The 'Ligea' Impulse in Theodor Storm's *Viola tricolor*." *Deutsche Vierteljahrsschrift* 65 (1991): 265–303.

Droste-Hülshoff, Annette von. *Historisch-Kritische Ausgabe: Werke—Briefwechsel*. Edited by Winfried Woesler. 14 vols. Tübingen: Niemeyer, 1978–.

Duroche, Leonard L. "Like and Look Alike: Symmetry and Irony in Theodor Storm's *Aquis submersus*." *Seminar* 7 (1971): 1–13.

Eisele, Ulf. *Realismus und Ideologie: Zur Kritik der literarischen Theorie nach 1848 am Beispiel des "Deutschen Museums."* Stuttgart: Metzler, 1976.

Evans, Tamara S. *Formen der Ironie in Conrad Ferdinand Meyers Novellen*. Berne: Francke, 1980.

Frenzel, Elisabeth. *Motive der Weltliteratur: Ein Lexikon dichtungsgeschichtlicher Längsschnitte*. Stuttgart: Kröner, 1976.

Freud, Sigmund. *Gesammlte Werke*. Edited by Anna Freud et al. 18 vols. 5th ed. Frankfurt: Fischer, 1973–78.

Freund, Winfried. "Annette von Droste-Hülshoff: 'Das Fräulein von Rodenschild'—Die phantastische Spiegelung einer Bewußtseinskrise." *Wirkendes Wort* 31 (1981): 11–17.

Gaier, Ulrich. "'Concurrenzstücke': Doppelstrukturen in Drostes Werken." In *In Search of the Poetic Real: Essays in Honor of Clifford Albrecht Bernd on the Occasion of His Sixtieth Birthday*, edited by John F. Fetzer et al., 135–49. Stuttgart: Heinz, 1989.

Geisler, Eberhard. "Abschied vom Herzensmuseum: Die Auflösung des Poetischen Realismus in Wilhelm Raabes *Akten des Vogelsangs*." In *Wilhelm Raabe: Studien zu seinem Leben und Werk; aus Anlaß des 150. Geburtstages (1831–1981)*, edited by Leo A. Lensing and Hans-Werner Peter, 365–80. Braunschweig: pp-Verlag, 1981.

Geppert, Hans Vilmar. *Der realistische Weg: Formen pragmatischen Erzählens bei Balzac, Dickens, Hardy, Keller, Raabe und anderen Autoren des 19. Jahrhunderts*. Tübingen: Niemeyer, 1994.

Girard, René. *"To double business bound": Essays on Literature, Mimesis, and Anthropology*. Baltimore: Johns Hopkins University Press, 1978.

Goedsche, Charlotte L. *Narrative Structure in Wilhelm Raabe's "Die Chronik der Sperlingsgasse."* New York: Lang, 1989.

Goldammer, Peter. "Animosität, Aversion und Aggression? Noch einmal zum Verhältnis Wilhelm Raabes zu Theodor Storm." *Jahrbuch der Raabe-Gesellschaft* (1993): 100–109.

———, ed. *Der Briefwechsel zwischen Theodor Storm und Gottfried Keller*. Berlin: Aufbau, 1960.

Gössmann, Wilhelm. *Annette von Droste-Hülshoff: Ich und Spiegelbild: Zum Verständnis der Dichterin und ihres Werkes*. Düsseldorf: Droste, 1985.

Graeffe, A. Didier. "Goethe's Faust: Ego and Alter Ego." In *Goethe on Human Creativeness and Other Goethe Essays*, edited by Rolf King, 179–98. Athens: University of Georgia Press, 1950.

Grimm, Gunter. "Theodor Storm: *Ein Doppelgänger* (1886): Soziales Stigma als 'modernes Schicksal.'" In *Romane und Erzählungen des bürgerlichen Realismus: Neue Interpretationen*, edited by Horst Denkler, 325–46. Stuttgart: Reclam, 1980.

Guerard, Albert J. "Introduction to the Issue 'Perspectives on the Novel.'" *Daedalus* 92 (1963): 197–205.

Guthke, Karl S. *Wege zur Literatur: Studien zur deutschen Dichtungs- und Geistesgeschichte*. Berne: Francke, 1967.

Hallamore, Joyce. "The Reflected Self in Annette von Droste's Work: A Challenge to Self-Discovery." *Monatshefte* 61 (1969): 58–74.

Haller, Rudolf. "Eine Droste-Interpretation: 'Das Spiegelbild.'" *Germanisch-Romanische Montatsschrift* 37 (1956): 253–61.

Hardaway, R. Travis. "C. F. Meyer's *Der Heilige* in Relation to Its Sources." *PMLA* 58 (1943): 245–63.

Hein, Jürgen. *Dorfgeschichte*. Stuttgart: Metzler, 1976.

Heine, Heinrich. *Sämtliche Schriften*. Vol. 1. Edited by Klaus Briegleb. Munich: Hanser, 1968.

Heldt, Uwe. *Isolation und Identität: Die Bedeutung des Idyllischen in der Epik Wilhelm Raabes*. Frankfurt a.M.: Lang, 1980.

Helmers, Hermann. "Die Figur des Erzählers bei Raabe." In *Raabe in neuer Sicht*, edited by Hermann Helmers, 317–37. Stuttgart: Kohlhammer, 1968.

Henel, Heinrich. "Annette von Droste-Hülshoff: Erzählstil und Wirklichkeit." In *Festschrift für Bernhard Blume: Aufsätze zur deutschen und europäischen Literatur*, edited by Egon Schwarz et al., 146–72. Göttingen: Vandenhoeck & Ruprecht, 1967.

Hertling, G. H. "C. F. Meyer's *Der Heilige*: Die *sortes Vergilianae* als Diviniation und symbolisches Kryptogramm." *Seminar* 25 (1989): 127–46.

Heselhaus, Clemens. *Annette von Droste-Hülshoff: Werk und Leben*. Düsseldorf: Bagel, 1971.

Hildenbrock, Aglaja. *Das andere Ich: Künstlicher Mensch und Doppelgänger in der deutsch- und englischsprachigen Literatur*. Tübingen: Stauffenburg, 1986.

Hoffmann, E. T. A. *Sämtliche Werke*. Edited by Walter Müller-Seidel et al. 5 vols. Munich: Winkler, 1960–65.

Hohendahl, Peter Uwe. *Building a National Literature: The Case of Germany, 1830–1870*. Translated by Renate Baron Franciscono. Ithaca: Cornell University Press, 1989.

Holub, Robert C. *Reflections of Realism: Paradox, Norm, and Ideology in Nineteenth-Century German Prose*. Detroit: Wayne State University Press, 1991.

Howe, Patricia. "Breaking into Parnassus: Annette von Droste-Hülshoff and the Problem of Poetic Identity." *German Life and Letters* 46 (1993): 25–41.

Jacobson, Manfred R., and Evelyn M. Jacobson. "The Idyll Besieged: *Tristan und Isold* and *Der Heilige*." *Journal of English and Germanic Philology* 81 (1982): 55–72.
Jameson, Fredric. *The Political Unconscious: Narrative as a Socially Symbolic Act*. Ithaca: Cornell University Press, 1981.
Jennings, Lee Byron. *The Ludicrous Demon: Aspects of the Grotesque in German Post-Romantic Prose*. Berkeley: University of California Press, 1963.
———. "The Model of the Self in Gottfried Keller's Prose." *German Quarterly* 56 (1983): 196–230.
Junge, Hermann. *Wilhelm Raabe: Studien über Form und Inhalt seiner Werke*. 1910. Reprint, Hildesheim: Gerstenberg, 1978.
Kaiser, Gerhard. "Aquis submersus—versunkene Kindheit: Ein literaturpsychologischer Versuch über Theodor Storm." *Euphorion* 73 (1979): 410–34.
———. *Gottfried Keller: Das gedichtete Leben*. Frankfurt a.M.: Insel, 1981.
Kaiser, Nancy A. "Reading Raabe's Realism: *Die Akten des Vogelsangs*." *Germanic Review* 59 (1984): 2–9.
Keller, Gottfried. *Sämtliche Werke und ausgewählte Briefe*. Edited by Clemens Heselhaus. 3 vols. Munich: Hanser, 1956–58.
Keppler, Carl Francis. *The Literature of the Second Self*. Tucson: University of Arizona Press, 1972.
Kinder, Hermann. *Poesie als Synthese: Ausbreitung eines deutschen Realismus-Verständnisses in der Mitte des 19. Jahrhunderts*. Frankfurt a.M.: Athenäum, 1973.
Klopfenstein, Eduard. *Erzähler und Leser bei Wilhelm Raabe: Untersuchungen zu einem Formelement der Prosaerzählung*. Berne: Haupt, 1969.
Komar, Kathleen L. "Fact, Fiction, and Focus: Their Structural Embodiment in C. F. Meyer's *Der Heilige*." *Colloquia Germanica* 14 (1981): 332–41.
Körber, Esther-Beate. "Zeitablauf und Zeitwahrnehmung in den Novellen Theodor Storms." In *Spuren: Festschrift für Theo Schumacher*, edited by Heidrun Colberg and Doris Petersen, 363–86. Stuttgart: Heinz, 1986.
Korte, Hermann. *Ordnung & Tabu: Studien zum poetischen Realismus*. Bonn: Bouvier, 1989.
Kortländer, Bernd. *Annette von Droste-Hülshoff und die deutsche Literatur: Kenntnis, Beurteilung, Beeinflussung*. Münster: Aschendorf, 1979.
Krauss, Wilhelmine. *Das Doppelgängermotiv in der Romantik: Studien zum romantischen Idealismus*. 1930. Reprint, Nendeln/Liechtenstein: Kraus, 1967.
Kreuzer, Helmut. "Zur Theorie des deutschen Realismus zwischen Märzrevolution und Naturalismus." In *Realismustheorien in Literatur, Malerei, Musik und Politik*, edited by Reinhold Grimm and Jost Hermand, 48–67. Stuttgart: Kohlhammer, 1975.
Kurscheidt, Georg. *Engagement und Arrangement: Untersuchungen zur Roman- und Wirklichkeitsauffassung in der Literaturtheorie vom Jungen Deutschland bis zum poetischen Realismus Otto Ludwigs*. Bonn: Bouvier, 1980.
Laage, Karl Ernst. "'Der Storm-Keller Briefwechsel ist ein unschätzbarer Besitz unserer Literatur' (H.Maync)—Zur Neuedition der Briefe." *Schriften der Theodor-Storm-Gesellschaft* 42 (1993): 7–13.

———. *Theodor Storm: Studien zu seinem Leben und Werk mit einem Handschriftenkatalog.* Berlin: Schmidt, 1985.
Lacan, Jacques. *Écrits.* Paris: Seuil, 1966.
Lecouteux, Claude. "Le double, le cauchemar, la sorcière." *Études germaniques* 43 (1988): 395–405.
Lenau, Nikolaus. *Sämtliche Werke und Briefe.* Vol. 1. Edited by Eduard Castle. Leipzig: Insel, 1910.
Lietina-Ray, Maruta. "Das Recht der öffentlichen Meinung: Über das Vorurteil in der *Judenbuche.*" Special Issue of *Zeitschrift für deutsche Philologie* 99 (1979): 99–109.
Lillyman, William J. *Otto Ludwig's "Zwischen Himmel und Erde": A Study of Its Artistic Structure.* The Hague: Mouton, 1967.
Limlei, Michael. "Die Romanschlüsse in Wilhelm Raabes Romanen *Stopfkuchen* und *Die Akten des Vogelsangs.*" In *Wilhelm Raabe: Studien zu seinem Leben und Werk; aus Anlaß des 150. Geburtstages (1831–1981)*, edited by Leo A. Lensing and Hans-Werner Peter, 342–64. Braunschweig: pp-Verlag, 1981.
Ludwig, Otto. *Sämtliche Werke.* Edited by Paul Merker et al. 6 vols. Munich: Müller, 1912–22.
———. *Studien.* Edited by Alfred Stern. 2 vols. Leipzig: Grunow, 1891. (Cited as S1 and S2).
Lukacher, Ned. *Primal Scenes: Literature, Philosophy, Psychoanalysis.* Ithaca: Cornell University Press, 1986.
Lukács, Georg. *Die Grablegung des alten Deutschland: Essays zur deutschen Literatur des 19. Jahrhunderts. Ausgewählte Schriften.* Vol. 1. Munich: Rowohlt, 1967.
Mare, Margaret. *Annette von Droste-Hülshoff.* Lincoln: University of Nebraska Press, 1965.
Martini, Fritz. *Deutsche Literatur im bürgerlichen Realismus 1848–1898.* Stuttgart: Metzler, 1962.
Mayer, Gerhart. "Raabes Romanfragment 'Altershausen': Grundzüge einer Interpretation." In *Raabe in neuer Sicht*, edited by Hermann Helmers, 211–28. Stuttgart: Kohlhammer, 1968.
McClain, William H. *Between Real and Ideal: The Course of Otto Ludwig's Development as a Narrative Writer.* University of North Carolina Studies in the Germanic Languages and Literatures, no. 40. Chapel Hill: University of North Carolina Press, 1963.
McCort, Dennis. *States of Unconsciousness in Three Tales by C. F. Meyer.* Cranbury, N.J.: Associated University Presses, 1988.
McInnes, Edward. "Analysis and Moral Insight in the Novel: Otto Ludwig's 'Epische Studien.'" *Deutsche Vierteljahrsschrift* 46 (1972): 699–713.
Merkel-Nipperdey, Margarete. *Gottfried Kellers "Martin Salander": Untersuchungen zur Struktur des Zeitromans.* Göttingen: Vandenhoeck & Ruprecht, 1959.
Meyer, Conrad Ferdinand. *Sämtliche Werke: Historisch-Kritische Ausgabe.* Edited by Hans Zeller and Alfred Zäch. 15 vols. Berne: Benteli, 1958–.
Meyer-Krentler, Eckhardt. "Stopfkuchen—Ein Doppelgänger: Wilhelm Raabe erzählt Theodor Storm." *Jahrbuch der Raabe-Gesellschaft* (1987): 179–204.

Mullan, W. N. B. "Tragic Guilt and the Motivation of the Catastrophe in Storm's 'Aquis submersus.'" *Forum for Modern Language Studies* 18 (1982): 225–46.

Neumann, Bernd. *Gottfried Keller: Eine Einführung in sein Werk.* Königstein/Ts.: Athenäum, 1982.

Nollendorfs, Cora Lee. "'... kein Zeugniß ablegen': Woman's Voice in Droste-Hülshoff's *Judenbuche.*" *German Quarterly* 67 (1994): 325–37.

Nuber, Achim. "Ein Bilderrätsel: Emblematische Struktur und Autoreferentialität in Theodor Storms Erzählung *Aquis Submersus.*" *Colloquia Germanica* 26 (1993): 227–43.

Oehlenschläger, Eckart. "Erzählverfahren und Zeiterfahrung: Überlegungen zu Wilhelm Raabes *Altershausen.*" In *Wilhelm Raabe: Studen zu seinem Leben und Werk; aus Anlaß des 150. Geburtstages (1831–1981),* edited by Leo A. Lensing and Hans-Werner Peter, 381–405. Braunschweig: pp-Verlag, 1981.

Onderdelinden, Sjaak. *Die Rahmenerzählungen Conrad Ferdinand Meyers.* Leiden: Universitaire Pers Leiden, 1974.

Osterkamp, Barbara. *Arbeit und Identität: Studien zur Erzählkunst des bürgerlichen Realismus.* Würzburg: Königshausen + Neumann, 1983.

Passavant, Rudolf von. *Zeitdarstellung und Zeitkritik in Gottfried Kellers "Martin Salander."* Berne: Francke, 1978.

Pastor, Eckart. *Die Sprache der Erinnerung: Zu den Novellen von Theodor Storm.* Frankfurt a.M.: Athenäum 1988.

Perkins, David. *Is Literary History Possible?* Baltimore: Johns Hopkins University Press, 1992.

Peucker, Brigitte. "Droste-Hülshoff's Ophelia and the Recovery of Voice." *Journal of English and Germanic Philology* 82 (1983): 374–91.

Pfandl, Ludwig. "Der Narzißbegriff: Versuch einer neuen Deutung." *Imago* 21 (1935): 279–310.

Pickar, Gertrud B. "The Battering and Mega-Battering of Droste's Margreth: Covert Misogyny in *Die Judenbuche*'s Critical Reception." *Women in German Yearbook* 9 (1994): 71–90.

Pongs, Hermann. *Wilhelm Raabe: Leben und Werk.* Heidelberg: Quelle & Meyer, 1958.

Por, Peter. "Verrätselung: Perspektiven eines poetischen Verfahrens bei Gérard de Nerval und Theodor Storm." *Deutsche Vierteljahrsschrift* 59 (1985): 422–44.

Preisendanz, Wolfgang. "Die Erzählsturktur als Bedeutungskomplex der 'Akten des Vogelsangs.'" *Jahrbuch der Raabe-Gesellschaft* (1981): 210–24.

———. *Humor als dichterische Einbildungskraft: Studien zur Erzählkunst des poetischen Realismus.* 2nd ed. Munich: Fink, 1976.

———. "Voraussetzungen des poetischen Realismus in der deutschen Erzählkunst des 19. Jahrhunderts." In *Formkräfte der deutschen Dichtung vom Barock bis zur Gegenwart,* edited by Hans Steffen, 187–210. Göttingen: Vandenhoeck & Ruprecht, 1963.

Puknus, Heinz. "Dualismus und versuchte Versöhnung: Hoffmanns zwei Welten vom 'Goldnen Topf' bis 'Meister Floh.'" In *Text + Kritik. Sonderband:*

E. T. A. Hoffmann, edited by Heinz Ludwig Arnold, 53–62. Munich: Text + Kritik, 1992.

Raabe, Wilhelm. *Sämtliche Werke*. Edited by Karl Hoppe. 20 vols. Freiburg i. B. and Braunschweig: Klemm, 1951–59; Göttingen: Vandenhoeck & Ruprecht, 1960–69.

Radcliffe, Stanley. *Der Sonderling im Werk Wilhelm Raabes*. Braunschweig: pp-Verlag, 1984.

Rank, Otto. *The Double: A Psychoanalytic Study*. Translated by Harry Tucker Jr. Chapel Hill: University of North Carolina Press, 1971.

Renz, Christine. *Gottfried Kellers "Sieben Legenden": Versuch einer Darstellung seines Erzählens*. Tübingen: Niemeyer, 1993.

Reuter, Hans-Heinrich. "Umriß eines 'mittleren' Erzählers. Anmerkungen zu Werk und Wirkung Otto Ludwigs." *Jahrbuch der deutschen Schillergesellschaft* 12 (1968): 318–58.

Richter, Jean Paul Friedrich. *Sämtliche Werke: Historisch-Kritische Ausgabe*. Vol. 1/6. Edited by Kurt Schreinert. Weimar: Böhlau, 1928.

Ritchie, J. M. "The Place of 'Martin Salander' in Gottfried Keller's Evolution as a Prose Writer." *Modern Language Review* 52 (1957): 214–22.

Roebling, Irmgard. *Wilhelm Raabes doppelte Buchführung: Paradigma einer Spaltung*. Tübingen: Niemeyer, 1988.

Rogers, Robert. *A Psychoanalytic Study of the Double in Literature*. Detroit: Wayne State University Press, 1970.

Rogers, Terence John. *Techniques of Solipsism: A Study of Theodor Storm's Narrative Fiction*. Cambridge: Modern Humanities Research Association, 1970.

Rölleke, Heinz. *Annette von Droste-Hülshoff: Die Judenbuche*. Bad Homburg v.d.H.: Gehlen, 1970.

———. "Erzähltes Mysterium: Studie zur 'Judenbuche' der Annette von Droste-Hülshoff." *Deutsche Vierteljahrsschrift* 42 (1968): 399–426.

———. "Theodor Storms 'Ein Doppelgänger' und Annette von Droste-Hülshoffs 'Die Judenbuche': Produktive Rezeption in der Novellistik des Poetischen Realismus." *Zeitschrift für deutsche Philologie* 111 (1992): 247–55.

Said, Edward W. *Orientalism*. New York: Vintage Books, 1979.

Sammons, Jeffrey L. *The Shifting Fortunes of Wilhelm Raabe: A History of Criticism as a Cautionary Tale*. Columbia, S.C.: Camden House, 1992.

———. *Wilhelm Raabe: The Fiction of the Alternative Community*. Princeton: Princeton University Press, 1987.

Schanze, Helmut. "Theorie des Dramas im 'Bürgerlichen Realismus.'" In *Deutsche Dramentheorien: Beiträge zu einer historischen Poetik des Dramas in Deutschland*, edited by Reinhold Grimm, 2:374–93. Frankfurt a.M.: Athenäum, 1973.

Schedlinsky, Walter. *Rolle und industriegesellschaftliche Entwicklung: Die literarische Vergegenständlichung eines sozialgeschichtlichen Phänomens im Werk Wilhelm Raabes*. Frankfurt a.M.: Rita G. Fischer, 1980.

Schneider, Ronald. *Realismus und Restauration: Untersuchungen zu Poetik und epischem Werk der Annette von Droste-Hülshoff*. Kronberg/Ts.: Scriptor, 1976.

Schönert, Jörg. "Otto Ludwig: *Zwischen Himmel und Erde* (1856). Die Wahrheit des Wirklichen als Problem poetischer Konstruktion." In *Romane und Erzählungen des Bürgerlichen Realismus: Neue Interpretationen*, edited by Horst Denkler, 153–72. Stuttgart: Reclam, 1980.
Schuster, Ingrid. *Theodor Storm: Die zeitkritische Dimension seiner Novellen.* 2nd ed. Bonn: Bouvier, 1985.
Seyhan, Azade. *Representation and Its Discontents: The Critical Legacy of German Romanticism.* Berkeley: University of California Press, 1992.
Silz, Walter. *Realism and Reality: Studies in the German Novelle of Poetic Realism.* University of North Carolina Studies in the Germanic Languages and Literatures, no. 11. Chapel Hill: University of North Carolina Press, 1954.
Staiger, Emil. *Annette von Droste-Hülshoff.* 2nd ed. Frauenfeld: Huber, 1962.
Steiner, Hans. *Der Begriff der Idee im Schaffen Otto Ludwigs.* Frauenfeld: Huber, 1942.
Steinmetz, Horst. "Die Rolle des Lesers in Otto Ludwigs Konzeption des 'Poetischen Realismus.'" In *Literatur und Leser: Theorien und Modelle zur Rezeption literarischer Werke,* edited by Gunter Grimm, 223–39. Stuttgart: Reclam, 1975.
Storm, Theodor. *Sämtliche Werke.* Edited by Karl Ernst Laage and Dieter Lohmeier. 4 vols. Frankfurt a.M.: Deutscher Klassiker, 1987–88.
Suttner, Christa. "A Note on the Droste-Image and 'Das Spiegelbild.'" *German Quarterly* 40 (1967): 623–29.
Szemkus, Karol. *Gesellschaftlicher Wandel und sprachliche Form: Literatursoziologische Studie zur Dichtung Gottfried Kellers.* Stuttgart: Metzler, 1969.
Tusken, Lewis W. "C. F. Meyer's *Der Heilige*: The Problem of Becket's Conversion." *Seminar* 7 (1971): 201–15.
Tymms, Ralph. *Doubles in Literary Psychology.* Cambridge: Bowes & Bowes, 1949.
Verstraete, Ginette. "Friedrich Schlegel's Practice of Literary Theory." *Germanic Review* 69 (1994): 28–35.
Webber, Andrew. "The Uncanny Rides Again: Theodor Storm's Double Vision." *Modern Language Review* 84 (1989): 860–73.
Weinsheimer, Joel C. *Gadamer's Hermeneutics: A Reading of "Truth and Method."* New Haven: Yale University Press, 1985.
Wellershoff, Dieter. *Double, Alter ego und Schatten-Ich: Schreiben und Lesen als mimetische Kur.* Graz: Droschl, 1991.
Wenger, Kurt. *Gottfried Kellers Auseinandersetzung mit dem Christentum.* Berne: Francke, 1971.
Wetzel, Heinz. "Der allzumenschliche Heilige: C. F. Meyers Novelle im Lichte von Nietzsches Gedanken zur Genealogie der Moral." *Études germaniques* 30 (1975): 204–19.
Wiese, Benno von. "Annette von Droste-Hülshoff: Die Judenbuche." In *Die deutsche Novelle von Goethe bis Kafka,* 1:154–75. Düsseldorf: Bagel, 1956.
Wohlfarth, Irving. "On the Messianic Structure of Walter Benjamin's Last Reflections." *Glyph* 3 (1978): 148–212.

Index

Adolphs, Ulrich, 129–30
Adorno, Theodor, 76–93 passim, 106, 139 (nn. 3, 6)
Alter ego, 2, 3, 60–75 passim, 113–32 passim, 134; defined, 2–3; as evil, 53, 58, 114; identification with, 113–32 passim, 134; juxtaposition with ego, 4, 9, 12, 18–19, 21, 42, 45, 55, 79, 92, 112, 128, 134; as narrated, 11, 75, 113–32 passim, 134; versus Double, 2–3, 115, 135 (n. 2)
Amphitryon, 1
Androgyny, 70–71
Angelus Silesius, 87–88, 93
Arendt, Hannah, 142 (n. 8)
Arnim, Achim von: *Isabella von Ägypten*, 25, 27, 66–67
Atterbom, Per Daniel, 136 (n. 6)
Auerbach, Berthold, 136 (n. 11); *Schwarzwälder Dorfgeschichten*, 7

Balzac, Honore de, 139 (n. 6)
Beaucamp, Eduard, 131
Becket, Thomas à. *See* Meyer, Conrad Ferdinand: *Der Heilige*
Benjamin, Walter, 77, 83–86, 139 (nn. 3–5)
Berger, John, 22
Bernd, Clifford, 5, 11, 40, 96–97, 99–100, 101, 136 (intro., nn. 6, 11; chap. 1, n. 1), 140 (n. 2), 143 (n. 14)
Bertschik, Julia, 142 (n. 4)
Bible, 38, 68
Bloch, Ernst, 139 (n. 5)
Brecht, Walter, 102, 140 (n. 2)
Brinkmann, Richard, 55, 85–86, 138 (chap. 2, n. 7)
Brockhaus, Friedrich and Heinrich, 136 (n. 6)
Buck, Theo, 130
Buck-Morss, Susan, 83–84, 139 (n. 3)
Burkhard, Marianne, 138 (n. 4)

Chamisso, Adalbert von, 9, 127; "An meinen alten Freund Peter Schlemihl," 125–26, 127; *Peter Schlemihl*, 26–27, 106

Coates, Paul, 2, 3, 60, 135 (n. 1)
Coenen, Frederic E., 99
Coleridge, Samuel Taylor, 41
Cottrell, Alan P., 137 (n. 12)
Cowen, Roy, 5, 74–75, 135 (n. 5), 136 (n. 6), 139 (n. 1)
Crook, Eugene, 135 (n. 1)

Daguerreotypes, 28
Darwinism, 82
Denkler, Horst, 123
Dialectics. *See* Enlightenment: dialectic of; Identity: dialectic of; Negative dialectics; Poetic Realism: dialectics of
Di Maio, Irene S., 142 (n. 6)
Divided self. *See* Split self
Doppelgänger: definition of, 2, 3, 13, 115; origin of term, 3, 12–14; used interchangeably with "Double," 18. *See also* Double
Dorfgeschichten, 6–8
Dostoevski, Feodor, 3, 4; *The Double*, 1, 2, 46
Double: demoniac aspects of, 4, 9, 12, 14–16, 111; and fungibility, 78–94 passim, 106; and heredity, 82, 98, 100–104, 111, 112; and memory, 28–29, 82–83, 87, 95–112 passim, 114–19, 131, 134; and Other, 2, 3, 10, 51–52, 55, 69, 82, 111–12, 137 (chap. 2, n. 4); pictorial representation and, 1, 16, 98–104, 111. *See also* Alter ego; Doppelgänger; Double ego; Dream image; Hallucinatory Double; Mirror image; Phantom Double; Twins; Water image; Youthful Double
Double ego, 34
Downing, Eric, 95, 99
Dream image, 25, 27, 62, 115
Droste-Hülshoff, Annette von, 5, 10–11, 18, 20–39, 40, 48, 52, 62, 112, 133–34, 137 (n. 1); *Bertha oder die Alpen*, 22–23, 24; "Das Fräulein von Rodenschild," 29–30, 32; "Das Spiegelbild," 21, 30–32, 36, 137 (n. 9); *Die Judenbuche*, 20–21, 26,

153

32–39, 105–6, 137 (chap. 1, nn. 11, 12; chap. 2, n. 1); *Die Schlacht im Loerner Bruch*, 27; "Doppeltgänger," 27–29, 32, 33; "Durchwachte Nacht," 28–29, 33; *Ledwina*, 22, 23–26, 32, 137 (nn. 6, 7)
Duroche, Leonard L., 140 (n. 4)
Dürrenmatt, Friedrich, 4

Ego. *See* Alter ego; Double ego; Narrating ego; Primary ego; Solipsistic ego; Superego
Eisele, Ulf, 136 (n. 12)
Enlightenment: dialectic of, 78, 83–84
Evans, Tamara, 62, 68
Expressionism, 98

Fantastic, the, 6, 9, 10, 45, 95. *See also* Supernatural, the
Farrère, Claude, 4
Feuerbach, Ludwig, 87, 88, 93
Fichte, Johann Gottlieb, 3, 9, 14, 20, 128, 135 (n. 2), 136 (nn. 8, 14)
Flaubert, Gustave, 66, 81; *Madame Bovary*, 135 (n. 2)
Fontane, Theodor, 143 (n. 14)
Fränkel, Jonas, 84
Frederiksen, Elke, 22
Frenzel, Elisabeth, 5, 135 (n. 1)
Freud, Sigmund, 4, 17–18, 19, 24, 26, 27, 34, 52, 70, 102–3
Freund, Winfried, 30

Gadamer, Hans-Georg, 140 (n. 3)
Gaier, Ulrich, 21
Geisler, Eberhard, 113, 114
Geppert, Hans Vilmar, 141 (n. 1), 142–43 (nn. 9, 10, 12)
Gerber, Paul, 127
Ghosts. *See* Phantom Double
Girard, René, 55–57
Goedsche, Charlotte L., 116–17
Goethe, Johann Wolfgang von, 42, 77, 81; *Faust*, 38, 135 (n. 2); *Westöstlicher Diwan*, 61
Goldammer, Peter, 114
Gössmann, Wilhelm, 37, 38
Gotthelf, Jeremias, 7–8; *Uli der Knecht — Uli der Pächter*, 7–8
Graeffe, A. Didier, 135 (n. 2)
Grimm, Gunter, 105, 107

Guerard, Albert, 1–2
Gustav Adolf. *See* Meyer, Conrad Ferdinand: *Gustav Adolfs Page*
Guthke, Karl S., 138 (n. 9)

Hagbert, Carl August, 136 (n. 6)
Haller, Rudolf, 137 (n. 9)
Hallucinatory Double, 56–57
Hardaway, R. Travis, 138 (n. 1)
Hardenberg, Friedrich Leopold Freiherr von. *See* Novalis
Haxthausen, August von: "Geschichte eines Algerier-Sklaven," 39
Hegel, Georg Wilhelm Friedrich, 9, 72, 73
Hein, Jürgen, 7–8, 136 (n. 10)
Heine, Heinrich: *Florentinische Nächte*, 17; *William Ratcliff*, 12, 16–17
Heldt, Uwe, 120
Helmers, Hermann, 130
Henel, Heinrich, 35–36
Henry II (king of England). *See* Meyer, Conrad Ferdinand: *Der Heilige*
Hertling, Gunter, 62
Heselhaus, Clemens, 25, 26, 38–39, 137 (n. 6)
Hildenbrock, Aglaja, 13–14
Hoffmann, E. T. A., 9, 17–18, 21, 27, 43–49, 58, 95, 98, 115–16, 137 (chap. 2, n. 4); *Das Fräulein von Scuderi*, 46–49; *Der goldne Topf*, 43, 44; *Der Sandmann*, 25, 142 (n. 4); *Die Elixiere des Teufels*, 12, 14–16, 17, 116; *Meister Floh*, 45
Hohendahl, Peter Uwe, 8, 9, 76
Holub, Robert, 61, 62, 64, 74, 97
Homer, 77, 81; *Odyssey*, 83, 89
Horkheimer, Max, 83
Howe, Patricia, 22–23, 32, 137 (chap. 1, n. 5)

Idealism: subjective, 3–4, 6, 12, 14, 40, 135 (n. 4)
Identity: confusion of, 1, 9, 12–16, 25, 26, 32–39, 44, 54, 67, 70–71; dialectic of, 36, 61–68, 71–73, 78, 92–93; logic of, 85; mythic, 77, 88, 92; subjective, 9
Irony: Romantic, 6, 9, 12–16, 25, 63, 133, 142 (n. 6)

Jacobson, Evelyn and Manfred, 69
Jameson, Fredric, 118

Jean Paul. *See* Richter, Jean Paul Friedrich
Jennings, Lee B., 46, 51, 89, 139 (n. 8)
Jesus, 68–69
Jung, Carl Gustav, 33
Jungdeutschland, 5, 6, 20, 133
Junge, Hermann, 116

Kaiser, Georg, 98
Kaiser, Gerhard, 87, 88, 89, 90, 101
Kaiser, Nancy, 124, 126, 127
Keller, Gottfried, 2, 5, 7, 9, 10, 11, 20, 37, 75, 76–94, 106–7, 134, 139 (nn. 6, 7, 10), 141 (nn. 8, 9); *Das verlorene Lachen*, 89–90, 139 (n. 9); *Der grüne Heinrich*, 79, 87–89, 90, 92–93; *Martin Salander*, 10, 76–94, 106–7, 139 (nn. 8, 10), 140 (n. 11), 141 (n. 8); *Pankraz, der Schmoller*, 10, 79, 139 (n. 1); reviews of Jeremias Gotthelf, 7–8; *Romeo und Julia auf dem Dorfe*, 76
Keppler, C. F., 3, 4, 135 (nn. 1, 3)
Kinder, Hermann, 8, 76
Klopfenstein, Eduard, 120–21
Komar, Kathleen, 62
Körber, Esther-Beate, 141 (n. 12)
Korte, Hermann, 49
Kortländer, Bernd, 21
Krauss, Wilhelmine, 2, 17, 135 (n. 4), 136 (nn. 8, 14)
Kreuzer, Helmut, 7
Kurscheidt, Georg, 58

Laage, Karl Ernst, 140 (n. 2), 141 (n. 8)
Lacan, Jacques, 121, 128
Lecouteux, Claude, 135 (n. 2)
Lenau, Nikolaus: "Anna," 25–27
Lietina-Ray, Maruta, 37, 137 (n. 11)
Lillyman, William, 55, 138 (chap. 2, n. 6)
Limlei, Michael, 123
Lingg, Hermann, 63, 68, 73
Ludwig, Otto, 4, 5, 6, 8, 9, 10, 11, 20, 39, 40–59, 62, 75, 79, 112, 118, 133, 134, 136 (n. 6), 137 (chap. 2, nn. 1, 2, 5); *Das Fräulein von Scuderi*, 46–49; "Der poetische Realismus," 6, 40–43; *Die Heiteretei und ihr Widerspiel*, 49–53, 55–56; *Die wahrhaftige Geschichte von den drei Wünschen*, 43–46, 53, 137 (chap. 2, nn. 3, 5); *Zwischen Himmel und Erde*, 53–59, 138 (chap. 2, nn. 6, 7)
Lukacher, Ned, 141 (n. 10)

Lukács, Georg, 76, 77, 83, 84, 85, 86, 139 (nn. 4, 5)

McClain, William, 137 (chap. 2, nn. 1, 3)
McCort, Dennis, 70, 138 (chap. 3, n. 6)
McInnes, Edward, 41, 43, 54
Mare, Margaret, 28
Martini, Fritz, 121, 122, 129
Marx, Karl, 142 (n. 8)
Matthew, Book of, 68
Mayer, Gerhart, 129
Merkel-Nipperdey, Margarete, 80, 93, 140 (n. 11)
Meyer, Betsy, 68
Meyer, Conrad Ferdinand, 10, 11, 20, 25, 42, 55, 60–75, 112, 134, 138 (chap. 3, nn. 1, 4, 6, 9, 11); *Der Heilige*, 10, 61–75, 138 (nn. 1, 2, 5, 9, 11); *Gustav Adolfs Page*, 69–70, 138 (chap. 3, n. 6)
Meyer-Krentler, Eckhardt, 114–15
Mimesis: Aristotelian, 8
Mimetic desire, 55–57
Mirror image, 2, 5, 9, 20, 22, 29, 30–31, 52, 53, 54, 55, 62, 99, 128–29
Mirror stage, 121
Mullan, W. N. B., 96, 100, 103, 140 (nn. 6, 7)

Napoleonic Wars, 133
Narcissism, 24–27, 34
Narcissus, 24
Narrating ego, 11, 113–32 passim, 134
Naturalism, 40, 58
Negative dialectics, 77–80, 89, 93
Neumann, Bernd, 78
New Testament, 38; Book of Matthew, 68
Nietzsche, Friedrich, 24, 138 (n. 10), 142 (n. 8)
Nollendorfs, Cora Lee, 22, 32
Novalis, 66, 137 (n. 6)
Nuber, Achim, 140 (n. 6)

Oehlenschläger, Eckart, 143 (n. 13)
Old Testament, 38
Onomastics, 10, 38, 39, 43–44, 110–11, 128
Osterkamp, Barbara, 138 (chap. 2, n. 7)
Other, the: as desired, 128, 130; as narrated, 11, 115–32 passim, 141 (n. 1), 142 (n. 9); in Orientalist discourse, 60–61,

64–68, 72–74; as willed, 128. *See also*
Double: and Other

Passavant, Rudolf von, 81, 93, 140 (n. 11)
Pastor, Eckart, 140 (n. 2)
Pater, Walter, 41
Perkins, David, 18
Peucker, Brigitte, 27, 137 (n. 7)
Pfandl, Ludwig, 24
Phantom Double, 15, 16–17, 29–30, 33, 110, 111, 131
Pickar, Gertrud, 33–34, 137 (chap. 1, n. 5)
Poe, Edgar Allan, 4, 41
Poetic Realism: dates of, 5, 11–12; defined, 4–5, 8, 49, 137 (chap. 2, n. 2); dialectics of, 10, 12, 18, 49–53, 112, 134; embrace of aesthetic totality, 6, 7, 8–12, 17, 22, 40–43, 51, 53, 55, 58–59, 75, 76, 77, 85–86, 93, 99, 112, 133, 134, 138 (chap. 2, n. 7); end of, 5, 11–12, 85–86, 113, 132, 134, 143 (n. 14); origin of term, 4, 40, 136 (n. 6); and Romanticism, 4, 6, 8–12, 20, 21, 30, 31, 40, 46, 113, 128, 133–34; Scandinavian roots of, 40, 136 (n. 6)
Pongs, Hermann, 116
Por, Peter, 106
Preisendanz, Wolfgang, 5, 8–9, 127
Primary ego, 3, 10, 18, 34, 38, 39, 42, 43
Puknus, Heinz, 44–45, 137 (chap. 2, n. 4)

Raabe, Wilhelm, 9, 11, 20, 113–32, 134, 141 (nn. 1, 2), 142 (nn. 6, 8, 11), 143 (nn. 13, 14); *Alte Nester, Zwei Bücher Lebensgeschichten*, 115, 119–23, 124, 126, 128, 142 (n. 8); *Altershausen*, 11–12, 115, 116, 120, 128–32, 143 (n. 13); *Der heilige Born*, 116, 142 (n. 4); *Der Hungerpastor*, 143 (n. 14); *Die Akten des Vogelsangs*, 113, 115, 124–28, 131, 142 (n. 10), 142–43 (n. 12); *Die Chronik der Sperlingsgasse*, 115–19, 120, 121, 127, 128–29, 130; *Else von der Tanne*, 126–27; *Im alten Eisen*, 142 (n. 11); *Keltische Knochen*, 141–42 (n. 2); *Pfisters Mühle*, 126, 127; *Stopfkuchen, Eine See- und Mordgeschichte*, 114–15, 122–24, 126, 127, 128, 142 (n. 9); *Unseres Herrgotts Kanzlei*, 126
Radcliffe, Stanley, 118
Rank, Otto, 24, 28
Renz, Christine, 93

Reuter, Hans-Heinrich, 50–51
Revolution of 1848, 5, 48, 49, 118, 133
Richter, Jean Paul Friedrich, 3, 9, 115; *Flegeljahre*, 128; *Siebenkäs*, 3, 12–14, 106, 116, 136 (n. 14)
Ritchie, J. M., 80–81
Roebling, Irmgard, 128
Rogers, Robert, 18, 135 (nn. 1, 2)
Rogers, Terence John, 141 (n. 11)
Rölleke, Heinz, 33, 38, 105
Romanticism, 2, 3–4, 5, 12–19, 20–22, 24–27, 29, 32, 34, 44, 46–47, 49, 53, 63, 66, 70, 95, 97–98, 106, 110, 115–16, 128, 133–34, 135 (n. 4), 136 (n. 8). *See also* Irony: Romantic; Poetic Realism: and Romanticism
Rydqvist, Johan Erik, 136 (n. 6)

Said, Edward, 60–61, 66, 73, 74, 138 (chap. 3, n. 7)
Sammons, Jeffrey, 124, 125, 142 (n. 3)
Santayana, George, 101
Schanze, Helmut, 48
Schedlinsky, Walter, 117, 118
Schelling, Friedrich, 3, 9, 27, 136 (n. 6)
Schlegel, Friedrich, 66; *Athenäum Fragment* 116, 6
Schmidt, Expeditus, 48
Schmidt, Julian, 5, 6–7, 8, 9, 11, 16, 18, 20, 41–42, 75, 76, 118, 133, 136 (intro., n. 11; chap. 1, n. 1), 138 (n. 11)
Schneider, Ronald, 137 (chap. 1, n. 4)
Schönert, Jörg, 53
Schulz, Bruno, 4
Schuster, Ingrid, 105
Second self, 2, 9, 10, 25, 49, 54, 117, 135 (nn. 2, 3)
Seyhan, Azade, 66, 72
Shadows, 5, 9, 26–27, 106, 117, 118, 126–27, 131, 142 (n. 11)
Shakespeare, William, 42, 79
Silz, Walter, 65, 138 (nn. 2, 5)
Socialist Realism, 84
Solipsistic ego, 3–4
Spectral double. *See* Phantom double
Split self, 41, 43, 47–49, 54, 58, 104–15 passim, 124–28, 130, 134
Staiger, Emil, 137 (chap. 1, n. 4)
Steiner, Hans, 42
Steinmetz, Horst, 137 (chap. 2, n. 2)

Stevenson, Robert Louis, 3, 4; *The Strange Case of Dr. Jekyll and Mr. Hyde*, 1, 2
Stifter, Adalbert, 5, 9, 77, 81
Storm, Theodor, 4, 10, 11, 20, 21, 29, 37, 75, 76, 95–112, 113–15, 134, 140 (n. 2), 141 (nn. 8, 9, 11, 12); *Aquis submersus*, 96–104, 106, 111, 112, 140 (nn. 4–7); *Der Schimmelreiter*, 95, 140 (n. 1); *Der Spiegel des Cyprianus*, 99; *Ein Doppelgänger*, 10, 96, 104–12, 113–15, 141 (nn. 9, 11); *Im Schloß*, 99; *Viola tricolor*, 95, 99; *Waldwinkel*, 99
Straube, Heinrich, 30
Strindberg, August, 24
Superego, 14, 22–23, 128, 135 (n. 2), 136 (n. 8)
Supernatural, the, 4, 10, 20, 49, 95, 133. See also Fantastic, the
Suttner, Christa, 31
Symbolists, French, 41–42
Szemkus, Karol, 78, 91

Thanatos, 137 (n. 7)
Thierry, Augustin, 61, 74, 138 (n. 1)
Thirty Years War, 69
Tieck, Ludwig, 9; *William Lovell*, 30, 48
Tolstoy, Leo, 24
Totality: epic, 83; negation of, 76–94 passim, 114–15; psychological, 2–3, 9, 10, 11, 18, 41, 42, 43, 51, 55, 70, 75, 79, 88, 94, 112, 119, 124, 134; temporal, 98–99, 120, 127; utopian sociopolitical dimension of, 8–9, 76, 86, 114, 118–19, 132, 133, 134. See also Poetic Realism: embrace of aesthetic totality

Tusken, Lewis, 68
Twins, 10, 80–93 passim, 106, 134
Tymms, Ralph, 14, 17, 98, 106, 107, 135 (n. 1)

Uhland, Ludwig, 108
Uncanny, the, 18, 20, 21, 25–28, 34, 52, 95, 140 (n. 1)

Verstraete, Ginette, 6
Village tales. See *Dorfgeschichten*
Vita activa, 122, 142 (n. 8)
Vita contemplativa, 122, 142 (n. 8)

Water image, 23–27, 32, 52, 62, 115
Webber, Andrew, 95, 140 (n. 1)
Weinsheimer, Joel, 140 (n. 3)
Wellek, René, 136 (n. 6)
Wellershof, Dieter, 135 (n. 2)
Wells, H. G., 4
Wenger, Kurt, 139 (nn. 7, 10)
Werfel, Franz, 4
Wetzel, Heinz, 138 (n. 10)
Wiese, Benno von, 34–35
Wilde, Oscar, 24; *The Picture of Dorian Gray*, 1
Wohlfarth, Irving, 139 (n. 4)
Wu Ch'eng-en: *Journey to the West*, 1

Young Germany. See *Jungdeutschland*
Youthful Double, 27–29, 31, 33, 116–23, 127, 129, 130, 131, 134

Zwingli, Ulrich, 89

www.ingramcontent.com/pod-product-compliance
Lightning Source LLC
Chambersburg PA
CBHW031314150426
43191CB00005B/227